There is in my heart as it were a burning fire shut up in my bones,
and I am weary with holding it in,
and I cannot.

Jeremiah 20:9

Fire
in My Bones

by

CHARLES H. KING, JR.

WILLIAM B. EERDMANS PUBLISHING COMPANY
GRAND RAPIDS, MICHIGAN

Reprinted, April 1983

Library of Congress Cataloging in Publication Data
King, Charles H.
 Fire in my bones.

 1. King, Charles H.—Addresses, essays, lectures.
2. Racism—United States—Addresses, essays, lectures.
3. United States—Race relations—Addresses, essays,
lectures. 4. Afro-Americans—Biography—Addresses,
essays, lectures. I. Title.
E185.97.K46A3 1982   305.8'96073'00924 82-13934
ISBN 0-8028-3570-8

The author and publisher wish to thank those who have granted permission
to reprint the following:
 Excerpt from "The Specter of Black Power," *Sign* (Feb. 1968).
 Excerpts from "Black News Cues a Philly Uproar" and "Program Re-
  view: Black Perspectives on the News," *Variety* (Oct. 1976).
 Excerpts from "White People Must Change," *Sojourners* (May 1981),
  P.O. Box 29272, Washington, D.C., 20017; edited for use here.

Contents

v

CONTENTS

Preface

*T*HERE IS FIRE IN MY BONES. IT IS THERE BECAUSE of the problem of race. I speak of race as a condition, not as a state of being. The black of me has now become the whole of me. It was not always thus. The flames of hate and hostility toward white America developed slowly—burning all vestiges of accommodation or subjugation to whiteness. I am now a man.

I am compelled now to confront whites eyeball to eyeball and dare them to suggest anything less of me than they see in each other. It is then and only then that they too will achieve manhood.

The journey to this stage of life is being repeated by a growing segment of black Americans. Robbed of the dignity of person and manhood, they now flare up in flames of resentment against those who have castrated their hopes and dreams.

Born as others in the melting pot of America, we did not melt. Instead, we were strung out to mature in the slime of ghettoes; denied equal opportunities, our flesh and spirits wasted away into nothingness. It was from that posture that blacks formed the first concept of their identity. The flames did not burn at that early stage because of the risk of complete consumption. We could not become men because manhood requires aggression. We were unable to fight because warfare demands legions with weapons.

Whatever fire existed in us was exterminated by welfare and handouts. Whatever dignity we assumed was obtained in the separate arena of blackness.

The tragic consequence of that existence became a lifetime of wasted potential. Even now, in my late-achieved manhood, I mourn for those years as a parent would mourn the loss of a child. What we might have become, we are not. What we are now is only half of what we might have been. A man who knows not the power nor feels the worth of his true identity is a crippled man. Support comes only from dreams; and for far too many, dreams were never realized.

Turn now and look at black America. We are not only separated by geographical and discriminatory containment, but also isolated in spirit. We have become a separate people—both in philosophy and in experience. That black experience is unknown to white America. Since whites have not shared that travail, they have become bewildered spectators of a growing army of blacks who now declare themselves to be free. This declared freedom is from within, for no black in any time or any place in America has been able to escape from the prison of color. This inner man, purged by the flames of his true knowledge of self, militantly shouts his disdain for the white man's chains and thus comes into his own.

It is this growing shout that now disturbs this nation. For whether from the ghettoes or from Wounded Knee, there is fire in our bones and it shall not be quenched.

This book is dedicated to the thousands of white people who have been seared by my fire and have started fires of their own.

—CHARLES H. KING, JR.

PROLOGUE
In Search of a Lost Identity

*T*HE WHITE RACE FOUND ITS EARLY RATIONALE for racism by creating myths. One was based on a manipulation of the story of Adam and Eve: their banished son Cain represented the beginning of blackness. In another, it was Noah's son Ham, who was separated from his family by a curse (imposed not by God, as some racists claim, but by an intoxicated Noah). This allegedly turned his skin black, condemning him to become a slave to his white brothers. Or whites could choose the belief that when Ham emerged from the Ark he was struck black by the charge that he had engaged in sexual impropriety during the forty days of rain. Or they might prefer the story of the tower of Babel—the scattering of the whites to the north and the blacks to the south. White racists can take their pick of a large assortment of myths, including the truly absurd post-creation story in which Cain, banished from the garden of Eden, marries an ape and thus fathers a lower form of man-animal life that results in the black man.

I am black, and I reject all of these racist myths to explain my blackness. The search we have made for the roots of the black past has produced a record of glorious achievement, far beyond what the white man has even grudgingly acknowledged.

Allow me, if you will, to place blackness in historical and biblical perspective. Forgive me for using the personal pronoun, but I am so proud of my ancestry that I beg to step back and view it in the first person.

I lived along the Nile and Euphrates rivers long before any man's skin was white, forming with crude hands the cradle of civilization. Diodorus Siculus, the first world historian, will inform you (confirmed by archaeologists) that blacks colonized Egypt; in fact, the earliest known Egyptians, the Bedouins, a neolithic people, were my black ancestors.

It was from that ethnic background that the Semitic races sprang, making me a blood brother with the Jews and Arabs. The whitening of the Jews came much later, when the Caucasians came down from the north and intermarried with them. There arose then a struggle for power, not about race but between races—the light and the dark—and the dark won. Yes, we did. In fact, in the eighth century before Christ, blacks dominated all of Egypt, Africa, and Asia Minor.

Though I hang my head as an early oppressor, I quickly raise it again. You see, war was not our only thing. In 2980 B.C. I existed in the person of a black man named IUM-HOTEP (Imhotep), the first physician to stand out clearly from the mists of antiquity. For a long time he was worshipped as a prince of peace *by early Christians*. A black statue to certify that fact resides to this day in the Church of Rome.

And to you who would ignore the virtue and dignity of the black woman, there was a black queen named HAT SHEP SOT: according to Egyptologists, she was the initiator of the concept of women's liberation. She consistently challenged the supremacy of males—from a throne.

1500 B.C.: a black pharaoh by the name of THOTMES III ruled Egypt wisely and well. 1350 B.C.: another black man, AKHENATON, the most remarkable of all pharaohs, preached and lived the gospel of perfect love, brotherhood, and truth—from a throne. 1100 B.C.: the most celebrated sage of the east, my ancestor was LOKMAN, whose fame equaled that of Solomon. In fact, Mohammed quotes Lokman extensively in the KORAN and named the thirty-first chapter of that book in his honor.

As a writer and storyteller, no one today can be compared to Esop (560 B.C.), a black who inspired Plato, Socrates, Aristotle, and Shakespeare.

Now, in the face of all this, to those who still contend that blacks are "cursed," here are a few insights. Since we now know that the Jews were held captive in Egypt by blacks, we can understand why rabbinical writers were angry and bitter enough to record curses in the Masoretic Text (Old Testament). Blacks had oppressed them. In fact, a black man, SHISHAK, was the one who plundered Solomon's temple and took Jews as slaves to Egypt. The curse was the same as saying "may you be damned"—not because of their skin but because of what they had done. The curse on Canaan could not have been because of skin color, for the Canaanites were of a lighter skin than the Egyptians and than many of the Jews themselves. Why, then? The answer is obvious: the Jews' claim was that Jehovah had given them Canaan; the curse was thus on those who occupied that land (Gen. 10:25). The Masoretic Text does not mention color. "Black skin" was a term added later. Could it be that white writers added that to the Bible? Well, somebody did, and I assure you it wasn't us.

Neither the Jews nor the early Christians were hung up on color. Moses chose as his wife a black beauty named Zipporah. Solomon exalted the black skin. Did he not proclaim that Makeda, the black empress and queen of Sheba, had stolen his heart? It was from the union of those two that Manetic was born, and Solomon himself crowned his black son king of Ethiopia. The black woman has had her hand and heart in history. Ask Julius Caesar or Mark Antony: it was Cleopatra, the black queen of the Nile, who shaped the Kingdom of Rome. She died just thirty years before Christ was born. And how can you ignore the color of Hannibal (247-183 B.C.), a black man, the father of military strategy?

One of the most ironic twists of history is that a black man, Abraha, Emperor of Ethiopia, became a Christian in A.D. 330. It was his black Christian armies that held out against the conquering march of Islam that swept through North Africa and Southern Asia on their way north to conquer the world. These black Christians ensured the continued strength of the Christian faith.

*   *   *   *   *

I have taken you on a brief march through ancient and biblical history. Can you now see how black men and women have been stripped of their heritage, their glorious past? Can you see how Christianity has theologized the black man out of step with the rest of God's creation?

Need blacks undergo that long journey once more through the wilderness? No more. We have searched for our identity and have found it. There is no turning back, no search for another land. We are here—and shall remain. The next move is up to white America: this so-called Christian nation must reorder the priorities of its institutions and theology, reverse the trend, and echo the philosophy of St. Augustine, who in his *City of God* proclaimed that all human beings are of "the stock of Adam's or Noah's sons," and that "whosoever is anywhere born of a man, that is, of a rational mortal animal, no matter what unusual appearance he presents in colour, movement, sound, nor how peculiar he is in some power, part, or quality of his nature, no Christian can doubt he springs from a single protoplast." He added: "All the varieties of mankind . . . unquestionably trace their pedigree to that one first father of all."

PART I
Roots of Fire

CHAPTER 1

The Quest for My Father's Roots

NOW—IN THE YEAR 1982—I LOOK BACK INTO MY childhood to try to discover when the fires of resentment began to burn. Pottsville, Pennsylvania, population 24,000 (with fewer than 300 blacks), was an ideal setting to cast me into the mold of whiteness. Like a fly in a bowl of milk, I endured those years without any notable traumas induced by my blackness. I was the class clown, the cutup, and it was not long before I discovered that humor would always make me a favorite of teachers and students alike. I learned to roll my eyes like Montand Moreland, Charlie Chan's "numbah one niggah," and to say like he did, "Feets, do your duty." I was apologizing then, at that tender age, for being black.

I did not know it then, but as I look back I can see that my actions and mannerisms in grade school and high school induced a quiet rage. Shining shoes on a downtown street, allowing white men to rub my head for luck, popping a shoeshine rag while grinning up at the man, doing a tap dance for a tip beyond the five-cent shine—those antics and others ingratiated me into the white world. The first indication of the true meaning of my blackness came to me from a strange source, and through an incident that still burns an indelible mark on my psyche. The source was my father, a deeply religious, gentle man.

My father had a deep fear of white people. He must have had an experience in early boyhood that had scarred him for life. But try as we might, we children could not get him to talk

3

about his youth or his family. It was as though he had sprung from nowhere, married my mother, and fathered a family of nine children.

He was as tall and stately as an African warrior. He was self-educated and had a booming voice, with which he trumpeted commands to his children. But when he talked with whites, his voice became soft—delicately soft. When I was in my teens, the house we lived in could scarcely contain us, and it groaned with the winds of winter. He called it his "roof": "As long as you are under my roof you will do as I say," he warned us. We did as he said. Yet he was delicate and nice to white folks.

The first car he owned was an Essex; it was the only car that put a smile on his face. He would sit for hours on the front porch, watching his car, admiring its contours. His disposition changed when he drove that car . . . until one day they took it away. Where the Essex came from, how he obtained it, or where it went, we never knew. The loss of the car caused the loss of the tangy smell of cigar smoke and the rare banter that Father would engage in while he took us on our Sunday drives. He seldom left home after that. We tried hard to make him smile—to be happy with the rest of us; but the best he could give us was a half grin.

One day I came home crying from eighth grade. My shop teacher had kicked at me when I was late for class. He informed me that I could not return to class until I went home to get a note from my parents. It was a brushing kick, like one that is playfully delivered, and I hardly felt it. But he was white, and so was the rest of the class that saw it.

As I related what had happened to me, I saw my father through my tears surging ahead of me back to the school. He walked tall, angrily tall, and strode into that classroom. Without a word, he seized Mr. Minabak by the lapels of his coat and pulled him out into the schoolyard. Three men, including the principal, had to restrain him, and out of my father's mouth came torrents of rage and obscenity.

That was my first exposure to black rebellion, and it came from a deeply brooding and gentle man—my father, who always talked nice to white folks. Whatever was locked in the bosom of his past came out that day. Later, many years later, when I had become a man, we talked of that day, my father and I. I tried desperately to explore his roots, his past, but was unsuccessful again. Eighteen years ago I was called to my father's bedside; he was slowly slipping away. On his face was a contented smile, as if death were a welcome visitor. What was the deep mystery of this man who would not give us his roots?

A few years ago, as I watched Alex Haley, his son, and his grandson recount the genealogy that led through five genera-tions back to an African village, I felt a tremendous pain, an envy of Haley, and a surging desire to relive my youth with my father, to try once again to wrest from him that secret of whence he came—and why he would not reveal it. The only key I had was that incident in the schoolyard. Somehow my teacher had rekindled the flame of his past, and he had dared to fight back at those who had sapped his manhood, his desire to live.

*　　*　　*　　*　　*

The deeply hidden and mysterious roots are, indeed, a metaphor of the black legacy in America.

In May 1982 a chance recognition gave me an insightful and deeply personal revelation of the meaning of that metaphor of black roots. My picture had appeared in a Kansas City newspaper announcing my visit there to conduct my racial awareness seminar. I received a phone call from one Frank Rembert, a man whom I had met once, thirty years before. He had recognized my picture in the paper and wished to get together with me. He said he had a story about roots to tell me. Here is his story.

Qually Rembert was a white plantation owner in the early 1800s in Louisiana. By all reports, Rembert was a humane slaveowner who was kind to his slaves and mingled with them. In fact, he "mingled" with one female slave enough so that she bore several of his children. One of their mulatto offspring, "Little Qually" Rembert, stayed on the plantation as one of the favored "nigrahs." He married Susan ("Suki") King, a half-breed Indian from the Louisiana Chickasaw tribe of chieftains. This triracial union produced seven sons and two daughters between 1870 and 1888. When "Big Qually" died, the plantation—as was specified in his will—went to "Little Qually" and his part-African, part-Indian, and part-Caucasian progeny.

One of the Rembert sons, Richard, grew up to be a dark-skinned and fiercely proud black man. When he was about thirty years old, around 1905, in an incident shrouded in the mists of family memory and Louisiana county history, Richard rose up and slew a white man. Why he did—what massive racial offense or injustice drove him to commit so heinous an act in turn-of-the-century Louisiana—is still hidden in folk memory and the annals of American racial violence. But Richard Rembert fled and became one of the few blacks of that era to escape the noose of the Southern lynch mob. Monroe County whites threatened to take all of the Rembert brothers and whip Richard's whereabouts out of them. But Aaron and Moreland King, their Indian uncles (brothers of Suki), put a stop to that notion. Eventually the killing faded from present consciousness into the past.

Little Qually had died when his children were still quite young, so the sons had not received necessary knowledge of land ownership from him. Eventually the Rembert mulattoes lost the plantation because they did not know enough to pay the taxes. The family drifted apart, some of them never to hear from one another again. It was said, though, that one of the brothers hated white people so much that he was in constant danger of assaulting them violently. It was also said that five of the brothers became ministers of the gospel.

As for Richard, the one who fled North to escape—he made it to New York to carry out an incognito existence. To avoid discovery, he had changed his name, his profession, even his age. Like a number of his brothers, he had become a minister. In an age-old story of romance, he married the organist of his church in Kingston, New York, a beautiful seventeen-year-old from Boston named Esther Dickerson. Richard told Esther nothing about his past. In fact, in 1922, when they were married, he said that he was twenty-eight—when he was at least forty-five years of age. In the ensuing years the couple had nine children together: Mary, Charles, David, Phoebe, Margaret, Alfred, Elsie, Diane, and Frank, who died at birth.

Richard Rembert was never free of his past: his act of violence had once again placed him into slavery. He could not live as a free man because he was perpetually peering over his shoulder, haunted by the fear of white mob vengeance. He never saw any of his brothers or sisters again, save for one. In 1946 he risked a return to Union Parish County in Louisiana. Time had erased white memory, and the law no longer sought out its vengeance. He found that he was too late to claim any of the land willed to the Remberts. In fact, it appeared that the Union Parish Courthouse now stood on at least part of the Rembert land. But in that courthouse Richard Rembert discovered the name and whereabouts of one of his brothers. Elated, he hastened to Kansas City and embraced his brother Frank, the father of the Frank Rembert who was telling me this story. Richard and Frank relived together the days when they were but children, and how they were out in the yard making mud pies on the day their father, Little Qually, died. They also talked of how and why Richard had run away; but these conversations were in low whispers so that Frank could not relate why Richard had killed the white man in 1905.

When Frank Rembert had completed his story, my heart ached once again for that gentle, brooding man who rarely smiled. For he had taken his Indian mother's name to escape those who were searching for Richard Rembert. He had called himself Charles H. King. And he had given me the name Charles H. King, Jr.

CHAPTER 2
Getting Religion

MY PARENTS PLANNED FOR ME TO "GET RELI-gion" in the fall of 1938. At that time I would reach the age of reckoning and responsibility for my own sins. Rev. M. W. Carter, evangelist from Harrisburg, Pennsylvania, had been scheduled to conduct a two-week revival at my father's church, the Mount Zion Baptist Church. Posters were printed and circulars hung from all telephone poles in the neighborhood surrounding the church.

Come See and Hear
REV. M. W. CARTER
Our Nation's Greatest Preacher
Hear Him! See Him!
A Truly Born-Again Man
Two Big Weeks
October 15-25
Come One—Come All!

The coming fall revival weighed heavily on my mind all summer long. At last, according to my father, I was to get religion. The process through which this "getting" was to come was not unknown to me. For years I had watched sinners on the "moaners' bench" "come forward" and accept Christ. For many years I had wondered where Christ was. He never seemed to appear when the sinners went forward. Sometimes they accepted him crying, other times they would come forth shouting. One young man actually accepted Christ angrily, pushed forward by his mother who insisted she was not going to allow her son to become "lost" because he was bullheaded.

As each month rolled around nearing October, I developed

pains in my stomach. Somehow I didn't want to accept Christ. In the first place, I didn't know him; secondly, church was more of a place of amusement to me, where I could observe the antics of its possessed members. I began to develop a fear of becoming a Christian, and I took my problem to my mother.

"It's not what you think it is, Son," she reassured me. "When you get it, you'll know it. You won't necessarily have to shout and fall down."

"How am I supposed to feel?" I inquired.

"You'll feel good, all over."

"But I feel good now."

"Yes, but not like you'll feel when you get religion."

As the month of October began, my father called me in to inform me what was expected of me: since I was his son, and he was the pastor, he didn't want me to embarrass him by not joining the church. I was to give up all my bad habits, like playing marbles for keeps; in fact, I was to stop playing marbles altogether. "We can't have folks thinking you're gambling," he explained.

The possibility that Jesus did not like boys to play marbles made me angry. What kind of religion would take away my pleasures?

"Religion was never designed to make our pleasures less," Dad informed me. "Jesus said, 'I came that ye might have life and have it more abundantly.' " Yet, his desire to take away my marbles seemed inconsistent with his sayings. Informed that I would understand it better by and by, I waited for the by and by.

Rev. M. W. Carter arrived in town on the bus before the summer heat had abated. I accompanied my father to meet him at the station. He was a typical evangelist: tall and fat with piercing eyes. As he handed me a suitcase that was tied together with ropes, he appeared to be sizing me up as a candidate. His pants were pin-striped to match his black frock coat, and his shirt was dingy from travel. Turning away from me, he shook hands with my father, and they immediately concerned themselves with the challenge of having a great revival.

"The town is ready for it," Dad told him. "This is going to be the best one yet."

How Dad had assessed the readiness of the town for the appearance of Rev. Carter I could not understand. One thing for sure, I was not ready. As soon as I saw Rev. Carter, I wondered how he could get me religion. The front of his shirt was stained with tobacco juice. As we climbed up into my father's Essex, I noticed that his pin-striped pants contained patches from former years on the sawdust trail. It was obvious to me that one of the "world's greatest preachers" had been ignored by his Jesus who was supposed to "make a way out of no way." As soon as we entered the house, Dad called Mother out of the kitchen to inform her that the speaker had arrived. Mother gushed out her welcome. Dinner was ready. Rev. Carter protested, saying that Mother should not have prepared anything special for him since he had already eaten; after that protestation he proceeded to eat everything in sight.

That night, after I had taken my bath and was ordered to wear my suit with the short trousers, I was driven to the church by Dad and Rev. Carter. Mother and my sisters and brothers were to walk down later. I received my final instructions from Rev. Carter. At the completion of his sermon, when he would extend his arm as an invitation to the sinners, he informed me, I was to get up (if I felt anything) and come to Jesus at the altar. I promised him that I would.

The church was filled. I took my seat on the front pew and noticed that I was the only sinner on the moaners' bench. I could feel the stares of the congregation boring into my back, as if they felt they could stare me into the church. Three women, white dressed, sat immediately behind me. They whispered to me that they would be praying for my soul. I thanked them.

The service began.

"Come ye that love the Lord, and let your joys be known," Deacon Hunt announced the hymn to be sung.

> Come ye that love the Lord,
> And let your joys be known,
> Join in the song with sweet accord,
> Join in the song with sweet accord,

10

> And thus surround the throne,
> And thus surround the throne.

And so they sang:

> We're marching to Zion,
> Beautiful, beautiful Zion,
> We're marching upward to Zion
> That beautiful city of God.

After the singing and the prayers had been concluded, Dad introduced the "world's greatest preacher"; he did not spare us a long introduction. "Dr. Carter" was known far and wide as a God-sent preacher. He was second to none in the pulpit and possessed a power that was truly from on high. The devil in hell trembled when he preached. There was no telling how many souls he had led to Christ. For two big weeks he would be with us. Any Christian who failed to bring sinners he knew in to hear the preacher would have that blood on his hands. Dr. Carter was there to preach; it was up to the members to provide the sinners. Dad said he was proud to have his son on the moaners' bench tonight, and as Dr. Carter came foward to speak, he was asking the prayers of the righteous that the soul of his eldest son might be added to the Church and to the Kingdom. Everybody was commanded to say "Amen." Amens chorused all around. Then we were asked to raise our hands to acknowledge the presence of the speaker of the hour.

As Rev. Carter approached to speak, I was confronted with a growing fear that judgment day had come. The speaker confirmed my fears:

"Young man," he spoke to me looking down from the pulpit, "this is the ouwuh that I hope yu'l always remembah . . . this is the ouwuh that peace kin come intah yo soul . . . this is the ouwuh that John viewed on the Isle of Patomouse . . . let the church say 'Amen' . . . when he looked up and saw the heavens open and saw the Son of God sittin' on the right han' side of the fathah . . . let the church say 'Amen.' . . . If ya don't come tonight, it jes' might happen that there won't be anodder night that you will be able to come . . . I'm askin', the church is askin', God is askin' you to come tonight."

"Come," he screamed out suddenly. "Come, while the blood is still warm in your veins." Then he added, "Let the church pray. . . ."

The suddenness of his appeal almost lifted me out of my seat in fear. I was aware that all around me people began to mumble. I realized that I was the focal point of all prayers and mumbles. I was overwhelmed with shame. Glancing timidly behind me, I observed that my mother and brothers and sisters had arrived. My sister Mary, who had joined the church in a revival the year before, was looking at me very seriously. Mother had her head bowed in prayer, and my younger brothers and sisters were glancing around the church hoping that the shouting would soon begin. I wanted to get up and run. I was sure that this was not my night to get religion. Outside the church, spectators began to gather at the windows. They were waiting for the show to begin. The majority of them were what Dad called "in the world" and only came to mock and poke fun at the Christians. In the beginning he had sent a deacon outside to shoo them away; but one year a spectator "in the world" had actually got religion while peeping in. Since that time Dad made no attempt to send the spectators away.

I became aware that a fly was trying its best to alight on my forehead; each time I brushed it away, it returned to torment me. Rev. Carter was deeply engrossed in a prayer prior to his sermon; he had already begun to sweat. He loosened his tie for more volume and called out to God for my soul. I bowed my head and tried to think good thoughts to give the spirit a chance with my life. With my eyes clenched shut, I waited for the end of the prayer. When it came, I was surprised that I felt no difference; whatever feeling I was supposed to receive, prayer didn't bring it.

It was time for the sermon. Rev. Carter, with practiced precision, took out two handkerchiefs and laid them on the Bible. He looked around as if to size up the crowd. He looked at me with the shadow of a faint smile. Already his shirt was wet; he calmly removed his coat and laid it on the seat behind him. Rolling up his sleeves to the elbow, he began his message:

"This is the ouwuh," he continued, "for somebody to make up his mind." It took no great perception on my part to know that I was the "somebody" he spoke of. After announcing his subject, "Be Ye Also Ready," he read from Scripture the word that man "knows not the day nor the hour in which the Son of Man cometh." The sermon remains in my mind to this day as typical of its kind:

When the mastah came back from his journey, and found that the steward had been loafing, he got mad . . . he got mad. I tell you, 'cause you see, Jesus don't warn nobody when he's comin' . . . he might come one day when you're feelin' high (and I mean drunk), he might come one day when you're gamblin' and having a good time . . . heah me tonight . . . you can't fool God . . . he sees you, he knows about you. Lotta folks goin' around talkin' about havin' religion . . . it jes ain't so, and ya know how I know: I kin tell by the life that you live. My God is a mighty God, and ain't no tellin' when he'll sneak up on you and find you in the midst of sin and corruption. I don't know about you, but I ain't takin' no chances; I'm goin' to be ready, and you oughta be ready. There is a sinner here tonight, and if I never have a chance to speak again, he better heah what I'm sayin'. God is love, but if you don't open up your heart and let Jesus come in, hell is goin' to be your home . . . and son, you cain't hide to save your life, no, no, no . . . you cain't hide, my God can dispatch the angels from Heaven with cover snatchers in their hands, he can send out the forked lightnin' and split apart your hidin' place . . . I tell you, Church, you gotta be ready. Jonah tried to hide one day . . . didn't he do it, Church . . . yes, he tried to hide, got on board a ship that was scheduled for Joppa but wound up on the sea of nowhere. Then the storms came up, the wind blowed the ship to and fro, the thundah crashed around them and the lightnin' streaked across the horizon like a mad man with twisted fingers, the waves piled up and smothered the ship. I tell you, you cain't hide 'cause God got your numbah. Religion, my friends, is nothin' to play with; either you got it or you ain't got it; everybody's name on the church book ain't goin' to heaven, 'cause too many folks hidin' behind religion, they hidin' behind the religion that Jesus died for. Jonah found out he couldn't hide when his ship's captain came down and separated the crew and found out that Jonah was hidin'; he commanded them to throw him overboard—yes, he did. They threw Jonah out in the squallin' sea and a whale came up and swallowed him whole . . .

13

oh, I know what you sayin', you don't believe that the whale swallowed him whole . . . oh, I know what you sayin', you don't believe that the whale swallowed him. That's what I say about people who call themselves educated, go on off to school and have the devil teach you that the whale's mouth ain't big enough to swallow no man. But let me tell ya, it says right here in the good book, and God don't lie, that a whale swallowed Jonah, and I believe, yes, I do. I believe that if the Bible says he was swallowed, he was swallowed. Do you believe this, young man, do you believe that God can do wonders right now if you want to come to Jesus? You gotta believe *this,* Glory Hallelujah, right now; God is asking you to come to Jesus, 'cause if a whale with a little mouth can swallow a whole man, God can save your soul. You gotta come 'cause Jesus is your only hope, Jesus is your only friend. Friends may leave you, but Jesus, Jesus, my rock, Jesus, Jesus, my shield, he's the lily of the valley, the bright and morning star, he is the rock hewed out of the mountain, he's bread when you're hungry, water when you're thirsty, he's my sword and he's my shield, Glory to God. . . .

Rev. Carter stepped from behind the pulpit, and with one leap he stood on the floor before me. The acrobatic movement seemed to ignite additional members into movement. During the course of the sermon his words had become almost inaudible because of the cries and shouts of the congregation. Standing in front of me, he took his handkerchief that was dripping with perspiration and flung it into the crowd while shouting, "He's all right!" I was aware that the three white-dressed women behind me were flailing their arms right and left. Blow after blow glanced off my back as the three women held each other in the spirit. Originally, one had begun to shout and the other two were holding her; now all of them were having a good time in the Lord. Rev. Carter went on:

"I don't know about you, but I'm goin' to be ready . . . I cain't take a chance and miss out on heaven, 'cause one day, when the wars are over, one day when I lay down my hymnbook and my Bible, one day, when the battle's fought and the victory's won, I'm goin' home. . . ."

My father was on his feet now, standing at the vacated pulpit and looking around at the confusion that was his church. He appeared to be well pleased: every now and then he would cry out to Rev. Carter, "Preach," and then in a louder voice, "Preach, suh!" Rev. Carter was obliging.

"You see, Church, a long time ago, when I was a boy in Mississippi, when I was walkin' in the cotton fields . . . Jesus spoke peace to my soul, and every, every, every day since that day—one Thursday it was—he put clappin' in my han's and runnin' in my feet, and I jes' cain't keep still 'cause he gits aaaalll ovah me."

Suddenly I began to cry. Rev. Carter proceeded to exhibit how Jesus got all over him by running up and down the aisle shaking his remaining handkerchief at the membership. The sight of the handkerchief waving produced additional shouts. One woman reached out and grabbed his shirt sleeve. He tried to shake her loose but she clung to him as if her life depended on it. Her eyes rolled back in her head and she appeared to be in a trance. I became aware that I was surrounded by officers and women of the church who stood with arms outstretched begging me to come to Jesus. For a while it appeared as if Rev. Carter had forgotten me; he continued to tell of his own conversion:

"Some folks said I didn't have it, but I felt a rumblin' in my breast and a stirrin' in my heart like it was some big stick diggin' out of my insides . . . and you know somethin', I wouldn't give a dime for a religion that won't make you cry sometimes, make you shout. . . ."

Then, as if he had suddenly remembered, he pushed his way through the small group that surrounded me and stretched out his hand.

"You bettah come tonight," he warned me.

"Amen!" encouraged the membership. I sat rooted to my seat. I seemed chained there by some spirit that defied the Holy Ghost. I was aware that my father's eyes had begun to narrow; he was looking at me as if he was about to disown me as his child. The obvious signs of his growing anger further glued me to my seat. I was feeling something, as my mother had said, but religion was not it. I was one lone soul pitted against the combined might of a church on fire. I refused to ignite. I wanted to cry out to them to leave me alone, but I feared that my outburst might be mistaken for the outward manifestation of getting religion. I sat and seethed. The three mothers fell down on their knees before me, with voices that begged and insisted that I come to Jesus. Failing in this respect, they turned back to God and asked him to bust open my heart of stone and let the Holy Spirit come in. One of them began singing:

> Come to Jesus, come to Jesus,
> Come to Jesus, right now, right now . . .
> Come to Jesus, come to Jesus,
> Right now.

The church took up the song, and it went far out into the night, out beyond the spectators and those "in the world," and up onto the street. I knew that it could be heard by Big Lizzie, who sold chitterlings on the sidewalk. Old Shoe and Po' Boy would hear it and refuse to give up their lives in the world. It would be heard by Pretty Sally in the house that we had been commanded never to look at. Her lovers were probably laughing at the foolishness going on at the church as they paid her for her favors.

> He will save you, He will save you,
> He will save you right now, right now. . . .

I wanted to tell them I didn't want to be saved, at least not right now. I was only twelve; I still wanted to play marbles—for keeps, and I still liked the movies and music from the jukeboxes. To get religion now meant I couldn't laugh at the shouters; I would have to bow my head while the others prayed in church.

> He will save you, He will save you,
> Right now.

Rev. Carter turned away almost in disgust. He was apparently giving up in his efforts to bring me into the church. My tears had originally been taken as a sign of repentance, but by now everyone knew better. I faintly remembered that the curfew hour was ten o'clock and by now it must have been at least nine-thirty. I decided to let the curfew hour save me if it

16

could. The church had quieted considerably. My mother came and sat beside me; I reached out for her hand and she held my own. I saw tears running down her face as she squeezed my hand tightly. Unlike the others, she had remained calm. But the full extent of her emotions poured out of her eyes, and I knew she was troubled. She cried there beside me, and I welcomed her tears.

> Feel the fire burning, in my heart,
> In my heart, in my heart,
> Feel the fire burning, in my heart,
> Deep down in my heart. . . .

As this song began, my father ordered two tables to be placed before the congregation—one for the church, the other for the speaker.

> It's a burning and a churning, in my heart,
> In my heart, in my heart,
> It's a burning and a churning, in my heart,
> Deep down in my heart.

I did not remain to ride home with my father and Rev. Carter. Instead, I traversed the streets of sin toward home clutching my mother's hand. The policeman who stood on the corner of Minersville Street ignored us; he knew where we had been. The stars were shining more brightly than ever and seemed to contribute to the heat of the night. Looking up at the sky, I felt as if I had just escaped from torment. I had a sudden feeling of being freed from a burning forest where men and women had been walking like trees. I hadn't spoken to Mother at all. Silently we walked toward home until I felt guilty about disappointing her and Jesus. I had to explain.

"Mother," I spoke quietly, "I didn't get anything because I didn't feel anything."

She did not speak; instead she turned back to my younger sisters and brothers who were lagging behind. She motioned them to walk in front of us. As soon as they had walked past, she looked down at me and with a knowing smile she said, "Don't worry, Son, you will."

And I did.

CHAPTER 3

Serving My Country

*A*FTER FINISHING HIGH SCHOOL IN 1943, I ENLISTED in the U.S. Navy. It was the place where all of my white buddies were going—to war, "to make the world safe for democracy." My white classmates joined the Marines, the glamour troops with the beautiful uniforms. I was turned down. At that time I could not comprehend why I was denied the opportunity to be seen in the Marine dress uniform; those were the guys the girls swooned over. I did not realize then that the Marine Corps was the one branch of service that found it extremely difficult to accept blacks. So I opted for the Navy with its bell-bottomed trousers. My basic training was in Bainbridge, Maryland: all blacks, no whites. The only whites at Bainbridge Naval Base were the officers and the instructors. My hope was to be assigned to a fighting ship, to man the guns aboard a destroyer, a cruiser, or a battleship. I wanted to be able to shoot "the yellow dogs" right out of the sky. God, how I hated those low-down Japs! Even after I was beaten up in Washington, D.C. in 1944 by two white U.S. Shore Patrolmen, I still considered the Japanese people as the enemy.

I became a highly trained member of the U.S. Navy: trained to serve white officers their dinners in the officers' mess. It was my initial hope that I would be called upon to rout the Japanese from their dug-in positions on those tiny islands where our troops were dying or dead—Guadalcanal, Bataan, Corregidor, the Marshall Islands. I desperately wanted to return home to Pottsville as a hero, even wounded. I would even sacrifice a leg or an arm; that would evoke pity. I wanted to do all that for my country. But peeling potatoes, pouring cof-

18

fee, serving meals aboard the *U.S.S. General John Pope,* a troop transport, was my war assignment, my battle zone.

During the summer and fall of 1943 the war was waging strong in the Pacific Theater of Operations. At night, while the other steward mates (all black) slept, I would go topside, sit down in the dark night on the fantail, and wonder why my country would not send me into battle. Pots and pans, meat and potatoes, shining the Captain's shoes, making up his bed —disgusting and demeaning assignments. The fire started burning in my guts, and I began to contemplate how I could protest, rebel, get back at the system.

It was aboard the *General John Pope* that I learned how to hide my anger, to smile when I felt like crying, to laugh when I wanted to shout obscenities into the teeth of the white officers whom I served. I realized then that I was a servant, a non-person—invisible. They would pay me no attention unless I would drop a plate or spill coffee in their laps. Back in the kitchen, the other blacks found ways of getting back at "the man." They would drink milk from the glasses (out of sight), then place them on the tables in the wardroom. When they served steaks, they would drop them on the dirty floor (out of sight) and then cover them over with gravy. It was a kind of black warfare, waged with a vengeance, and it was my first awakening to the salient fact that I was a black man, separate and apart from white men. I had known that before, to be sure, but I had never felt it as strongly as I did on the *General John Pope.*

It was also during that period that I learned of the massive injustices that were heaped upon my race throughout the South. In Pottsville I had been sheltered from overt segregation and knew nothing of the denial of voting, the lynching, and the extent of black dehumanization. The awareness of America's denial of equality to blacks brought into sharp focus for me my selfhood, an identity, and a sharing of the frustrations and fully developed hostility echoed by my black brothers. The stories and incidents related by my fellow mess boys from Mississippi, Alabama, and Georgia were at first unbelievable to me. Tucked away in Pottsville amid all of my white friends, I had

had my feelings of race diluted, quashed, submerged. I was not who I thought I was. Shame, guilt, denial of reality came upon me; I had lived on a cloud.

One day a white noncommissioned officer called me a black nigger, and I struck him. I was placed on report and had to appear before the Captain. It was a trial—Captain's Mast.

"Why did you strike him?" the Captain asked.

"Because he called me a black nigger," I replied.

"What else do you think you should be called?" the Captain asked me.

There it was. I dared not speak. I choked back the tears. The Captain had represented to me a hope of vindication, a man who would uphold my dignity and manhood.

"Seven days, bread and water," he sentenced me, "and while you're serving this sentence perhaps you'll realize who you really are." Deep down in the bowels of that ship was the brig. I sweated out those seven days and became actively aware that I was a black man. I swore that never again would I retreat from that awareness.

CHAPTER 4

Searching for the Fire

ISCHARGED FROM THE NAVY AFTER D-DAY, I
went home to a new city. My family had moved to
Steelton, Pennsylvania, a steel town adjacent to Harrisburg.
My chest was full of ribbons; the *General John Pope* and the
U.S.S. John COTTLE APA 110 had transported me to virtually
all the ports in the Pacific Theater of Operations. From Austra-
lia in the Pacific to England in the Atlantic, troops had em-
barked onto and disembarked from the bowels of those ships.
On both ships I was the Captain's boy. Two and a half years,
and I was unable to attain the status of a hero. Cleaning toilets
and serving food was all the Navy had taught me. But upon
discharge I was less bitter than I was confused.

I looked for a job, and I found one. It was a job in which I
could use the skills that I had been taught so carefully: a waiter
at the Harrisburg Hotel. Once again I became invisible to
whites.

It was during the summer of 1945 that something happened which propelled me out of that waiter's job and into a
new awareness. Riding the bus each day between Steelton and
Harrisburg, I began to be curiously affected by a black statue
that stood on the curb of a two-story house. This art object was
the well-known grinning black jockey, with full red lips, holding the reins in his outstretched hands to the white occupants of
the house. It was the place to tie up the white man's horse. At
first I considered it funny. But as those bus trips went on, I
began to identify with the statue. White man's nigger. My
stomach churned each time the bus approached that stop.

21

One day, when I related my feelings to my sister Phoebe, she suggested that I ask the white owner to remove it since it was offensive to black people. I did.

"Who the hell do you think you are!" screamed the white woman at the door of the house.

A waiter at the Harrisburg Hotel. That's who I was. I was a statue too, grinning that perpetual grin, striving to please, to give good service, to live on tips.

I became determined from that moment on to fight back at whites, to use my feelings to activate the fire in my bones. I returned to that house one night after dark and stealthily pried that statue from its concrete moorings. I deposited it on the woman's doorstep.

We laughed that night, my sister and I. And Daddy laughed that night. All up and down that street, when the other blacks heard the story, the whole neighborhood laughed. The word had spread: by that one simple act I had given my people pride. To them I became more than a grinning waiter at the Harrisburg Hotel; at last I had established an identity. I sometimes think that had it not been for that grinning statue, I would probably be writing about my life as a head waiter at the now defunct Harrisburg Hotel.

*   *   *   *   *

That autumn I entered Virginia Union University in Richmond, Virginia. My first flexing of my blackness was to upset train porters by not riding in the segregated coach on the switch from Washington, D.C. to Richmond. The conductor glared at me, but, strangely enough, he did not make me move. When I arrived on campus, there was no dormitory space, so I decided to board with a family close to Lombardy Street. I felt that, despite my boldness on the train, trouble would come if I refused to ride in the back of the bus. So I walked to school.

But I was a poor student. Mathematics, science, biology, French—I hated them all. And my grades reflected it. All around me were blacks who excelled in those subjects, and I became ashamed of my poor standings. Even though I loved

English composition and literature, I decided after two years that I had had enough.

I joined the Air Force in 1948 with the promise of a commission, but my scores were too low. I began studying those subjects that I had flunked at Virginia Union, and my blackness began to ebb away as I steadily rose through the enlisted ranks to become a staff sergeant. Each military station to which I was assigned—Lackland Air Force Base, Smoky Hill Air Force Base, Salina, Kansas—found me taking correspondence courses or attending a university in the vicinity. It was at Kansas Wesleyan University that I regained the confidence I needed by removing the past shame of my scholarship.

There were virtually no blacks at Kansas Wesleyan in 1949. I learned how to debate, studied and memorized much of Shakespeare, and won that school's annual McGurk oratorical contest. Robert Cardwell, a black teacher and fellow Kappa Alpha Psi brother, suggested that I was beginning to sound like good preacher material. But since I still desired a commission, and the Army had a special program that offered commissions to those in other branches who completed specific requirements, I passed their test, transferred to the Army, and was sent to Officers' Training, Camp Chaffee, Arkansas.

It was a mistake. Being barked at by uneducated, rough, and arrogant whites made me feel that my life was reverting, once again, to the Captain's boy role. My fighting back mood returned, and finally I couldn't take it anymore. I requested and was granted a return to the Air Force. My ego was restored.

I remained in the military, including the Navy stint, for a total of ten years. I do not regret those years. Those were years in which I was struggling for a self-concept, a way out, a focus on life. It was a time when most blacks were at the stage of thinking of or developing solutions to the problems of race. No black leaders had emerged to give us direction or hope. We were floundering in a white world, being accepted or rejected with mixed reviews. It was a period for black individuality. No surging cries for freedom for the black masses were heard. It was the postwar era of the Tucker Car, the newness of television, the hand-chopping speeches of Harry Truman. These were the Douglas MacArthur years, with the Marshall Plan for Europe. The back of the bus still held us in the South, while the ghettoes were expanding in the North. Nobody ever even imagined that blacks would revolt, burn, and loot the cities. We were too newly out of war and still clutching the vestiges of patriotism, still believing that we had a stake in making the world safe for democracy. During that time we considered only the KKK and White Citizens Council the enemy.

It was a time for me as a black to cast about for what to plan for and what to do with the rest of my life. Historically— up to that point—most successful blacks had become so by either teaching or preaching. Both professions kept us in a black environment, free from adapting and adjusting to whites. I consider the ten years I spent between high school and the ministry as a refuge from those things and events that were unclear or undefined. It was a time in which my blackness was in a holding pattern, a vacuum. The occasional fire came forth as sporadic flickers, lacking intensity or overall purpose. It was a time of self-indulgence and a search for myself—of who I was and where I was going.

PART II
Ecclesiastical Fires

CHAPTER 5

Serving God

*M*Y EVENTUAL DECISION TO ENTER THE CHRIStian ministry was an easy one. Early exposure to life in the black world did not offer many alternatives. No dramatic event brought on this decision, but collective experiences that emphasized a need to serve the purposes of God. My entrance into the ministry was fortified by the nature of the black church. Its position in the social order not only served as a refuge from a world that was too much with us, but also as a creative instrument to fortify its people against the unbearable social conditions with which they were surrounded. Few other institutions indicated promise for future hope commensurate with the overwhelming needs of a ruptured society.

I had come to see why my father and Rev. Carter were so anxious for me to "get religion" back when I was a boy of twelve or thirteen. The black church represented the one area of life in which black people could be free—could be themselves. The fires in the bosom of a young man or woman could be channeled to burn for God and the body of his believers rather than in the much more dangerous realm of white society.

Entrance into the black church carried with it a soothing effect. All my inhibitions vanished, and it became my purpose to bring to the institution of the church the best that I could offer. I chose it as my life's vocation because I felt that it was worthy of full-time service. Yet, in relationship to the history of black ministers who told of their call, I suffered by comparison. A review of the traditional call is in order to set in perspective the origin of the black minister and the black church.

27

The ambiguous nature of the black church's structure and ministry has a perplexing history. Recognizing it as an intensely emotional institution, some historians have attempted to trace its characteristics back to the African culture from which the early slaves were taken. W. E. B. Dubois, one of America's earliest black scholars, wrote in 1898: "The Negro Church is the only social institution of Negroes which started in the Africa forests, and survived slavery." The implication is that the earliest black minister was an offshoot of the transplanted African priest—the man who interpreted the supernatural and who, by his rituals, became interpreter of the unknown.

Other historians claim that there is no connection between the rituals of Africa and the early characteristics of the black church. They advance the argument that the black church is a development of the assimilated culture of the white religionists. Carter G. Woodson, an authority on early black history, traces the emotional church back to the "Dawn of the New Day." This movement began in New England during the latter years of the eighteenth century. The white Methodist and Baptist churches during those years had mounted an intense program of conversion among the slaves. Typical in these New England revivals of the white masses was the expression of emotion through faintings and convulsions during the revival meetings. When the Methodists and the Baptists began revivals in the South, large numbers of blacks, attracted by this free form of religious behavior, were converted into those two denominations. The ministers of these white churches, lacking the training of their counterparts in the established Episcopalian, Presbyterian, and Lutheran churches, had greater appeal to the poor and ignorant slave. The sermon emphasis strove for "feeling" as a sign of conversion; and this emphasis found ready response among black slaves.

The "dangers" associated with the "aroused" religious slave, who, upon being exposed to the gospel, began forming a new image of himself, led the slave masters to take steps to curtail this fervor. Black code laws were established. One such code read as follows:

Meetings or assemblies of slaves, or free Negroes, or Mulattoes mixing or associating with such slaves, above the number of five, in the daytime or at night, under whatsoever pretext, shall be deemed an unlawful assembly. And any Justice of the Peace of the county, or Mayor or Chief Magistrate of any incorporated town, whenever such assemblage should be held, either from his own knowledge or on information from others, may issue his warrant, etc. . . . and all slaves offending therein shall be tried in the manner hereinafter provided for the trial of slaves.

This code reveals that the slave had evidently begun to constitute a problem of control, induced primarily by his religious activities. His new identity as a child of God had been given to him by proselytizing white ministers. These conditions and restrictions were later to give rise to the birth of the established black churches. The black church in its infancy was called an "invisible institution." Wherever blacks gathered for worship, isolated from white people, they imitated the white worship order but observed it in their "own way." In their own way they gave full vent to their emotions, unrestricted by the presence of the white people. The services were characterized by shouting and other ecstatic forms of behavior. As these "invisible institutions" progressed in form, they spurred the growth in numbers of black preachers, who naturally encouraged their revivalistic energies.

These men, like the white ministers who first introduced them to "Jesus," had little or no training at all. Some could not read. Yet, to support their claims to leadership, they told of their "call" to preach. This call assumed mysterious proportions, such as being "struck by a bolt out of the blue" or "hearing a voice that said 'go preach!' " This mysterious call was a qualifying stamp of being accepted by other blacks as a man of God.

The natural result of this call was to encourage others to "feel" the presence of God. In order to enter the church, one had to offer evidence of a startling religious experience—to "feel the fire burning," to "get religion." The psychological result was an emotional dramatization to justify one's entrance into Christianity. The joyous aspects of these experiences were the results of "becoming a new creature." The slave, separated from his blood ties, seldom could identify with a family that he could really call his own. To meet in church with those who had similar deprivation was the highlight of his week. The strong emotional pull of religion shaped his life into one of tolerable acceptance.

To say that the emotional nature of the black's worship is a carryover from his African background is questionable. It was taught to him by his masters on the soil that made him a prisoner not only to the white man's customs but also to his religion. His exuberance is recognized by the loss of restraints that his religion offered. His trials were more pronounced; consequently, the freedom of expression was emphasized to match his condition. There was fire in his bones. The black church called for the minister to completely readjust his values by minimizing the theological concepts and emphasizing the customs and emotions of the people he was called to serve. Today this difficult adjustment between training and serving the emotions of blacks is a difficult stream that black clergymen seldom cross. If one is able to ford this stream, he does it at the risk of alienating his followers.

Thus, many a black minister is trapped in the black world and must perform the traditional functions as the primitive medicine man until he tires of his task. It does not take him long to discover that one sure path to mass popularity and acceptance is to deviate as little as possible from the traditions set up by his forefathers. The emotions of his people are volatile, and he must do his best to "carry on" as if he still lived in the dark days of slavery. With practice and precision, he introduces the congregation to the theme that he must always use as a frame of reference in every sermon that he preaches: the tragedy of the cross, which is, of course, identifiable with the plight of his listeners. He dramatizes the mistreatment of Christ, who was spit upon, despised, and whipped. The spark that he ignites sets up rhythmic patterns that are designated to "set the church on fire."

The necessity of continuing on in the mold of traditional behavior, then, is clear. In fact, the longer these ministers cling to the techniques of the past, the more popular and imitable they become. Black associations, conventions, and other gatherings fortify the traditions. Those who are called upon to preach at these gatherings are selected on the basis of their ability to arouse.

As I have illustrated above, the getting of religion was expected to be accompanied by emotional behavior. Potential church members were asked to sit in the "moaners' bench" and there await the power of God. The presence of a sinner on the moaners' bench served to electrify the membership into anxious expectancy, and few souls indeed could run the risk of refusing to accept Christ. Consequently, those on the bench came forward to join the "converted" either out of fear or shame. From this conversion arose a new vocabulary for the new soul: "changed," "born again," "soul set on fire." All of this was induced by the fiery sermons and songs that ministers brought out of the past. From this time on, such a black convert lived through the rigors of continual emotional upheavals that were part of the church's life. The minister was asked to continue to "preach the word," but more often than not the word became senseless ramblings tacked on to the end of a weak theology. Since God is never clearly understood until he makes someone "happy," or when shouts fill the church, these became the strongest manifestation that the "Lord is surely with us."

The black minister then makes a frightful discovery: religion offers release from life. Now that he has brought to the surface the raging torrent of the emotional needs of his people, he must keep them there. Unless someone in his flock gets "happy," he has failed in his task. He discovers that people who have been battered by life must lean on him for support, and he dares not refuse them the crutch they sorely need. From that point on, he commends them in a loud voice to God. Because no one else can, God becomes a "way maker," one who will "make a way out of no way." The Son of God becomes a "heart fixer" and a "mind regulator."

All of these expressions of escape are skillfully interwoven in sermon, song, and prayer. Many a black minister, whose conscience informs him of the irrevocable damage that is inflicted on the emotional makeup of his parishioners, nonetheless dares not deviate from the path that he has chosen to follow. The membership demands that he bring them in word and song to the foot of the cross. They demand it from their position of need. The world has offered them nothing because a segregated society offers no hope. Battered lives must find stability in the promise of religious experience. Their joy must abound in the essence of seeking; if God has no immediate solutions, at least they will have a good time hearing about it from the man they have chosen to lead them. So on they sing: "I got a home up in that Kingdom, ain'ta that good news?"

Each Sunday the black minister mounts the pulpit with the realization of the task that he has before him. The high point of his message comes only when he reminds his listeners of their own hard times. He develops in time a chain of references which, each time repeated, paradoxically makes his worshippers happy. Then he must identify himself with the troubles of his people, for he too must "climb up the rough side of the mountain," he too has "friends that forsake him," he too must "bear the burden in the heat of the day." From this central theme of despair and loneliness his sermon moves on to the cross. The cross is successfully projected as the symbol of the black man's suffering. It has all the ingredients of self-identification: the futility of the struggle, the Garden of Gethsemane, the torture of carrying it. It is at this point that a song is remembered and sung:

> Must Jesus bear the Cross alone and all the world go free?
> No, there's a cross for everyone and there's a cross for me.

It is not long before the black minister finds himself so immersed in these patterns that he becomes hypnotically enthralled with his own power to manipulate the emotional behavior of the congregation. The pattern thus established may create a kind of righteousness that cannot be argued away. The visible evidence of his power of persuasion magnifies the black minister's feeling of self-importance, and this feeling is shared by his flock. It is not unusual for blacks to feel that they are highly favored by God. Many openly admit skepticism concerning the validity of the "white man's cold religion."

The Black Muslim movement, founded upon racial ex-
clusivity, is a radical extension of this philosophy. It is a black
religion that has no room for the white man. The black church
itself does not put forth such outlandish claims, but lurking
beneath the surface is a subtle black hostility that has encouraged such movements.

In the church of my childhood, my father's pastorate in
Pottsville, my Sunday School teacher taught me that Christ
was black. He submitted his proof on the basis of the Bible's
descriptive reference to Christ's hair as resembling "lamb's
wool." It was not long before I discovered that worship, within
some black churches, invited biased interpretations of the Bible
to support the need for required dignity. Under the influence of
these interpretations, they did not find it difficult to assume a
kind of spiritual superiority. The story is told of a white minister who in a paternalistic spirit visited a black church. The
black minister called upon the visiting minister to pray. The
white minister prayed thus:

> Oh Lord, we are so happy to be worshipping with our Negro
> brethren, and Lord, we understand the problems they face in this
> life. But they are good Negroes and Lord, when I get to heaven, I
> pray that our Negro brethren and sisters will be given a seat
> somewhere in the back of the Kingdom.

When this prayer of racist concern was concluded, the
black minister, with eyes blazing, responded: "Let *us* pray."
He began:

> Lord, you have heard the prayer from our white brother, and
> Lord, you know all about him. In your own way, Lord, let him
> know that *if* he gets to heaven, all of us Negroes are going to sit
> where we damned well please!

This story and others similar to it have circulated freely in the
black church, and its underlying motivation is not quite as
humorous as the anecdote portends.

Stratification of religion into caste and custom places the
black minister in a precarious position: either he must proclaim
the gospel of the church as a social support system for the op-

pressed, or he must reject it. There is virtually no middle
ground. The black church, then, is a product of injustice. It is a
living symbol of this nation's social failures.

*   *   *   *   *

I entered the ministry, and once I found myself there, the
black church held me to its bosom, filled me with its fire, and
then thrust me out into the white world. Prior to that thrust, I
accepted the call to my first pastorate, the Fifth Ward Baptist
Church in Clarksville, Tennessee. Clarksville was a segregated
town.

Segregated schools.

Segregated hospitals.

Segregated U.S.O.

Segregated lunch counters.

Segregated cemeteries.

Segregated Austin Peay State University.

I sounded no protests; I did not know how. I had never
fought or challenged white society in behalf of my people
before. I had always reserved that fire for myself, for individual
acts of personal "heroism." So I preached Jesus and him
crucified, and the promise of being born again. I imposed upon
myself a blindness to the black condition. Fifth Ward was a
small church, and all my people demanded of me was that I
give them Jesus.

In 1956 I accepted a call to the Liberty Baptist Church in
Evansville, Indiana. The scales on my eyes were gradually
loosened as I began to really see and feel the black condition.
Each day of the week for the next ten years I lived for that moment when I could stand in the pulpit before my people and
propel my feelings into their lives. That decade of pastoring the
Liberty Baptist Church was one of inner and outer turmoil; but
the turmoil was not within the church. I experienced the love of
my people and their acceptance of me as their spiritual leader.

A startling idea had come down from the President of the
United States: the dream of a Great Society. It was as if the
gospel were about to be fulfilled. The people that I led and their

children were shackled to the present and, without dramatic change, would be to a racially restricted future. My sermons to them were mixtures of Jesus' gentleness and my fiery condemnations of the structures and forces outside of God's house that were steadily draining away their dignity. I blessed their newborn babies, prayed publicly for their sick, buried their dead, and comforted their bereaved. That was the inner turmoil.

The total black experience from the cradle to the grave, a mixture of laughter, pain, and tears, was for me an indescribably shattering experience. The pain in the lives of black people comes far too often, and the laughter helps only to minimize the flow of tears. Stillborn babies, cancer, tuberculosis, murder, jail, alcoholism, drugs, unemployment, underemployment, welfare, discrimination—all of these were a part of my ministerial task to deal with, to pray for, to help erase with the spiritual healing waters. To be sure, there was no uniqueness in my experience—merely the historical record of all black people. None escapes entirely from the rope of injustice, the religious foundations that defy and confront it. Black ministers find themselves absorbing the full load of both personal and communal oppression. The more they love the people they pastor, the more they begin to develop hostilities toward the destructive white forces that deny them an equal existence in a free society.

But institutionalized white racism, as such, was not known to me then; each hurt was a personal, private occurrence that I could not see as a link in the collective chain of massive white racism. During those years I was also blinded by the good will of whites who worked for better race relations. Whatever fires of resentment I felt concerning what was happening to black people in Evansville were quelled by my working with whites for better race relations. Improving race relations, as I now see it in retrospect, was actually a device they used to curtail black protestation. "Niggers, keep quiet," "do not penetrate beyond our comfort level," "help us to feel good about ourselves," "minimize our guilt" were their unspoken feelings. I preached of love in their churches on Brotherhood Sunday. On other occasional visits I was asked to pray, read Scripture, give invocations, and pronounce benedictions. I performed well, like a robot responding to a button, for the total concept of blackness had not yet emerged in me. I was caught in the conflicting pulls of trying to be a spiritual leader, an emerging protestor, and a balm to the whites. I joined their councils of churches and ministerial associations. I must have diluted my blackness completely when they elected me vice president of the Evansville Ministerial Association. What happened next completely shocked them, for the inner fire in my bones was beginning to come forth.

CHAPTER 6
Rebirth in a Barbershop

*I*T HAPPENED IN A WHITE BARBERSHOP CALLED
Emory's. Three chairs, one bootblack stand; three white
barbers, one black bootblack. Sit-ins had not yet engulfed
America, the nation had not yet heard of Martin Luther King,
Jr., and the back of the bus was still the place for blacks
throughout the South. Rosa Parks was still riding the buses in
Montgomery, Alabama, consenting to be degraded, not yet too
tired to sit down. I had no role models to imitate; I was just a
Baptist preacher in a sleepy little city, burning with a desire to
help and comfort my people. The bootblack in that shop was an
occasional visitor to the Liberty Baptist Church. He had been
paroled from prison the year before and had visited my office
seeking employment. Without employment he would be sent
back to prison to serve out the rest of his term. His problem
was just one of the thousands that exist in every city in the
nation.

As I walked by, I didn't really see the barbershop. I was
not interested in getting a haircut; and even if I needed one,
white barbers were not trained to cut black people's hair. But I
did see in that shop a black man who was reluctant to come to
church, struggling to survive, and smiling at me as I walked
by. I stopped, smiled back, went in, and shook his hand. We
conversed. Yes, he was doing all right; yes, he would begin attending church. Mission accomplished. I glanced at my shoes,
and they were dirty. So I climbed onto the shoeshine stand.

"Get out of that chair!" It was the voice of the shop owner,
Mr. Emory. I was shocked not only by the command but by
the tone of the voice: it was high-pitched and threatening.

37

"Why?" I asked, controlling my voice. "All I want is a shoeshine."

"Not in here! We don't shine Negroes' shoes in this shop." The fact that he said "Negro" instead of "nigger" surprised me, because his drawl and tone were of the deep South. He was poor white, poorly educated; the contrast to my background, education, and grooming was a ludicrous one.

"But I want a shoeshine," I objected, "and this is a public place."

"Not for you, it ain't. And if you're not out of that chair in ten seconds, by God, an ambulance will be here to haul you away."

Through the years, as I look back on that scene, I realize that it was really the first time I stared death in the face. Because as Emory spoke, he pulled out a drawer and put his hand inside as if to draw out a gun. The shoeshine man ran out onto the sidewalk. But I sat frozen to my seat because there was no strength in my legs; they were stiff with fright. Emory's eyes were like pits of fire, and his hand outside the drawer was trembling. The other two barbers, as I remember, were looking at Emory in shock.

Each second that I sat there, my manhood, pride, and self-concept were draining away. I tried to find something to say, but nothing would come out of my mouth. I foolishly began to wonder how I would look dead, who would come to my funeral, and why I had to die in a shoeshine stand. Who was this white man before me? What had blacks done to him in the past? Did I remind him of the failures in his life, the lost opportunities to achieve success like millions of whites before him? I had spent seven days on bread and water for hitting a white man who had called me a "nigger," but that was when I was in my teens, when nonviolence was not yet in vogue and not yet a working theological concept within me. In those few seconds Emory was deciding my future; it was a magic moment to decide what I was to do in the future, a moment to decide the end of me or, worse yet, the end of my manhood.

> Once to every man and nation,
> Comes the moment to decide,

In the struggle for the future,
For the good or evil side.

I now thank God for Mr. Emory, that scrawny, rednecked white man in Evansville. He, more than any other person, conceptualized my growth and stoked up the fire that had been flickering in my bones for years. I was coming to grips in that chair with the noble meaning of a shoeshine, of how one's spilled blood could become a process of conquering evil. This thought comes now only as a reflection after the fact; it certainly did not come then, for in the space between Emory's words and my eventual decision, time stood still. No philosophy was in play—only a draining, hollow emptiness, like a gas tank with no station in sight. I made a decision. It was not to be a hero, for heroes do not emerge from shoeshine stands but from the heat of battle where the stakes are high. Heroes are made by the masses, who admire their courage and their sacrificed offerings for others, not for a pair of dirty shoes. It would have made better sense and public press if, instead, I would have sat down in Mr. Emory's barber chair and commanded him to deal with my person, rather than asking his "boy" to shine my shoes. I would have then entered his shop with a sense of purpose, a defiant mission that would have earned me a fitting epitaph on my plaque in the black hall of fame.

"To thine own self be true" I had learned from Shakespeare in a white English class. Mr. Emory did not know it, but he was facing down a black man who had studied all of Shakespeare's works, taught to him by a bigoted white teacher at Kansas Wesleyan University in 1951. My thoughts went back to that year, the year I married Annese; it was she who had held my book and checked out my meaning. As the only black in that class, I was determined to memorize pages of Shakespeare, to quote his plays and sonnets as if I were an Oxford scholar. The white students at that university marveled at my ability to memorize, but Dean Stanley Trickett (later to become president of Kansas Wesleyan) reluctantly awarded me first place in the school's annual oratorical contest, and my teacher's final reward for my class efforts was a grade of "C." And now the orator was to die over a shoeshine.

"And it must follow as night the day, thou canst not then be false to any man." That day in Emory's barbershop I knew who I was, that I had allowed myself to be false to white people. I had learned how to skillfully compromise my blackness, to smile quaintly at racial jokes as long as they came from whites engaged in "better relations." It was the tacit acceptance of white liberals as the best you could get out of the white race. They were the ones who would later denounce Emory's threat on my life, only later to inquire of me privately why I had gone into a place like that—an unmasking of their own subtle white racism. I speak of these things now for I can look back at that chair with a crystal gaze. I can milk my thoughts for all the implications that that moment gave me, the steadfast determination from that moment onward to free the fire locked up in my bones. My decision of that moment has been washed away by the tide of black protestation that would soon sweep the nation. Individual acts of protest were multiplied all across the nation, but the white press buried them under the indicting title of "disorderly conduct." The liberal press in those days was not advocating justice but "better relations," while the barbershops, hotels, buses, drinking fountains, voting booths, and five-and-dime stores were rejecting black people.

My decision was to remain in that shoeshine chair. I had to remain. The black man who was witnessing my human debasement deserved to witness the stiffening of a black backbone. This was his moment also. I was doing what he would never be able to do; he was out of prison but still in chains. His opportunities to become somebody had been erased.

So I sat. I had called Emory's bluff. I stared at him almost hoping that he would shoot me—perhaps in the shoulder for I did not want to die. Something within me told me he would not shoot, but I could not completely trust that something.

> Shoot if you must this old grey head,
> But spare your country's flag, she said.

The words of Barbara Fritchie marched into my thoughts from out of white history. A white woman, so full of love for her flag, had invited death for the sake of saving the old rag from burning during the Revolution. "How stupid!" I thought. "I only regret that I have but one life to give for my country," said the patriot Nathan Hale.

"I'm going to sit here until I either get a shoeshine or an ambulance hauls me away," I found myself saying to Mr. Emory. As I look back, if I would have been shot, it would not have been to save a flag or even Nathan Hale's country. If I had died, those dirty old black shoes would at last have shined, stained red by my blood.

Emory called the police. Two burly cops, Evansville's finest, came to take me away. A crowd had gathered outside, summoned by the flashing red lights and the blaring siren. Emory had reported that a black man was being disorderly in his shop. The cops came in with nightsticks in hand, ready to crush a black skull. It would not have been the first. I had politely complained to Mayor Vance Hartke about the brutality of the Evansville Police, but he had done nothing to stop it. Some of the officers—the ones whose beat ran through the ghetto—were worse than others. Acting as policemen, judges, jury, and executioners combined, and seeking to devour, these men meted out justice on behalf of the entire judicial system. Operating out of a "them versus us" mentality, they drew guns more quickly, their trigger fingers were itchier, and their nightsticks were more ready against blacks than against whites. I was later to learn that every major civil disorder that was to occur in the 1960s was a consequence of the interaction between blacks and white policemen, working in pairs, like the two officers who were now ordering me out of Emory's barbershop.

> Just like a tree,
> Planted by the waters,
> I shall not be moved.

The refrain from the old Negro spiritual ran through my mind as I refused the order to disembark from the shoeshine chair.

"I have a right to be here, officer; this is a public place, and the Indiana statutes protect my right to be served," I stated, quoting the appropriate law. But my knowledge of the law was to no avail in the face of these "officers of the law." After declaring me a "f---ing smart ass," they seized me—a veteran of ten years' service in Uncle Sam's Navy, Army, and Air Force, the pastor of the Liberty Baptist Church, and almost elected vice president of the Evansville Ministerial Association —by both legs and arms and carried me out through the crowd and thrust me headfirst into the back seat of the patrol car.

It was my first civil rights jailing. In the years to come I would become accustomed to the dirty cells with crawling roaches, the clanging of steel doors, the dispassionate look on the faces of white jailors, and the perpetual question of jail drunks and criminals-in-residence: "What are you here for?" But in the late 1950s jail had not yet become honorable for an honorable black man. It was soon to receive the stamp of approval of Martin Luther King, Jr.; but at the time of my first arrest, my mentor was still studying about Gandhi at Crozier Theological Seminary.

What bothered me the most was that my name would appear in the morning paper, and what I had been charged with was not only a lie, but lies heaped on lies.

DRUNK!
DISORDERLY!
CAUSING A PUBLIC NUISANCE!
RESISTING ARREST!

Sweet Jesus, what had I done to deserve this? The truth, the real story—please God!—let it be known. I sat in the corner of that urine-stinking cell weeping copious tears that only innocent men can shed. Those damnable shoes! I thought of the many things I could have done—should have done—that might have saved me from this disgrace. I envisioned my church disowning me, my white friends deserting me. It was a strange feeling, this first jailing. I certainly was not proud of my actions now that it had come to this.

However, the black grapevine was at work, and the news spread quickly. My people, my beautiful people, bailed me out. A mass meeting was held that next night, and the church was full. Black people—angry black people—came in droves.

CHAPTER 7

The Social Gospel

*I*T WAS OUT OF THE CONTEXT OF THE SHOESHINE
episode that I ran for the office of president of the Evansville Chapter of the NAACP. I won. From that moment, the
gospel that I preached was almost entirely a social gospel. No
more "heaven is my home," but rather the gospel of earthly
social redemption. Full employment was one key to current
black despair. Beyond Emory's barbershop was an issue that
called for instant attack. Job discrimination. One of the largest
employers in the city of Evansville was the Mead Johnson
Company. Using the Liberty Baptist Church as a meeting
place for plans for active protest, we devised a plan to picket
Mead. Out of their thousands of employees, Mead Johnson at
that time had one black employee: Alonzo Cooper was Mead
Johnson's personal chauffeur. I held a news conference deploring that fact and announcing at the same time that the NAACP
would protest Mead's hiring practices by establishing picket
lines outside their plant. Howls of protest emerged from press
editorials and my white liberal friends. Their arguments were
based on Mead's philanthropic endeavors in the city. Every
worthy civic cause was supported by Mead Johnson dollars.
Why pick on such a fine company that had a proven record of
civic endeavor?

We picketed.

The *Evansville Press,* which had just completed a series of
penetrating articles on black unemployment, editorialized
against our actions, calling for a "quiet approach" as the "bet-

ter way.'' I responded to that editorial with the following letter to the editor:

To the Editor of The Press:

This letter is being written in sincere appreciation for the fair and accurate reporting in regards to Negro employment. Edna Folz and Tom Ryder are to be commended for their comprehensive report: "Jobs Are Negroes' Number One Problem" (Friday, June 7, 1963). The research and analytical summarizations were informative and enlightening.

It was written in a manner that all sides were represented and enabled us all to better appreciate the vast scope of a difficult problem. In fact, it might well be that it served in a measure to temper the issue into one of intelligent presentation that neither side could accomplish alone. All of us needed that.

However, your editorial on the same date, "Quiet Talk Is Better Way,'' left most of us surprised. Surely you must be aware that this is the story of our lives. Your better way has been walked by the Negro for years. In this way since Emancipation, he has begged, pleaded and implored society for his rights.

Quiet talks did not persuade Governor Barnett and apparently will not dissuade Governor Wallace. Let's face facts: Every effort to achieve our rights has been as a consequence of the Negroes' insistence. The same is true of our advances in Evansville.

The Negro has learned that if he is to receive his equitable share in a democratic society, he must stand up within the structure of that democracy and utilize his right of protest. His dignity requires it, his condition demands it. For every advance made in the conference rooms of quiet talks, ten others are being made by the therapeutic necessity of our voices crying out in the wilderness.

The Negroes of Evansville, assisted by the Ministerial Association, Council of Churches, church women, interracial committees, Interdenominational Civic Committee, NAACP, and even the Mayor's Commission, have been communicating with local industry for several years in the arena of your "better way.'' The carpet to the mayor's office and major industry has been worn thin by our feet.

Together we have breakfasted, lunched and dined over the problem, with the only resulting benefit that of a good meal. Indeed, while we were talking quietly, our Negro youth who could not hear nor understand the language of diplomacy, just as quietly reached for their suitcases and left our "Valley of Opportunity'' for greener pastures.

Today, the only evidences left of those quiet talks are the astronomical soaring of the Township Relief program and our memories crammed with broken promises.

Ironically, while you are advocating the quiet talks continuing, President Kennedy, speaking to Mayor McDonald and other U.S. mayors in Hawaii, stated, "It is clear to me that the time for token moves and idle talk is over. Justice cannot wait for too many meetings."

What has brought about these urgent demands? The truth is, the same so-called "flamboyant approach" that you beg we resist the temptation to use. To use the words of John A. Hannah, chairman of the Federal Civil Rights Commission, in your editorial was proper, warning that the current struggle for equal rights was dividing the nation. But you failed to quote additional parts of his speech:

"Philosophically, a slow tedious advance toward equality in employment, etc., is best, but the individual Negro cannot afford to be that philosophical. Instead of being critical of Negro leaders who now demand action, we should be grateful to the American Negro for their patience, forbearance and tolerance."

If picketing was not the answer, at least it raises the question. A question that even you had not raised until the picketing began. We have discovered, Mr. Editor, that one sure way of opening doors to industry and all other rights is to stand at the door and pound away until our knuckles bleed. If any other way can bring the results that we are now experiencing all over the nation, please tell us now and spare us the pain.

If Evansville Printing Corporation and other industries can lead us into the haven of employment in fulfilling their moral and ethical responsibilities to the disinherited few, perhaps this will serve as a catalyst for a great awakening. When this happens, we shall gladly burn our picket signs and return to quiet talks. We agree, this is the better way, but it has not been best for us.

God grant us the courage to do that which is right—rather than that which is quiet and expedient. After all, quiet talks did not make America. It was because of the voices raised in protest that the Negro now echoes, "No taxation without representation."

To ask the Negro now to resist the temptation of the flamboyant approach is the same as requesting the slave to remain on the plantation—and wait. To say that our approach is dangerous is to say that cancer is best treated with patent medicines.

As far as community responsibility is concerned, no community will grow any larger than its weakest minority. Consequently, Evansville, led by men of vision, should deplore its schizocarpous existence.

We cannot afford to have two images—one to attract new industries and another to deny its citizens a fair share of its progress. We want our city to move ahead, but please take us with you.

Therefore, we have stored away our picket signs, and we shall temporarily "resist the temptation of the flamboyant approach." The move on the checkerboard of equal rights is up to those who can do something about it. And as they ponder, it would be well to keep before them the concluding remarks made by Dr. Hannah, which also were omitted from your quotes from his speech:

"The Negro has just one lifetime. Who can blame him for wanting to enjoy those rights within his own lifetime?"

Frankly even this is a conservative statement. As one Negro student said to me recently, "We not only want our rights now, today, we also want them yesterday."

Rev. Charles H. King, Jr.
Liberty Baptist Church

*   *   *   *   *

Next came a challenge to an old, established Evansville tradition, the annual St. Ben's Minstrel Show. Each year the town was overrun by black-faced whites who posted signs all over town announcing the minstrel show. It was held at St. Benedict's Catholic Church and sponsored by the Catholic laity. As far as I was concerned, Mr. Bones and his charcoaled white brethren had to go. As President of the NAACP, I sent an angry letter to the Bishop. The Bishop arranged for me to meet with the men of St. Ben's. It was a hot meeting. The press sat outside while we debated the issue. The following day's *Press* headline indicated the outcome:

Minister Wins Battle;
Last Year for Blackface

The white press once again expressed its displeasure with my tactics. This time the defense of the racist practice came from a close friend of mine, a daily columnist named Bish Thompson of the *Evansville Press.* He wrote:

Dan Emmett, one hundred years ago this month, gave the world a great spirit-booster.

It was a song. He wrote it on 24-hour notice as a "walk-around" for a minstrel show he was in.

The jubilant lilt of the melody and the exuberance of the lyrics lifted it from its original use and spread it across the land.

"Dixie" was one of several beloved products of the blackface minstrel show, one of the few purely American forms of entertainment.

It is an odd quirk of circumstance that on the centennial anniversary of "Dixie" the curtain goes down for the last time on blackface minstrel show in this old river town.

As I understand it, the permanent boom was lowered on this long popular and time honored type of entertainment by one man, the Rev. Charles King, local president of the National Association for the Advancement of Colored People.

He called upon the men of St. Benedict's Catholic Church, told them he was racially embarrassed by publicity and promotion attending their seventh annual blackface minstrel show.

They promised to never again so offend if Mr. King would withdraw his objection to this year's show, then in final rehearsal.

The reverend was magnanimous.

I talked to my friend Charlie King about this the next day and told him I thought he was wrong. He said in his opinion I was wrong. I stated I thought such a move, right or wrong, had probably lost for his cause more ground than it had gained.

In my opinion, the American people as a whole are getting too blasted touchy.

Recording vocalists must sing watered down lyrics to avoid offending someone. "Hear the banjos ringing, the people are singing. . . ." Little Black Sambo got the heave-ho.

What's it coming to?

No comedy scenes featuring a country bumpkin. The Farm Bureau might rise up and boycott the show.

No jokes about the Scotch being tight with their money . . . no Swedes, no Lo, the Poor Indian, no smartalecky remarks about fat girls. . . . A white Protestant politician is just about the only fair game left. . . .

I could not let Bish Thompson get away with that unanswered. The following was my personal response to him.

Dear Bish:

For Shame! Just think, I was one of your original boosters for Mayor. It was surprising to learn that Dan Emmett gave birth to the minstrel 100 years ago, for this same type of minstrel has caused concern among Negroes for just as many years. The only possible way for you to feel this concern would be to live as a Negro.

The spread of "Dixie" and several other "beloved" black-faced minstrel shows has made its mark upon a people who have strived for years to erase the blight of stereotype; surprisingly enough, there are just as many varieties and "types" of people in our group as there are in yours.

It was no "odd quirk of fate that on the centennial anniversary of 'Dixie' that the curtain goes down," but it goes down because intelligent people were able to sit down at a conference table and discuss the pros and cons of said entertainment and arrive at a conclusion in an amiable and democratic way. This curtain goes down in the future in tribute to the men of St. Ben's who realized that: the boom was not lowered by one man, it was lowered by Americans' awakening conscience that should ensure the inculcation of belief in and respect for the inherent worth and dignity of human personality, irrespective of racial identification, religious belief, or political affiliation.

Your beautiful lament for the minstrel written from your Ernie Pyle-winning desk was a moving masterpiece; frankly, it almost made a believer of me. But after wiping away the tears, I was able to see that one by one you cited arguments for the end of the minstrel and stereotyped jokes: "It is a disappearing aspect of America's humor." Thank God for America! It is a disappearing aspect because America realizes that blackface buffoonery, Jewish dialect jokes, and other performances made at the expense of any racial or religious *minority* threatens if not actually destroys the dignity of that minority. "Little Black Sambo" and, for that matter, "The Merchant of Venice" are fast disappearing from the classrooms of our children because of the indelible imprint that it *could* make upon their growing minds.

Weber and Fields may make America howl, but *all* America will not howl with them, for intelligent sponsorship realizes that where some howl in laughter, others cringe in disgust. You see, Bish, it boils down to this: the smiles of a group of people should never ignore the tears of another.

Remember how we enjoyed playing together in the same scene in the local production of "Sunday's Child"? You were the judge and I the slave. I was not nor shall I ever be sensitive of my skin. I was proud to depict an honest and historical account of America's history. The Negro is a part of that history, and he is not ashamed of his racial heritage. Never would I, nor should you, portray any dialect rendering prototype that runs the risk of permanently capturing the mind of a child who seeks to know man as he really is. No Bish, America is not getting touchy—it's getting wiser and more American.

There seems to be a misunderstanding as to the future of the minstrel in Evansville. There is no law barring its presentation; have one if you wish. Raise the curtain and let Mr. Interlocutor and Mr. Bones break forth in the best tradition of Dan Emmett. After your laughter has subsided, walk out of that auditorium and question the Negro doctor, teacher, lawyer, scientist—and don't forget, question the grade school, high school and college Negro student, and you will find out what I have found. A few of them will see no harm in the minstrel, but the overwhelming majority will agree that whereas your esteem for the Negro is not lowered, the Negro's esteem is lowered for anyone who would portray him in any light not complimentary to his God-given individual personality.

P.S. I still think you would make a good candidate for mayor, but please omit from your political platform the time-worn plank of the minstrel.

CHAPTER 8

The March on Washington

*I*N THE INITIAL STAGES OF THE BLACK REVOLU-
tion (or the "Negro Revolt") the quest for equality not
only caught this nation by surprise in its intense suddenness
but also led from initial white resentment to acceptance as a
necessary part of racial progress. Laws were slowly enacted to
rectify some of the gross injustices against black people. White
lawmakers, responding to an aroused electorate who had witnessed the use of police dogs, horses, and cattle prods as instruments of repression against blacks, reluctantly but decisively
placed legislation on the books of cities and states which legally
certified that the revolt had a basis of legitimacy. In those days,
black men had their unquestioned heroes. Chief among them,
of course, was Martin Luther King, whose Southern Christian
Leadership Conference, with its theology of passive resistance,
held full command of the black quest for equality. The SCLC
often found itself at odds with the NAACP, the historic champion of black people, because during the "Negro Revolt" it
found the latter's position untenably conservative. The direct
action approach of SCLC, CORE (under the leadership of
James Farmer), and SNIC (engineered by John Lewis) caught
the court-oriented Roy Wilkins behind the times. The leadership mantle that had been his never returned because of his initial foot-dragging. The Urban League, directed by sophisti-
cated Whitney Young, never became an integral part of direct
action. Its emphasis on employment opportunities, with built-
in rapport with white industrial and business complexes, was
not geared for the revolt. Consequently, King and his followers
stood head and shoulders above other identifiable black leader-

ship. However, King wisely recognized that a "go it alone" stance would not serve the best interests of the masses. In fact, King magnanimously left room for his slower colleagues by identifying and aligning himself with Wilkins and Young.

The events that led up to the March on Washington can now be considered the glory days of the revolt. The contained and dignified control of black leadership caught the imagination of the nation. Only John Lewis, the young turk of the black leadership ranks, rebelled at the Lincoln Memorial procession. Lewis was primed to utter the harsh realities of white supremacy, as he exemplified in his anger at the absence of President John Kennedy. He was urged by others to water down his speech, and the march eventually found itself pricking the conscience of the nation. This conscience was best expressed by the late entry of white liberals from the vocal stage of support to active participation in the full sweep of events. White racism had not yet been fully identified and excoriated; but against the backdrop of the Goldwater days, Southern recalcitrance, and hobbling attempts at legislation, the black revolt reached its highest peak.

*   *   *   *   *

The March on Washington. The church was there!

On the day blacks and whites marched on Washington, Dr. Eugene Carson Blake, stated clerk of the Presbyterian Church, stood at the foot of the Lincoln Memorial and announced to 300,000 freedom seekers: "The white church is here, but we came too late." He was right.

Somewhere in that throng stood my mother, and beside her was my seventy-nine-year-old grandfather. Both of them had ridden a special train from Connecticut to Washington to march with their son and grandson. I came by car, driving alone—fatigued yet expectant. At a Howard Johnson's rest stop I met a young man named Mike, a student at Queens College, New York. He and a carload of friends were also on their way to Washington. Noticing that I was very tired, Mike offered to ride with me and share the driving. I accepted his offer.

As we rode and talked, I discovered that Mike was an atheist. When I asked why, his answer was revealing:

"I can't believe in a church or synagogue that makes it necessary for me to go to Washington. The sight of clerical garb and stained-glass windows makes me sick."

At each rest stop along the way, we met new friends. The highways were crowded. Time after time we locked arms with strangers and sang freedom songs at those rest stops. We were on our way. Buses loaded with blacks and whites thundered down the turnpike. As we drew near to Washington, Mike rejected my attempts to present the church in the light of its historical weaknesses, but maintained that it was now alerted to perform the will of God.

"I won't buy it," he insisted. "It will never happen."

We separated at dawn at the foot of the Washington Monument. I never saw Mike again. But later in the day, when Dr. Blake expressed the lateness of the church, Mike's words came back to haunt me. Was the church too late?

It was obvious that the white church was present in Washington. It came from every stratum of organized religion —came as if summoned by the pope for council. This time the church was there in ecumenical might. The blacks' cry of "Now" had cracked the sound barrier of the white church. It was represented in the March by the glistening white collars of Episcopal priests, the skullcaps on the heads of rabbis, the crosses hanging from the necks of Lutherans that were blinding as the sun struck them. We all marched together, weeping to feelings that were inexpressible. The black church, with calmly determined images, had newly awakened out of the deep slumber of hopelessness. I shall never forget Ernest Levels, a black dishwasher from Boston, and Josephine Warner, a white schoolteacher from Brooklyn, joining hands with a Catholic priest from Arkansas. Together they sang, "We shall overcome!" Was the white church too late?

Its priests, ministers, and rabbis had been firmly entrenched behind stately architectural structures, mouthing words of concern—but caution. Its members had denied that any problems existed. They were a people who boasted of good race relations, unaware that the term "good" expressed the fact of an uneasy peace. Nothing had shaken them to row the boat in the black man's sea of bondage and misfortune. The white church, prior to the March on Washington, contained the mayors and city officials who had shuttled the "Negro question" between boards and commissions like a hot potato. Its worshippers came from suburbia, passing through black ghettos on their way to jobs that were labeled "for whites only." As they left their Sunday worship services to the strain of "Blest Be the Tie that Binds," they were unaware that the same song sounded to blacks like, "Blest Be the Chains that Bind."

Yes, the church was too late.

It was too late to save six million Jews during World War II. The most emotional appeal to America was made by a Jewish rabbi who, upon relating the atrocities and suffering in Nazi Germany, said: "It was the silence of the church, the people of religion, that was the sin much greater than the Nazi atrocities."

My mind went back to events that preceded the March on Washington. . . .

When President Kennedy made his epic appeal to the nation in behalf of black people, it came as a soothing balm to a nation that was trembling in the wake of an ignited fuse. Once before, on the heels of James Meredith's entrance into the University of Mississippi, the President had addressed the nation. While white-helmeted U.S. marshals tried to control the growing anger of students at "Ole Miss," Kennedy spoke in measured tones. His recitation of the past glory of the South (including a roll call of its heroes) left little to be added. His was an appeal to conscience, for the good of the nation and for white law and order. He appealed particularly to the students of Ole Miss; unfortunately, the majority of them did not hear him. They were gathering rocks.

The white uproar on the night of President Kennedy's speech was awesome. Secreted in a dormitory room, guarded by marshals, Meredith sat out the riot scene that was breaking beneath him. The militant, half-crazed leadership of deposed

General Walker added to the confusion. The nation was stunned when it learned that this former army commander who had put down the Little Rock "crisis" was engaged in leading a pop bottle brigade against the government. More was present at Oxford that night than the segregationists. There, for the roll call of hate, was a sickness.

Oxford contained the dying throbs of a degenerate system. It was a Jericho whose walls had been shaken by the marching feet of black progression. The seams of the garment made by "King Cotton" were being ripped apart. Denuded of its "past glory," the South stood naked and exposed under the glaring light of truth. The campus of Ole Miss was plowed up as a graveyard to receive the skeletons of segregation. The flesh had been picked clean, and only the stinking white bones remained. The stench of the Oxford madness even turned the stomachs of many white citizens. They awoke the next morning to discover that they had been through hell. History wrote of the night and closed the book in disgust. But it was no nightmare, for sitting and breathing in the halls of Mississippi's seat of culture was a black man who dared. James Meredith, in spite of his later defection, was a symbol of black might in right.

Governor Barnett became a prophet of bloodshed, while Governor Wallace damned all the Kennedy clan and boasted a Klan of his own. Crosses will burn, he predicted, and so will the nation. He said this at the hearings held by Congress on the President's civil rights bill. But Congress was charmed by the sophistication of Roy Wilkins and amazed at Dean Rusk of Alabama. It was the latter who promised to demonstrate also if only the gods had made him black.

Then came the March. Dr. Joseph Harrison Jackson, leader of the black Baptists, was against it. So were Eastland and Thurmond. The AFL-CIO refused to endorse it, but ten other organizations gambled and won. They won the respect of a nation that trembled at the spectacle of the power of combined purposes. From the mountains of freedom Martin Luther King related his dreams. James Baldwin was angry and promised the "fire next time," and Wallace took him at his word and ignited the fuse. Rednecked storm troopers stood in school doors and forbade entrance to the sons and daughters of the revolution. Kennedy stood up, and Wallace sat down. But the damage had been done.

On September 16, 1963, fifteen sticks of dynamite were planted in hate in Birmingham—in the house of the Lord. The blast left lifeless four children who were deprived of their right to mature, even if in a segregated society. They did not have the time to forgive their enemies; they died instantly. Those torn and mutilated daughters of the revolt were not old enough to rebel. Governor Wallace, too late to stem the tide, offered a $5,000 reward for the capture of the killers he had indirectly hired with his inflammatory speeches. Blood money! Shots rang out again, and two black boys died.

From the throat of America came the gurgling sound of a nation choking on its own blood. The President was outraged. The consciences of white supremacists began to prick them to reassess their prejudices: the price was beginning to be too high. "How long, O Lord!" cried black men as they picked up rocks and bottles. Their weapons were inadequate to dent the insidious hatred. The missiles glanced harmlessly off the hide of the South.

White churches stood like specters in the hot sun of the South while the blood of their black brothers cried to God from the ground. As the nation approached those crises, once again the question came forth: "Has the church been too late?"

It was too late to put the glint of hope back into the eyes of those who remained in the grips of the gutter. Too late for those who had turned to drugs and alcohol. Too late for those in prison because they had to steal bread they could not work to obtain. Too late to feed the malnourished monstrosities made so by the absence of early sustenance. The toll of black twisted lives with distorted values will never be assessed. The chains struck from the ankles of the oppressed were struck from too few, too late. And the healing would take too long; hate had already begun to fester into riots. Had the church arrived sooner, a generation of people might have been rescued from the trash heaps of mediocrity. Fathers would have been granted to illegitimate offspring sired by the ghetto.

The concert of the March on Washington was a fleeting sweet symphony that has long since disappeared. For a while its music contained the strings of life, the flutes of peace, the bass notes of power. The music from the collective churches of Washington on that 28th day of August, 1963, flooded the cities and hamlets from which the people of God had come. But the sound was too late even then. The glistening collars and swaying crosses of the clergy could not bring life back to Medgar Evers. Nor could freedom's songs convince his fatherless children that he had "overcome." Alone he had stood in his blackness, a man who had trudged up to white Calvary bearing the cross of race. It was too late for the church whose voice had been clogged with the phlegm of caution while its hands clasped its rosaries, crosses, and itself to its bosom. When the church gathered at the foot of the Washington Monument and prostrated itself before the fathers of this nation, too long had it ignored the Father of its creation.

It was there that it falsely pledged to continue the struggle it had never begun—until then. The sun was already high in the heavens, and the dawn could not be brought back. The ministry of the church was late. It had failed to convert the Wallaces and Barnetts. It was too late to save the ghettos that would soon burn with fire. Where was the church when Arthureen Lucy braved the spittle and the rocks? When the butts of rifles cracked the skulls of God's people? The black man was sold by Judas for the coinage "good race relations." Try as it may, the white church will never wash off those stains.

When blacks fought through the integration of the schools, swimming pools, and other accommodations, the church was silent. When blacks struggled to be protected from the police brutality and dogs of Birmingham, they were forced to depend on the government, the FBI, and the federal courts. Meanwhile, the vast majority of Christendom sat in the bleachers, deploring the upheaval that was being caused. The church trembled at marches and wished them away. They frowned at sit-ins and continued to voice the refrain over and over, like a broken record: "You're going too fast." The church was pleading for time, even though the striking clock was showing them that time had run out. Prior to and after the March on Washington, the church was too late.

White Christendom had ignored its mandate: it had thrust out from its midst black men who no longer would be content to be robbed of their dignity. The time had come when they refused to be satisfied to live in a state of limbo, submissive to the heel of the oppressor, denying themselves the expression of righteous and indignant hate. Too long had they languished in the state of Nowhere and drunk from the fountain of Welfare. Again and again black hostility was to rise up and damn the white man.

The march on Washington appeared at that time to be the answer. I could not help but feel that the mysterious power of God was beginning to work in us all. The March served as a brief catalyst to confront the church with its destiny. From black voices all over America came the cry "Now!" It came from the hearts of an untapped reservoir of power, the people of God. I hope that my friend Mike heard that sound. I did, and it brought tears to my eyes and hope to my heart. The issue was clear, and the cause was just. The church united briefly under the banner of that cause.

The sound of "Now!" that came from a gathered church in Washington has faded into the past. The hope for the humanity and dignity of all men remains in white pews—the synagogues of Judaism, the cathedrals of Rome, and the churches of the Reformation. Mike, wherever you are, I now confess that you were right. For a few moments we marched with the church, but it could not keep pace. The last two decades have still found the black man saying, "Perhaps we must go it alone."

CHAPTER 9
A Vacation in Nashville

*I*WENT FOR A REST TO NASHVILLE, TENNESSEE,
late in the spring of 1963—and was arrested. Prior to my
departure from my home in Evansville, Governor George
Wallace came to tour Indiana. Armed with picket signs, we
met him. With the smallest police escort our mayor dared to
provide, Wallace met the press, orating on how much he loved
freedom. For the information of those in our city who might
have thought him to be a racist, he reminded us that during his
inaugural address he had "asked God to bless all, black and
white alike."

He was reminded that his prayers must have fallen through
(or else the Almighty was not in the mood to integrate Alabama). Instead of blessings falling upon the blacks, stars fell on
their heads—courtesy of Bull Conner.

He promised us that a primary vote of Hoosiers in his
behalf would cause the liberals' eyeteeth to drop out. His actual
garnering of 29.5% of the votes served in a measure to loosen
our wisdom teeth as well. The cause, everyone said, was
"northern white backlash."

Sickened at this turn of events, I decided to go south to
Nashville. Someone had informed me that it was an "open
city," a place where integration really worked; the "Athens of
the South" they called it. The first day I arrived in Nashville, I
was met by the headlines proclaiming that high school students
had begun demonstrations anew. Not content with the incar-
ceration of their older brothers and sisters in 1960, they were
determined to open up the city completely. I trembled when I
thought of the effect this news would have on the white back-

lashers back home. As a race, we had narrowly escaped lashing when the "stall-ins" were threatened, and (some of us thought) fortunately for the World's Fair (and the Mets), this colossal pile-up of traffic fizzled out beautifully.

In the struggle for civil rights, the specter of the so-called backlash affected all of our movements. It infringed upon our "-ins" and took the steam out of our demonstrations. For those wondering what was meant by the "-ins": they were the creative means of protest used by those who are *out*, namely, the American black. My first acquaintance with an "-in" was the solo one I performed in the barbershop in Evansville in 1959—in the days before demonstrations became popular.

Now, since I was in Nashville, away from the backlashers, I decided to exercise my last right to demonstrate before the passage of the Civil Rights Bill. Our leaders had already promised a "long hot summer of discontent." Thanks to the coalition of Southern filibusters, the young people of Nashville were determined to sit in the street until all places of public accommodation were opened.

Meeting at The First Baptist Church (where I was guest minister for the week), the demonstrators conferred with the Chief of Police, who came down to plead with their leaders. He warned them that if the demonstration proceeded, all of the adults would be arrested for contributing to the delinquency of minors. Finally, the demonstrators and the police arrived at a compromise. Yes, the Chief understood that the youngsters were determined to demonstrate. As an officer who believed in law and order, he would provide escorts for their marches. But if they sat down in the street, he said he had no other alternative but to arrest them. In response to this kind offer, the demonstrators promised that if they were arrested, they would go along with the arrest peacefully—provided all demonstrators would be arrested together. "If one goes to jail, we all go to jail" was the theme. The Chief promised that he would oblige.

Starting out with this gentlemen's agreement, we marched to our destination, sat down, and waited. As the cameras converged on the scene, Chief Barton motioned to his men to remove us. They did.

I was herded into a paddy wagon that was built for eight prisoners; I was the sixteenth person shoved in. In order to make room, the officer had to virtually corkscrew me in onto the laps of my fellow demonstrators. This action he accompanied with short pokes in my ribs with his nightstick. To my chagrin, those within the wagon began to protest, insisting vehemently that I return back to the street and find another conveyance to jail.

"Too many in here," they complained to me and to the officer who was poking my one remaining rib that had not yet cleared the door.

I made a quick decision to remain where I was. This decision was prompted by a swift kick in the rear by the arresting officer, who was determined to remove me from the streets of the coming long, hot summer of discontent. Rubbing my wounds, I glanced at my companions and was pleased to discover that I was sitting in the lap of John Lewis, the president of SNCC. After the proper introduction, he politely asked me to find a new space for my 240 pounds.

In the wagon I noticed that several of the arrested demonstrators were white. Throughout the black revolt, white people have always asked the question, "What can I do?" Although most of them ignored the answer given by the Black Muslims, they began to actively demonstrate with their ebony friends. Initially they were eyed with suspicion; later, however, no demonstration was complete without the status symbol of a number of white friends. As such, they served the dual purpose of providing visible targets for rotten eggs and lending color to the "pinkish" charge so vitally needed for the speeches of Governor Wallace. Who can forget Mrs. Peabody, probably the most distinguished ex-convicted one among us? She set a wonderful pattern for graceful jail-going that our more liberal white friends had formerly shunned.

As we rode toward jail, the question was raised about how long we would remain incarcerated. One of the problems involved in jail-going is obtaining sufficient money to free demonstrators pending their trials. At one time, remaining in jail was a badge of honor. Students enjoyed remaining in jail; not only did it relieve them of classwork, but most sympathetic professors gave them an "A" for the quarter in the subject of American Problems. (It was not unusual to find that most of the students who preferred to remain in jail were bordering on flunking that subject.) We decided to hold the question of bail until we came to that bridge; then those who were financially able would cross it.

Thirty-nine of us were placed in a cell that measured twenty feet by forty feet. No water, no air.

"What charge are they holding us on?" asked one of the demonstrators, gasping for breath.

"Disorderly conduct and contributing to the delinquency of minors," came the answer from a head-bandaged demonstrator.

"What happened to you?" I asked him, wondering how he had been bandaged so neatly and quickly.

"Oh," he explained, "I was arrested yesterday, got out on bail, and here I am back again."

"What was the charge against you yesterday?"

"I don't know," the bandaged one replied.

I could not avoid venturing a guess. "From all visible evidence, it must have been 'failure of the head to yield to a nightstick'." No one laughed. After an initial loud outburst on my part, I also decided it wasn't funny.

"I want to make a phone call!" yelled another demonstrator (out through the solid door to the jailer) and, in the diction of the more militant freedom seekers, he added, ". . . and I want to make it now."

After being informed by the rest of us that President Lyndon Johnson and Bobby Kennedy had already been notified of his predicament, he returned to his seat on the floor and sulked.

It was John Lewis who proposed the "bust out." He told us that the Nashville jail was one of the worst ones he had ever been in. Four hours had passed. The air became so contaminated with our beings that it really seemed necessary to escape —if only to get away from each other. Sweat poured from our bodies as well as from the floor and the walls. We decided to attract the attention of the jailer. This was done by four men in relays, who slammed the slack of the steel door until the sound reverberated and shook the jailer's teeth. The door was opened.

Fresh cold air rushed in.

"Listen," Lewis pleaded in his best voice for kind policemen, "we don't mind not having toilet facilities. We don't mind not having water to drink . . . but please, how about a little air?"

All thirty-nine of us were gulping down the air that the jailer provided when he opened the door to hear our complaints. That sight must have unnerved him. He slammed the door in our faces; at the same time he promised that he would investigate the possibilities of having the heat cut off. He waved a sympathetic farewell and disappeared. It was at this point that Lewis proposed the "bust out" plan.

"Men," he informed us, "we have a right to ventilation, if nothing else. The next time that door opens, let's all of us rush out in that passageway and sit down." Noticing the fear on the faces of most of us, he reassured us of the validity of the plan. "We're not trying to escape," he cautioned, "we just want to breathe."

We debated the "bust out." We were reminded by one of the more reflective demonstrators (a Ph.D. candidate at Vanderbilt) that the walls of the jail did not have ears, while all of the policemen were armed with guns. All thoughts of "busting out" were filtered out by this thinking man.

We considered other methods of protesting our quarters. We were finding it increasingly difficult to be creatively resistant in jail. The only other possibility left to us was a suggested hunger strike. "We're already on that," Lester McKinny, the leader of the student rebellion, observed. "We've been here eight hours and no food has been offered us yet." Freddie, the most militant one among us, contended for the strike if and when the food arrived. Gradually he worked up a hard core of dinner resisters. I was not among them.

When dinner finally arrived, we were ordered by the jailer to line up against the wall in order to be counted. I moved reluctantly. The evening before, I had witnessed a scene in a late, late war movie in which a machine gun had popped up out of nowhere and burpingly exterminated prisoners of war who had provided lining for the walls at the command of a German officer. However, the smell of spaghetti and meat balls reassured me that this lining up was for real. I lined up.

Freddie, subject to the same pangs of hunger as the rest of us, decided to relieve his men from the hunger strike pledge. He rationalized to them that it would be better to start the hunger strike the next day by not eating breakfast. So we all dined.

After dinner, word came to us that it was bail-out time. The leaders were to be bailed out first. A mass meeting was to be held that night, and they were needed to explain the conditions of the jail and to raise enough money to bail the rest of us out. As a visiting demonstrator, I was hurt because I was not considered a leader. Pulling out my NAACP membership card, I implored the departing leaders to take me with them. The only recommendation I could offer for my own release was that on occasions when I made speeches, I could move an audience to tears. I wept to prove my point. No soap—just tears.

By this time I insisted to the jailer that I should be given the one phone call that is permitted to all prisoners. I placed a long distance call to Dr. Fred Coleman, a friend in Clarksville, Tennessee, forty miles away. I reversed the charges.

"Hey Doc," I called.

"Who is this?"

"King," I answered, and added with the proper emphasis, "I'm in jail!"

"In jail?" he asked incredulously. "What are you. . . ?" he paused as he thought of my passion for protests. "Are you there demonstrating?"

"Not now," I answered truthfully. "Earlier I was just observing the demonstrations and they picked me up because I looked like a leader," I lied.

"What do you want from me?" he inquired sympathetically.

"Out," was the unhesitating answer. He provided the bail.

I hastened to the Clark Memorial Methodist Church, where the mass meeting was to be held. I was directed by a student to the educational wing of the church, where, he informed me, the meeting was already in session in the upper auditorium. When I entered, I was met by the strangest assortment of people I had ever seen in all of my demonstrating days. Approximately fifty people were in the room. A bearded one was behind a table speaking. As I was being motioned to a seat by an usher, the speaker was evidently concluding his oration: "And I say," he spoke with blazing eyes, "I say we ought to come out from among them. Right now, there is a bill pending in the House that will send all of you folks back to the richest land in the world." His face contorted in anger. "The white folks won't tell you that," he opined. "They won't tell you that the government has already set aside four billion dollars to allow us all to go back home to Africa. The money is there and it's yours for the asking . . . I say, let's go back."

I discovered that I had mistakenly stumbled in on a meeting of the Black Nationalists. Right church, wrong floor. Politely tiptoeing out of the room like an elephant, I descended to the auditorium where the freedom fighters were meeting. At the time it struck me as ironic that upstairs they were planning separation, while downstairs they were plotting integration.

The strategy that evolved out of the mass meeting was simple. No more arrests for the time being. It was decided that all following demonstrations would be confined to picketing. There would be no more sit-ins or stall-ins—only walk arounds. We were reminded by our lawyers that all adults arrested in the future would have great difficulty being released unless they had personal bail money. The funds were running low. We were asked to avoid arrest at any cost. Those who needed the extra hours of jail in American Problems, of course, were given the green light to finish out their credits.

The next morning, Nashville policemen were staked out at all of the black high schools and warned the students that if they continued to demonstrate they would be picked up. However, to obtain new students, the demonstration leaders "bused" in those on the outskirts of town. Rev. Grady McDonald, one of the Nashville leaders of the Southern Christian Leadership Conference, met with these students on the lawn of the American Baptist Theological Seminary, where they had gathered to catch the bus. He informed them of the courage that they would need for the demonstrations that were yet before them.

"What you'll need," he told them, "is that rare kind of fortitude that will enable you to stand up, sit down, and protest regardless of the consequences. To do this, you must be willing to face police dogs, police brutality, or . . ." He broke off abruptly in the middle of his pep talk. Out of the corner of his eye he had detected a police squad car approaching. The car drew menacingly near and stopped. Remembering the warning in relationship to bail, Rev. McDonald made his next move in accordance with the desires of the organized leadership. His retreating form down the hill prompted me to wonder how he had been overlooked as a candidate for the 100-yard dash in the 1964 Olympics.

The students assured the policemen that they were on their way to church. I crouched down in the middle of them and assumed my juvenile look. We were allowed to proceed to the buses. Arriving at the church, we did everything else but pray. Orders were given for the day: we were to picket the places of discrimination in relay groups of fifteen. Then we were to proceed to City Hall and meet other demonstrators, who would be praying for the city on the steps of City Hall.

My squad of youngsters and three adults was assigned to picket the Tic-Toc Cafe. As we approached, one of the students bolted out of the picket ranks and burst into the cafe. (Normally, when seeing demonstrators approach, restaurant owners would lock their doors and allow only their trapped customers to depart.) Taking advantage of this new open door, we followed our brave student inside and filled up all the seats. The manager and the one waitress on duty observed us with bewilderment. Noticing that we were enjoying the air-conditioned comfort of his segregated haven, he not only refused to serve us but cut off the air conditioning as well. So we sweated out our protest. His next move mystified us: he left and informed the waitress to lock the door behind him. After he had departed, however, she found it difficult to bolt the door. Politely turning down our offer to assist her, she pleaded with a white bystander on the outside to enter and bolt the door for her. He entered, bolted the door, and was rewarded with a cup of coffee. He drank the coffee while looking daggers at us.

Twenty minutes later, the street outside of the cafe became thick with policemen, including Chief Barton. They made no move to enter or arrest us. Suddenly we thought of the reason why. The manager was evidently following a precedent established a few days earlier by another discriminating restaurant: he was obtaining John Doe warrants for the arrest of all sit-inners. We held a brief consultation, and after determining that among the fifteen of us there was only $21.33, we decided to leave before the manager returned.

"We would like to leave now," I said, smiling at the waitress.

"What's your hurry," she answered with the same smile. She did not move.

"We want to leave, and we want to leave now," another demonstrator broke in with a voice sounding like Martin Luther King's.

The man drinking the coffee shook his head at us. When we continued to insist that he open the door, he took another swig and nastily informed us:

"Look, no one asked you to come in here. If you want to get out, you'll leave when we get good and damned ready to let you out!"

This constituted the first "lock-in" movement in the entire history of demonstrations. Not to be outmaneuvered, I went to the plate-glass window and motioned frantically to the chief of police. Ordering his men to stand by with billy clubs out of their holsters, he cautiously approached the door. I yelled out at him:

"We want to come out, but they won't let us."

The chief, both surprised and pleased by our request to curtail our sit-in, ordered with his facial muscles that the door be opened. We were able to enter once more into the clean hot sun. As we left, the waitress, fearing the loss of her job because of her inability to detain us, gave us a caustic invitation:

"Do come again," she said bitterly.

We promised her that we would.

The hour was now at hand when we were to converge on City Hall for prayer. On the steps of City Hall, we were met by clergymen, deans of colleges, and even a president of a religious seminary. Each took his turn praying for racial justice while we were on our knees. The prayers were long and the pavement hard. When we finally stood up, it was enough to turn us all into atheists. No word had been received about the removal of any barriers while we were on our knees.

Failing to move the Almighty, the demonstrators then attempted to move Mayor Bailey. Someone had spotted him peeking from between his blinds at the demonstrators below.

"We want the mayor, we want the mayor," we chanted. The mayor was not to be had. Since none of the leaders had made an appointment with him to air grievances, he refused to come down and pacify our demonstrating spirits. As we departed from the steps of City Hall, it appeared that both the Lord and Mayor Bailey had failed us.

It was now the hour of our arraignment on the charges stemming from the arrests of the day before. The courtroom was filled. Every spectator's seat was occupied by those who had been arrested (200). Attorneys Alexander Looby, Avon Williams, and John Vincent constituted our battery of lawyers for the defense. Each case was to be tried separately. The judge smiled as he handed down a ten-dollar fine and two days in jail to the first man in the alphabetical order of arraignment. I made a quick calculation: if all of us were found to be similarly guilty, the fines should provide the city with an adequate excuse to cut the next year's tax load. At 11:00 p.m. the trials had not yet proceeded through the G's, and the K's were informed to return in three weeks.

By now my demonstrating muscles were tired. I firmly resolved that the cause of freedom would be minus my presence in future demonstrations. Not that I loved first-class citizenship less, but as one sage has said, "He who fights and runs away lives to fight another day."

I went back home to Indiana, and just as I suspected, the news of the demonstrations in Nashville brought on the feared backlash. Some of my best friends had become backlashers. Most of them were removing their NAACP buttons and re-examining their restrictive covenant clauses. An alarming number of them were beginning to build swimming pools in their back yards while clutching their daughters to their bosoms. In vain did I show them the bruises I had as a result of police brutality. In an effort to rearouse their sympathy, I informed them of the newest "in" that was initiated in Nashville during the demonstrations. It was the "sip-in." Of all the "ins," this one afforded the white demonstrator freedom from the more militant posture of his black brother. In Nashville, 200 white students from Vanderbilt University and Scarret and Peabody Colleges entered into the largest restaurant that discriminated against blacks at dinner time. Having taken all the seats, they all ordered coffee; for the next two hours they sipped on one cup of coffee. Customers who wanted to enter for their customary meal had to go elsewhere for dinner. The manager of the restaurant counted his dinner receipts (from which he had to pay nine waitresses): a grand sum of $20.00 (no tips were left). It can be safely said that soon after that this culinary haven was open to blacks, Chinese, Japanese, and Puerto Ricans.

Still, the white backlashers refused to be impressed. And it is only in desperation that I proposed the most radical "in" of all: the "pass-in." This proposal was sorely needed. For years blacks had been in the forefront of the "ins." Wade-ins, ride-ins, kneel-ins, sit-ins had placed us on the firing line for civil rights. Now that the backlashers had withdrawn into the cocoons of Birchism and Wallacism, it became apparent that the black needed a rest from all his "ins."

I have been tried and sentenced to many days in jail. The days in jail I welcomed; however, jail accompanied by white backlash was the last straw. The only solution I could see to hold the white backlashers was to make them victims of the "pass-in." Its administration was easy. All the black needed was a cultured voice and a telephone (some of us had both). He made a call to an exclusive restaurant that denied entrance to blacks, informing the manager that a Negro passing for white was planning to dine there in an effort to break down their policy of discrimination. Of course, no such "Negro" was known by the caller. However, if the discriminating manager bit at the bait, the arrival of some innocent white customer who would sit at the tipped-off table would possibly set up a chain reaction that would lead to one or more of the following consequences:

A. Refusal of service
B. Spilled soup in lap (with half apologies)
C. Summoning of police when they refuse to leave as ordered
D. A combination of A, B (with apology withdrawn), and C.

So, you see, the backlashers might very well become the victims of their own lashes, brought on by their inability to prove that they had no black blood.

CHAPTER 10
"God Cried on Us"
in Alabama

*T*HREE PRIESTS FROM ST. MEINRAD AND FATHER Terrence Gerken of St. Benedict's Church invited me to accompany them to Selma, Alabama. In Selma we traveled in pairs—never alone, but no more than four to a group.

Father Camillus Ellsperman became my constant companion. The first night we entered Browns Chapel we witnessed the most incongruous sight of our lives: children filled the chapel to the balcony; we had to step over their bodies as they attempted to find a space in which to sleep. Others would not sleep; they sang instead. A Catholic nun in the rear of the church made the sign of the cross as a 16-year-old black boy prayed so fervently that sweat ran down his face in rivulets. And then we all learned the song of the Berlin Wall, composed by a student to fit the Selma situation:

> Hate built up the Berlin Wall
> in Selma, Alabama,
> Love is going to make it fall
> in Selma, Alabama.

We sat there and absorbed the spirit of freedom. The hope of it and the agony of its searching were in the faces of the children. We walked out of that church toward the object of the song—ten yards away; and at the wall more children were singing. Clergymen of all faiths stood in front of the youngsters facing the harsh glare from the state troopers' cars. In those cars and standing behind them seemed to be amassed the whole State of Alabama police force.

71

We stood there on Sylvan Street, the one paved street for blacks in Selma, and sang about the wall that separated us.

> We're going to stand here till it falls,
> in Selma, Alabama.

The roaring engines of the troopers' cars tried to drown out the meaning of our songs and prayers, but we continued them far into the night.

* * * * *

I learned another song in Selma: "God is Love." It was taught me by Catholic priests during a mass. I could not understand the order of worship, but I did not feel out of place—until communion. Fathers Camillus, Terrence, and Sippian went forward to take the sacrament; they invited me, but I remained seated. How strange that the body of our Lord should separate us at that point when we had shared all other things together! I sat there in the foolish traditions of doctrines and creeds. I joined these white Catholic priests as they arose to walk to the Selma Wall. They sang Baptist spirituals taught them by a black Baptist minister, and they were willing to offer their bodies as a sacrifice for oppressed black people. I wept there on the line as we sang, and asked God to forgive us all.

So we stood there staring into the eyes of the city of Selma and its way of life. It was an impasse. The first two days it rained intermittently as if God were weeping at the sight of us.

Sunday the sun came up bright and early, freeing us from two days of cold and rain. It was the day that people worship in the church of their choice. The church that we chose to worship in was the First Baptist Church of Selma, Alabama. At 9:30, Dr. Homer Jack, national officer of the Unitarian Church, Dr. Lemuel Peterson, executive minister of the Seattle Council of Churches, and I approached Mr. Baker, the Director of Public Safety at the Selma Wall, and requested permission to go into Selma for services.

"Kneel and pray where you are. Why go into Selma?" he both commanded and inquired.

We prevailed upon him. Finally he relented and commanded the troops to allow us to proceed in groups no larger than three at a time. But along with his permission he gave an accompanying ominous warning: "I cannot assume any responsibility for your safety once you leave this area." His warning was not without foundation.

Outside the phalanx of state troopers we were joined by a white Baptist minister, a white girl, and a black girl. As we walked silently toward the church, the people of Selma watched us closely. A dozen or so followed behind us, and we dared not look back; it was as if they were pressing us forward. As we began to cross the street toward the church, a car shot off the curb where it was parked and bore down upon us *on the wrong side of the street.* The intent of the driver was obvious. Dr. Jack shouted a warning, and all of us leaped back onto the sidewalk as the car zoomed by. Momentarily disturbed, we held a short conference there on the sidewalk and decided to proceed.

We were met at the church by ten men standing at the top of the steps. The chairman of the council identified himself and served as their spokesman.

"We are the officers of this church. We don't want any trouble, and we know why you are here."

"May we enter?" Dr. Peterson asked quietly.

"This church is not integrated . . . never has been and never will be," the chairman informed him. "I suggest that you go back where you came from and worship," he stated with finality. One of the other officers vehemently broke into the conversation:

"Git! Get gone, you hear! If you're lookin' for trouble, by God, you'll git it right here."

That remark stirred the other deacons into apparent agreement. And it made me realize what we were really facing: not the officers of a church but the full depth of hatred contained in Selma. The ecclesiastical officials were threatening us with violence on the very steps of the church. Behind them stood the parishioners with clenched fists and trembling lips. Not one sympathetic face could be seen. Even the youths, some of them with Bibles in their hands, edged forward with that look.

"May we pray here on the steps with you?" Dr. Homer Jack asked in an effort to find some common ground and to relieve the tension.

"No, you can't." The chairman spoke more harshly now. He recognized the mood of the people behind him. "Go out on the street and pray. That's where you came from."

"You're not as good as that nigger there," the threatening one said to Jack, pointing at me. "At least he knows better." I swallowed hard and did not speak. I never did. What could I say? Dr. Peterson moved back and asked us to follow him. Standing back on the sidewalk, we linked our arms together, bowed our heads, and prayed. As we closed our eyes, we knew that the hate of the South was boring into our circle. We heard footsteps and voices as they moved toward our circle.

"Hurry up with that prayer . . . you ain't prayin', you're playin'!"

"Forgive them, Father," prayed Dr. Peterson, "for they know not what they do."

"We know what we're doin' and if you don't hurry up with that prayer . . ."

At that, profane remarks were directed at the white girl in our group. Suffice it to say, all of us were relieved when Dr. Peterson concluded with "Amen." We knew we had to leave— and leave quickly. We walked rapidly back to the city, where the state troopers allowed us to return to our places behind the Selma Wall. We stood there and looked out into the city that had denied us entrance. A man of God had died out there. We had attempted to carry our witness to the one last bulwark of Selma's conscience, the house of God. We had failed, and I know why. During the exchange between Dr. Peterson and the chairman of the board, Peterson had asked:

"Isn't this the house of God?"

Someone in the background had shouted the incredulous answer: "No! It's our house; we built it."

I wept, now again, in the face of the undeniable fact that he spoke the truth—of all of our houses.

* * * * *

On Friday morning Father Camillus and I went back to the Selma Wall. Over and over we sang the song "Hate built up

74

the Berlin Wall in Selma," along with a mixture of nuns, priests, rabbis, and students. As we all swayed back and forth to the music in one harmonious natural movement, a very strange thing happened. Suddenly, a large, portly man who was in one of the police cars facing us leaped out of the vehicle and ran toward us with a knife in his hand. He headed directly for Father Camillus, who was standing in the front of the line behind the rope that separated us demonstrators from the police.

Father Camillus did not move; he kept right on singing. The hulk of a man reached up and brought the knife down decisively—to cut the rope. It was our first meeting with Mr. Baker, Director of Public Safety in Selma. His is one of the amazing stories of the Selma crisis.

Baker was an enigma who commanded the respect of all the blacks of Selma who realized that it was his duty to uphold the segregated patterns of the South. Thus it was necessary for him to confront the demonstrators with all the power that he could muster to restrain them from reaching their goals. The day he cut the rope indicated to us his growing frustration and the internal conflict that his actions could no longer belie. "I got tired of looking at the rope," Mr. Baker said later.

At the cutting of the rope, a shout of victory went up from the demonstrators, and the children surged forward. Suddenly we discovered that there was no one in charge of the scene. We restrained those who were straining forward as best we could until the local leadership could analyze the significance of this apparent invitation to march.

"Stand where you are; the cutting of the rope means nothing," cried the Rev. Hosea Williams, aide to Dr. Martin Luther King. "There is still an invisible wall before us. It separates us from our rights, our dignity, and the door of the courthouse." Not sure of the significance of this cutting of the rope, a few of us faced the demonstrators and urged them not to move forward. It was a spur-of-the-moment decision that later proved to be correct. The Selma Wall was more than a rope or a barricade erected to separate the marchers from the police. It was a sounding board for our challenge to the segregated patterns of the entire South. Two powerful forces faced each other: the spiritual force of right, the secular force of might. The Selma Wall provided the place where an "eyeball to eyeball" confrontation could take place.

The plan of the civil rights leaders was for this confrontation to become continuous, to overwhelm the hostile forces with the spiritual power of songs, prayers, and spoken words. The plan was not to march over the police but to stand there day and night until the right of the courts and the power of justice could be obtained without violence. So we stood there looking into the eyes of the city of Selma and its way of life. It was an impasse. Once we had become aware of the true significance of the wall, our voices became louder, as if we were trying to break down the barrier by sheer lung power. After the rope was cut, we sang louder still. Father Camillus' voice could be heard above the rest:

> We're going to stand here till it falls,
> in Selma, Alabama.

And he did.

The meaning of that impasse gave birth to one of the strangest ecumenical scenes in America. A Catholic priest wept when he learned that a black Baptist minister was barred from worshipping in the First Baptist Church of Selma. And I was filled to the brim when I was told that the white Catholics of Selma rejected not only the blacks but also the priests and nuns who had come to offer their bodies for the blacks of Selma. And so we all went back to Browns Chapel and heard a Catholic nun speak from the pulpit of an African Methodist Episcopal Church. And a Unitarian minister said "Amen." The wall outside the church was still up, but the walls inside were falling. And God was weeping.

* * * * *

Mrs. Lucy Brock is black. She was a high school graduate, and she had never been allowed to vote. Her number was 520: that was the number of all persons whose names were on file at the Selma courthouse—waiting to be called to register even though the court had recently ruled that 100 individuals should be registered. She had been waiting for that call, but on the day we met she had not yet been called. The last time she had attempted to register, she was rejected because of a minor mistake on her application form. Her husband worked in a downtown store. Every evening when he came home he told the same story: the stores were empty. The blacks' boycott of the downtown establishments was having its effect. Since Lucy's home was the most popular one on the line, it became a gathering place for demonstrators, reporters, and TV cameras from all over the nation. They loved her coffee, and she had it ready at all times. She had little time for her twin eight-year-old daughters, who observed the comings and goings of strange people from the North with wonder. Ann and LeeAnn had never spoken to white people before; they had never been close enough in Selma. When the phone rang it was never for Lucy but for one of the newsmen or students from far-flung states who mingled in the crowd in front of her house. She never made any calls; she didn't have the time. Cooking food and answering questions afforded her little opportunity for social amenities. When she tried to sleep, it would not come; the songs on the line kept her awake. But she did not complain, for the name of the song was "We Shall Overcome." Many demonstrators slept on the Brocks' lawn, on their porch, on their floors. Lucy gently stepped over those who had collapsed from fatigue, for she knew why they were there and was glad.

Lucy Brock had recently won a color television set in a raffle, and it was on this set that all of us watched President Lyndon Johnson speak to Congress and the nation. We waited anxiously for the words we hoped to hear—and they came. At the end of his speech, the President said, "We shall overcome!" and shouts of victory rang through the house and out into the streets. The sound echoed through the entire housing project at the news that the President had joined our march.

Mrs. Brock ran into the kitchen and grabbed a napkin to wipe her eyes; I followed and wiped mine with her. No one came in for coffee that night. It was no longer necessary to stand on the line that night, for the watch on the Selma Wall was over. I shall never forget the shouts of relief and joy from the throats of Selma's people on that historic evening. The troops had withdrawn, and the people were marching.

"Let's go out for a while and mingle with the people," I said to Father Camillus when the house had emptied.

"No," he replied softly, "I am going to pray tonight. I haven't had time to say any prayers since I came here."

So I walked out alone, out of the house where we both had lived during our Selma sojourn. The beloved community was about to return to the rituals of its religions. I reflected on how the good priest had stood up in the face of events that would cause most men's knees to tremble. I did not say it then, but I can say it now: how strange are the ways of religion! Some of us can only say our prayers, while Father Camillus and the monks of St. Mcinrad went to Selma and lived theirs. I looked back at the house and remembered that I too had not prayed. But God had heard someone, somewhere, and it would not be long before the dirt in Selma turned to grass and the mud into concrete sidewalks.

*   *   *   *   *

"Good-bye," we were saying to Mr. and Mrs. Brock. It was time for us to leave. We were all sorry it was ending, and yet we were glad that the Wall had fallen. We packed our bags and walked down Sylvan Street for the last time.

"We're so glad you came," Lucy Brock called after us. Neither Father Camillus nor I was ever to return. Like everyone else who arrived in that race-torn city, we came thinking that we had something to give and left knowing that we had received more than we could ever give in a lifetime.

Once we were airborne back to Evansville, we were both troubled with the same thoughts: What will happen now to the Brocks and the other folks of Selma? Had the peace of that city been disrupted beyond repair? Were all of us indeed "outside agitators" who had sown seeds of hatred between the blacks and whites of Selma? I continue to resolve that question in good conscience: we could not have left them worse off than they were when we arrived.

Father Camillus and I recalled some of the unforgettable people and scenes of those six days in Selma. The small, unknown black lady—Lucy Brock—who couldn't put it into words but let her umbrella speak for her when she gave it to us to protect our heads from the rain. The joyous singing of the little children who had witnessed more violence than most of us see in a lifetime. We would never forget the woman reporter from Belgium who had come to gather news but who, after witnessing the spirit of Selma, tore off her press pass and marched to the Selma Wall shouting "Freedom. . . ." The tears in the eyes of a sympathetic state trooper who did not relish staring a nun in the face at the wall of confrontation, his knees trembling visibly when the Reverend John Cavanaugh of Notre Dame resoundingly read the 87th Psalm to his comrades. And the graciousness of Director of Public Safety Baker, who offered transportation to four ministers enabling them to return to St. Elizabeth's mission in safety. The demonstrators paused in their songs that night and applauded him for his magnanimous act, and Mr. Baker smiled and bowed to acknowledge their applause.

The lessons of Selma go beyond the accounts of the tear gas, hoses, and brutality. They are found in the aftermath that caused Governor George Wallace to open his office door for the first time to the petitions of black people. To shake the bleeding hand of a bombed black youth in Birmingham. The Selma story took men of the cloth out of their pulpits and placed them in the middle of the misery of people. The people will never be the same again; nor will the men of the cloth who were there. Each major faith was present in Selma; they came as if beckoned by a catalytic agent of justice. It was the hand of God; and the fingers of that hand, like Sheriff Clark's cattle prods, would probe our customs and religious separations until the body of our churches would heave with acute indigestion.

What did Selma accomplish? Congress heard the voice of the people and would soon deliver into their hands the ballot. The mud streets would soon be paved with concrete, and lights would illumine the now-darkened walkways. The children of Selma would soon sing songs of America with the same passion with which they sang "We Shall Overcome." Selma will never be explained in the stern logic of reason, for the six days that we spent there were illogical and unreasonable times. To those who worried about the future of that city, I could find no answer to give. But one thing is for certain: if Selma never rose to the heights we prayed for or the fondest hopes of our democracy, at least for a few days the mud of that city baptized us forever into a common pool of concern. The Protestants, Catholics, and Jews who came to and left Selma all asked the same question of each other when it was over: "Where do we go from here?" No one seemed to know.

CHAPTER 11
The Black Church in Transition

D R. JOSEPH HARRISON JACKSON IS A SPELL-BIND-ing orator. Friends and critics alike acclaim him to be one of America's greatest preachers. And Dr. Jackson success-fully used his talents to lift himself to the highest office of the black religious world. He is president of the National Baptist Convention. When he won the presidency after a stormy all-night election in 1953, it was conceded that his election, at that time, gave promise of a new day among black Baptists.

"We want Jackson!" was the cry of the delegates, and they got him. The past thirty years they have had him have been years of struggle and black division. In the early years of his leadership, Jackson followers were some of the strongest black ministers in the nation: the Reverends J. Pious Barber, J. Raymond Henderson, Gardner Taylor, Martin Luther King, Sr., Marshall Shepherd, and Benjamin Mays, President of Morehouse College. But one by one, black intellectuals deserted his camp.

Among the many reasons for their departure were the issues of tenure and civil rights. At the time of Dr. Jackson's election, a small, wiry youngster named Martin Luther King, Jr., was developing at Crozier Theological Seminary in Philadelphia, Pennsylvania. Unknown to him and to others at that time, his name would soon challenge the very structure of the black church and its leadership. Today, the cleavage of two black civil rights philosophies is complete.

After the Montgomery, Alabama, Bus Boycott and the subsequent rise of Martin Luther King, Jr., to international fame, a new, hard look was in order for black leadership. Initially, Jackson's voice was one among many raised up in eloquent protest against injustice perpetrated against blacks in the South. None could say it like Joseph Harrison Jackson. The activist movements and philosophies of King, however, soon divided black ministers into two camps. The first issue that brought schism into the ranks was the issue of tenure, and the tragic story of that issue in the National Baptist Convention is thus closely allied with the blacks' fight for civil rights.

From the organization of the Baptist Convention in 1880 until 1953, only eleven men had served as president. Of these eleven, five had served one year, one had served for two years, and one had served for three years. The remaining sixty-three years found four men in strong control at the helm of black Baptists: Rev. W. J. Simmons, 1886-1890; Rev. E. C. Morris, 1894-1921; Rev. L. K. Williams, 1923-1940; Dr. D. V. Jemison, 1941-1953. During the late years of Dr. Jemison's term, a movement was begun to install young and progressive leadership. Joseph Jackson was the man. After the forced retirement and eventual death of Dr. Jemison, Jackson was elected. One strong plank presented in his campaign was that, if elected, he would only serve four years. This modern approach to leadership was accepted by thousands of black ministers who had desired for years to free themselves from one-man dominance. A new article was placed in the constitution as insurance against betrayal. The revised constitution read as follows:

ARTICLE IV, OFFICERS, . . . ELECTION

Section 2. A president of this Convention shall not be eligible for re-election after he has served four consecutive terms, until at least one year has elapsed.

In 1955, the delegates were stunned when a minister stood on the floor to make a motion that that revision of the constitution be declared null and void. President Jackson responded by selecting a committee to examine the constitution in light of tenure and report back to the convention. Already at that time, thundering voices began to be raised, among them Dr. L. K. Jackson, the fiery minister from Gary, Indiana. L. K. Jackson condemned the administration as being "immoral" for tampering with the constitution. Dr. Martin Luther King, Sr., still a strong supporter of Dr. Joseph Jackson, demanded that L. K. Jackson apologize to the convention for the strong language he had used. L. K. Jackson refused.

In Denver, on September 4th, 1956, the auditorium where the convention met was a tempest. The speaker's platform was crowded with ministers from both sides—those who wished to retain tenure and those who wished it to be declared null and void. As the argument rose in fury, President Jackson rapped for attention. He was ignored. With a rare display of emotion, the president declared that they could "have the convention," and made an angry exit. The lights were turned off. In pitch darkness the delegates began stomping and yelling for the president to return and restore order. The session ended in a stalemate: Dr. Jackson would not return.

In September 1957, the convention met in a dingy auditorium in Louisville, Kentucky. This was the session that would decide the issue. The lines were clearly drawn. The question of the hour was, Is Dr. J. H. Jackson eligible for re-election, or is another leader to be chosen? Both contentions were set forth. Jackson's men insisted that the tenure revision was null and void, that the convention had voted for it illegally: it was voted on the wrong day. The wrong day vote, they claimed, caused the constitution to remain as it was originally. The president could succeed himself as many times as possible. They pointed to the constitutional article that supported their stand:

ARTICLE XIV

This constitution may be altered or amended at any annual session by a two-thirds vote of the members present, provided that such a vote is taken without regard to total enrollment, and provided further that *no amendment may be considered after the second day of the session*. . . .

This was the legal clincher that the Jackson forces held. While conceding the fact that it was voted on in violation of the constitution, the progressive forces contended that the "spirit of the constitution was as the majority directed. It was the majority's wish to have tenure." It was not the legal issue, they argued; it was a matter of ethics. Furthermore, a promise was a promise, and Jackson should declare himself ineligible as a candidate and rule on the validity of tenure. As the convention waited with hushed voices, Jackson promised to settle the issue once and for all. First he quoted from the opinion of Attorney A. T. Walden, convention attorney:

> Based upon my understanding of the ordinary meaning of the word, we should think that the amendment [tenure] would not be adopted. . . .

Then President Jackson referred the Convention to Roberts' Rules of Order. He quoted:

> Any measures adopted contrary to the constitution of the body are null and void.

"Therefore," said the ambitious president, "in light of the 1952 record, which shows that the so-called revised constitution was adopted on the wrong day . . . I rule that the so-called Revised Constitution is null and void and the only valid constitution that the convention has is the constitution of 1951."

All hell broke loose, and no one could stem the tide. Amid cries of "No, no, no," ministers broke down and wept. The Jacksonites broke forth into cheers and shouts. Fists were raised and the air shook with rage. Virtually all delegates were on their feet propelled by the tension and disorder. The Rev. Q. L. Jones, pastor of the 4th St. Baptist Church, Owensboro, Kentucky swung into action. Trucks had been waiting outside with banners for Jackson. With a trained crew of delegates, Rev. Jones swept into the auditorium with banners proclaiming Jackson for President. Preceded by a bass drum, the marchers snaked their way through the crowd. Amid cries of protest, Jackson's army marched victoriously. There was a struggle for the microphone, and the Jackson forces commandeered it.

"I move that we suspend the rules and re-elect our president by acclamation," shouted Dr. T. S. Harten of Brooklyn.

"All those in favor say aye," directed one of the vice presidents.

A second wave of anger came upon the anti-Jackson forces. *The election was being called for a full day before it was programmed.*

The Jackson people were going to take advantage of the noise and turmoil and declare a re-election by acclamation. It was an old convention trick. So strong were the voices raised on both sides that the "ayes" could not be distinguished from the "nays." Both blended into an indistinguishable roar.

"The ayes have it," screamed the moderator of disorder. And have it they did. Jackson had broken the back of tenure.

What had brought about this bid for power on his part? Critics point to a messianic complex, a desire to be considered the deliverer of the black masses. As pastor of the great Olivet Baptist Church in Chicago, J. H. Jackson lived for power and recognition. Enter Martin Luther King, Jr.

In September 1956, a beaming President Jackson had led a shy young man down the aisle of the auditorium to the strains of "Onward Christian Soldiers." It was an inspiring sight. President Jackson introduced young Martin Luther King to the convention in glowing terms. King was beginning to soar in popularity, and he captivated his audience. His brilliant address on that occasion, "Letter to America," was masterfully delivered. His father, Martin Luther King, Sr., strode with pride at the back of the auditorium as he listened; his pride in his son would not allow him to sit down. He glanced around at the delegates to see the effect that his son was having on them. What he saw there was the same thing that Joseph Harrison Jackson saw—a black Moses.

"I must close now. . . ," the young King was saying, ready to conclude his speech. But the entire delegation was caught up in hypnotic rapture, and they did not want him to stop.

"No, go on," they cried as with one voice, "speak on. . . ."

However, King did finally end his speech and took his seat. From that moment on the black Baptists had an idol. Martin Luther King, Jr. had added the National Baptist Convention as another one of his conquests.

Critics of Jackson point to this moment as the time when Jackson made his decision to remain at the helm of the National Baptist Convention. "Jealousy was written all over his face," reported one minister. The fact that King posed a threat to Jackson's popularity was unquestioned. A new day was dawning in the struggle for civil rights, and the technique of active protest was beginning to bear fruit and capture the imagination of the world. The black world was burning with a new fire, the fire of protest. It was in its bones. King had done what no other black man up to that time had been able to do. He stood as the symbol of black solidarity.

One of Jackson's critics, Rev. Joseph Kirkland, remembers:

> In Denver, after listening to King, Jackson felt power slipping from his grasp; that plus the issue of tenure warned him that he was facing oblivion.

The late Rev. Owen D. Pelt, statistician of the convention and a long-time Jackson supporter, rejected this sort of thinking. On the contrary, he once told me, King merely echoed the philosophy that Jackson had been preaching for years. Jackson was too intelligent to become a victim of petty jealousy.

Whatever the reason, the impact of King was sufficient to cause a ground swell toward new black leadership. The indecisive status of tenure helped to create the swell. The supporters of King, recognizing the potential political hold that he could exercise within the convention, jockeyed him into position for leadership. The next year, at the annual Sunday School and BTU Congress, his name was offered in nomination for the vice presidency of that body. His popularity became clear when all candidates for the office withdrew in his favor. It was apparent to all that King was being groomed to take over Jackson's leadership. Neutral observers declared that it was unfortunate that King and Jackson were thus pitted against each other. Many men who backed King were bitter, fading ministers who feared that Jackson would destroy their own ambitions for leadership.

The young supporters of King began a campaign against Jackson on the basis that he was like "Uncle Tom" compared to King. Jackson's leadership was discredited as being weak on civil rights and strong on dictatorship. Martin Luther King likewise came in for criticism. His role, some contended, was too large to enable him to enter factional denominational considerations. As a world-renowned figure, he was diminishing his standing by playing the part of a "conventional" churchman. He did not need the convention, and the convention did not need him. In the years after the re-election of Jackson, a separation of philosophies concerning the black struggle for rights broke out. Even Jacksonites were surprised when Jackson made a public statement condemning sit-in demonstrations.

While there had always been supporters for Jackson, as well as supporters for King, a third group of ministers were loyal only to the administration. It was this third group that began to drift away from Jackson. Jackson, in an effort to gracefully retreat from his anti-sit-in statement, insisted that he had been quoted out of context. What he had really said, he argued, was that "protest was not enough."

"Excellent," responded the Jacksonites to their president's timely clarification. "Nonsense," retorted the progressives. Jackson's slap at the activists was nothing more than a slap at Martin Luther King. Jackson had miscalculated the mood of the day. The angry reaction that set in upon him shook the foundation of his administration. A steady stream of progressives began to develop. Nineteen sixty was the year the entire nation was caught up in the black rebellion.

Jackson was not focusing on the immediate problems of the day. His proposals, coming at any other time in history, would have probably met with unanimous approval. However, considering the intense struggle taking place in the South with virtually no support from the Jackson administration, he was exhibiting a masterful flair for bad timing. Leadership was lying heavy upon his shoulders.

In June 1961, he amplified his position on "protest is not enough" with his now-famous "The American Struggle in the American Way." It was called by the progressives "A Masterpiece of Tomism."

Below I cast excerpts from this document alongside a compendium of statements and events that came prior to and after its release:

> "All America must unite in the struggle to render this nation free . . . but in this struggle, we must employ American techniques. . . ."

February 1st, 1960: four black students in Greensboro, North Carolina took seats in a Woolworth store. They were arrested.

> "While we are in revolt against segregation wherever found, we must not allow ourselves to be in rebellion against state and federal laws."

Chain stores, supermarkets, department stores, libraries, and movies were hit by picket lines, stand-ins, sit-ins, and boycotts. By February 10th, the movement had spread to fifteen Southern cities in five states. By September, more than one hundred cities in twenty states had been affected. At least 70,000 black and white students had participated. Most of these were in violation of state law.

> "To undertake to force the states to conform to federal law is a task too great for civilians. . . ."

The Southern Regional Council estimated that 3,600 students had been arrested by September 1961. At least 141 students and 58 faculty members had been expelled by college authorities.

> "Protest must be carried on within the confines and according to the methods prescribed by the Federal constitution. . . ."

Finding nothing in the constitution prescribing sit-ins, Marzette Watts, expelled student from Alabama State College, replied: "We have made up our minds to be free. If the road to freedom leads through the jails of the South, to the jails we shall go."

> "But protest is not enough," droned Dr. Jackson in his document.

"You weigh the situation, you take the counsel of caution," said the leader of A & I sit-ins in Nashville. "You listen to the voices that say don't rock the boat, but the time comes when a man finally has to stand up and be counted.''

Barbara Broxton, Florida A & M student, after serving forty-eight days in the Tallahassee jail, predicted: ''There will be more sit-ins, more boycotts, until integration at lunch counters is won. We shall continue to go to jail because we feel we are right.''

So on they marched. March 13: 2,000 students met at Yale to map support for sit-ins. March 15: 350 student protestors arrested and herded into stockades in Orangeburg, South Carolina. March 16: San Antonio, Texas integrated its lunch counters in the first major breakthrough in the South. Meanwhile, thirteen were arrested in Savannah, and seven were arrested in a library in Greenville, South Carolina. ''If your son or daughter telephones you and says that he or she has been arrested in a sit-in,'' thundered Rev. Martin Luther King, Sr., ''get down on your knees and thank God.''

March 19th, the public libraries in Memphis were invaded by seven blacks. They were jailed. March 22: blacks tried to appreciate art in the Art Gallery in Memphis; they joined the book lovers in cells. March 29: four blacks were arrested in Houston because they refused to pay $2.50 for a cup of coffee in a white restaurant. On March 24, a *New York Times* editorial spoke out: ''This growing movement of peaceful mass demonstration by Negroes is something new to the South . . . let Congress heed their rising voices, for they will be heard.''

March 26: 600 students staged a protest demonstration in Hampton, Virginia. Seventy-one were arrested in Marshall, Texas. On Good Friday, while ten blacks were arrested in Birmingham, the White House Conference on Children and Youth endorsed sit-ins. The Passover was celebrated by thirteen whites and seven blacks who were convicted of breaking bread together in a black restaurant in Montgomery.

Dr. J. H. Jackson continued his ''protest is not enough'' position:

> ''In our racial struggle, we must welcome and work with allies in the white race who also believe in the American way of life. . . .''

"Liberty won by white men would lose half its luster; who would free themselves must strike the blow," Frederick Douglass had once predicted. And Lillian Smith remarked: "Let us not forget that these students are going to jail not only for their freedom, but for yours and mine. Not only because they have been hurt by the indignities of segregation, but because we all have been hurt."

"In these days of crisis, American Negroes must do more than seek their rights. . . ."

Dr. Jackson was not considering that blacks were not in a position to do more than seek their rights. The *Southern News* reported that in 1960, 94 percent of the black population was still in segregated schools. On April 19, the second Youth March for Integrated Schools drew 30,000 students to Washington. The next day, the home of Z. Alexander Looby, civil rights lawyer and counsel for 163 Fiskites in the Nashville movement, was bombed and destroyed. Two thousand students marched on the city hall in Nashville to protest.

"We must move from protest to production," prophesied the president of the National Baptist Convention.

"You may bomb our homes and spit on our children, but we will still love you. Be assured that we will wear you down with our capacity to suffer," said Martin Luther King, Jr.

The suffering continued. May 1: two faculty members dismissed from Kentucky State College; May 7: forty-seven arrested in sit-down demonstration in Durham, North Carolina. It was reported that Woolworth's also suffered. Sales were down 8.9 percent due to the march picketing. May 18: Woolworth's stockholders decided they would not be able to suffer much more as they urged the company to integrate lunch counters. "Lunch counter segregation is morally wrong," said Governor Leroy Collins of Florida.

The students of Nashville, Fisk, and A & I were filling the jails. A statement was sought from the president of Fisk: "As President of Fisk, I approve the ends our students are seeking by these demonstrations. They have conducted themselves peaceably and with poise and dignity."

Dr. Jackson was still speaking:

"Production itself will prove the kind of constructive protest that will help move the barriers that a protesting people confront. . . ."

Production was not the theme of Marvin Robinson, who was expelled for demonstrating. He was given the ultimatum of remaining in school to learn how to produce or be expelled if he continued to lead in demonstrations. His answer was: "We feel that we must bring to the attention of the world the condition of the Negro in the South. Which is the more important, the University or human dignity? I feel it is human dignity." He was expelled. "We cannot adjust to the Southern way of life," said Bernard Lee of Alabama State College, Montgomery. "We have to move, to work with the white man until we become not a minority, but a part of the whole."

"Through production, we can develop more self-reliance, more self-respect. . . ."

"We plan to continue in accordance with our common ideal: equality for all through nonviolent action,", said Edward Rodman of Norcom High School, Portsmouth, Virginia.

"The church cannot be used as a rubber stamp for every method employed in the name of democracy and freedom. . . ."

"The sit-in is one of the best things since the Boston Tea Party," said Dr. Kenneth B. Clark. "It is so wonderfully American and has jolted American students out of their complacency. It can only be successful."

"The church must not wait until others begin movements for human betterment. . . ."

But the church did wait. At least the National Baptist Convention waited. By July 17, 1960, 250 lunch counters had been integrated since the start of the sit-ins. It waited while CORE opened its interracial training institute on nonviolence in Miami, Florida. Nine Southern states reported forty-three cities with integrated eating facilities by mid-August.

Dr. Gardner Taylor, preparing for the big push to oust Dr. Jackson, added his voice to those of the militants: "Tomorrow, libraries, parks, theatres will face the same choice, integration or disintegration.''

It appeared that the doctrine of patience was passé. After successfully riding through his second four-year leadership cycle, Dr. Jackson prepared to make his stand for another term. Philadelphia, the "city of brotherly love," was to be the scene of the next election. The progressives, conceding that Jackson would run again, searched for and found a new candidate. Gardner Taylor, pastor of the Concord Baptist Church, Brooklyn, N.Y., was their man. Taylor made an attractive candidate. Pastoring a church of over 10,000 members, he, like Jackson, was a gifted orator. Jackson supporters tried in vain to get Taylor to withdraw as a candidate. They warned him that if he was defeated, his chance of ever becoming president was gone. You are young, they informed him; you still have time. Let Jackson have another four years. Your day will soon come.

Gardner Taylor was cast in the mold of a fighter. He was the first black member of the New York City Board of Education; he was also the first black president of the New York State Council of Ministers. Tall, handsome, and militant, he was "tailor-made" as a Jackson opponent. A major attraction was his identity with Martin Luther King. By this time the younger King was the leader of the Southern Christian Leadership Conference, and the talk of him as a possible president of the National Baptist Convention had long since diminished. Prior to the annual session in Philadelphia, Jackson and Taylor skirmished briefly at the Sunday School and BTU Congress. Once again Jackson was expounding on his favorite theme—"patience." He told of an incident when he was a boy picking cotton in Mississippi. The gist of the story was that when he missed one train, he would "wait," for he knew that another train would be coming in the future. Gardner Taylor seized upon this analogy to set in contrast the mood of the new blacks. He attacked Jackson's reasoning by saying:

> Some people might find it easy to wait for the next train, but the Negro wants his freedom . . . now! He is not going to wait for any other train, he wants the one at the station . . . now.

As the delegates flocked to the new battlefield in Philadelphia, it soon became apparent that the Taylor forces were strong. Philadelphia was the political stronghold of the Reverend Marshall Shepard, former state legislator and recorder of deeds in Washington. Shepard was an avid worker and arranger for Taylor; he worked against Jackson with a passion. He had his reasons: Jackson had disposed of him as chairman of the Foreign Mission Board. Taylor likewise was supported by Dr. Sandye Raye, President of the New York State Convention. These large Eastern voting blocs, far removed from Jackson's political strongholds of the South and Midwest, the Jacksonites watched with deep anxiety.

Both sides immediately sought ground rules for the election. The electoral procedure that had become customary was deplored by the Taylor team. This procedure worked in this manner: after the president had made his annual address, someone would make a motion that the rules be suspended and that the president be reelected by acclamation. The progressives claimed that this method was unfair, undemocratic, and had steamroller elements. Give all the delegates the right to cast ballots, they contended, and let their votes be recorded as they vote by states. It was reported that an agreement had been hammered out. All delegates were informed that the election would be conducted by states. The ground rules worked out by both parties likewise included an agreement that the nominating committee, selected by the president, would bring in two names: Taylor and Jackson. The delegates would then vote for the man of their choice.

The Taylor team was ready; the Jackson forces were waiting. The events that were to follow were almost unbelievable.

On Wednesday, contrary to the alleged agreement concerning the dual submission of names, the nominating committee reported one name—J. H. Jackson. The Taylor forces were caught off guard. Moving quickly, before the delegates could regain their balance, the committee went on. Without asking for nominations from the floor, they moved that their report be adopted as a unanimous vote for the reelection of Dr. Jackson.

This maneuver must be viewed from two positions: 1) the body had voted earlier that the election would be by states; or 2) the report was made prior to the time of the scheduled election. Outmaneuvered, the Taylor team resorted to bedlam.

"We want Taylor, we want Taylor," they shouted in unison.

"We want to vote, and we want to vote by states," they chorused.

Someone cut the microphone cord. Turning to the large choir, Dr. Jackson ordered them to sing. The chanting grew louder, accompanied by the songs of the church. Churchmen were on a rampage. Dr. Jackson, facing a dead microphone, attempted to read his annual address. The election was to follow his address.

"Sit down," the Taylorites yelled, "we don't want to hear you."

"We want to vote, and we want to vote by states," they screamed out in the middle of his opening statement.

The premature report of the nominating committee had set up this tempest, and it was clear to the Taylor team what was to follow.

As Dr. Jackson attempted to deliver his annual address, Taylor supporters brought in a bass drum and marched behind its noisy booming with Taylor banners. They released Taylor balloons. The president struggled on to be heard, but after a few sentences he realized the utter futility of proceeding. In desperation he skipped to the end paragraph and read it with a flourish; but it was unheard. Then came the betrayal.

Immediately after the few sentences of Jackson's address had been delivered, a motion was offered in the midst of the bedlam that the report of the nominating committee be received and adopted. What followed this motion was never clearly determined. Those who were standing close to the platform heard the motion, but many of the delegates were meanwhile still shouting, "We want Taylor." Considering that the mike was dead and the delegates were in turmoil, it was surprising to everyone when the news came out that Jackson had been reelected.

Alice Dunningham, reporting the scene for the *Pittsburgh Courier*, described the proceedings as follows:

> The place was in such a hub-bub that no one knew what was going on. Martin Luther King approached the press table to inquire about the re-election of Jackson. He was startled when reporters sitting directly in front of the platform replied that there had been no election.
>
> "There must have been," retorted King, "I just met Rev. Jackson leaving the hall and he told me he had just been reelected." This sent up an inquiry among reporters on how and when the president had been elected.

When the news sifted back to the masses that the election was over, Dr. Jackson was rapping the convention adjourned until the evening session. The angered Taylorites increased the fervor of their demonstration. It was at this point that Jackson left the hall and notified King that he had been reelected. Gardner Taylor, standing tall in the midst of his supporters, yelled out:

"The worst days of Hitler never matched this. If Negroes stand for this, they will let the world know they are not prepared for leadership. But they will not stand for this . . . they *will* have an election!"

"God help us," prayed an old minister. The Taylorites, with Jackson gone, moved quickly.

"This meeting is not adjourned," shouted Dr. Sandye Raye. "Please hold your seats; this meeting is not adjourned," he repeated over and over again. "We're going to have an election, and we're going to vote by states." A roar of approval went up from the delegates.

Dr. Jackson, meanwhile, had locked himself in his convention office. Reporters seeking to interview him were hustled off by his "bodyguards." Alice Dunningham further reported:

> Some persistent reporters hung around the door and buttonholed the self-appointed president as he departed for his hotel. He assured reporters that this election had been conducted legally under the terms of the convention's constitution. He blamed Dr. Marshall Shepard, a Philadelphia councilman, for the disorder implying that the disgruntled minister was angry after being dismissed from the convention for filing a suit against the president

95

some years ago. He claimed that the police officers, working with Shepard, declined to keep order in the hall. Declaring that this city of brotherly love was the most inhospitable city in which the convention had ever met, he declared that the convention would never come to Philadelphia again as long as he was president.

While Jackson was making this declaration, the convention itself was coming to order. The delegates were filing in and arranging themselves by states. They were determined to have an orderly election. Rev. C. V. Johnson, Illinois state president and one of the National Convention vice presidents, was selected to conduct the election. The election results were not surprising. 1,864 voted for Taylor; 536 voted for Jackson. The convention now had two presidents.

When the time for the evening session approached, Dr. Jackson entered the hall to preside; Dr. Taylor was standing beside him. The police were called. Neither side would yield. When the police inspector remarked that the situation was embarrassing to him, one of the delegates yelled up to him:

"If you had stayed out of here you wouldn't be embarrassed. We're Baptist," he argued. "We have a right to fight among ourselves without your help."

In spite of this brief moment of humor, which was appreciated by both sides, the wound in the side of the Negro Baptist Church went deep into the heart of its church. The year 1960 found two men claiming the presidency. The conclusion to the affair, with elements of tragedy, was to come in Kansas City the following year.

The 1961 convention was called to order by Dr. Jackson. The Taylor team had decided to fight with the use of another method—the courts. However, Taylorites could not contain their anger while Jackson was presiding. Disorder again broke out. It began when Dr. E. C. Estell of Dallas presented a resolution that requested Dr. Jackson to allow his name to be voted on again as president of the convention. Stomping and yelling, the Taylor forces became so disorderly that the director of the auditorium begged the mayor of the city to appeal to the convention.

Typical of the mood of black people then was the story that was making the rounds. It involved the traditional Uncle Tom who was ordered by the white folks to go on television and report that the Negro had nothing to complain about. They handed him a prepared script and commanded him to read it. The old black man took the script the white folks handed him; it was full of lies concerning the good treatment the Negro was getting in the South.

"White folks, am I on ABC?"

"You are," they assured him.

"CBS?" he inquired further. They assured him he was.

"Am I also on NBC?" By this time the white prompters were losing patience: they had paid for this time on the air and Tom was wasting it.

"Tom," they informed him. "You can be heard all over America. You are on radio and T.V. stations in the land." Reassured that he could be heard all over, Tom stepped in front of the cameras, looked dead at the red light, and screamed, "Help!"

This was the mood of the day. The black church and many black ministers entered the fray with enthusiasm. It was against this backdrop that J. H. Jackson began his own program of freedom. First, he presented to the convention a plan to buy farmland in Tennessee. This was during the "Tent City" crisis. The purpose of his plan was to buy farmland so that blacks would not have to depend upon the white man. But the plan was labeled a "Booker T. Washington approach" by the progressives.

"Let down your buckets where you are," said Jackson. His critics seized upon this new venture with mirth.

"Old man Jackson had a farm. . . ," they chanted. It was ironic, they contended, that in an age of sit-ins, pray-ins, wade-ins, and stand-ins, Jackson would stage a "farm-in."

The next venture by Dr. Jackson, in support of his "protest is not enough" approach, was his plan to buy land in Liberia. The purpose, he explained, was to import black families to Liberia to teach the Liberians by example how to live and farm as Christians. More followers deserted him as he

97

seemed to focus his attention on blacks in other nations rather than on the black condition in America.

> As Christians, we must accept and employ those methods that are just, seasoned in love, and based on the brotherhood of man and the fatherhood of God. The church cannot be used as a rubber stamp for every method employed in the name of democracy and freedom. The church must not wait for others to begin a movement for human betterment. The church is a revolutionary movement, and God's prophets and God's ministers have historically been "those who have come to turn the world upside down."

True, responded his critics. However, even though these words were directed against the militancy of the blacks' march toward freedom, they can more wisely be applied to the National Baptist Convention itself. Dr. Jackson, with his ministers and prophets, had indeed turned it upside down.

* * * * *

Today, thirty years after promising a new day for black Baptists, Joseph Harrison Jackson is still president of the National Baptist Convention. The 1982 Convention will be held in the plush Fontainebleau Hotel, Miami Beach, instead of the dingy halls and auditoriums of earlier years. Dr. Jackson is an old man now, doddering and feeble; his oratorical voice of old has vanished, and so have thousands of black ministers who initially looked to him as a beacon but long since have seen him as a light that failed.

I will attend that convention as an observer, not as a delegate. I will seek hard to find, once again, a young, bold, and militant black preacher who will electrify the Convention into social concern. I will seek in vain.

The bullets that pierced the body of Martin Luther King, Jr. killed something in me with regard to the institutional church. That is, the institutional church died in me when Martin died. I followed and loved Martin with a passionate and deep respect. I was proud to have often been mistaken for his brother. And so we were, albeit not by blood kinship. So little time did we have with him . . . so little time did this nation have with him. His advice, his theology, his disillusionment still remain with me.

In the year 1982, a strange black silence has emerged. The traditional protesting voices have become silent. In a year when Reaganomics has imposed itself on black dreams and aspirations, black militancy has disappeared, and in its place have come only sporadic mutterings concerning this nation's policies and directions. The black caucus, composed of this country's thirteen lonely black congressmen submerged in the milky white lake of Congress, has reduced its rhetoric and demands to meet with the President. The yearly hot fires of anger have turned slowly into ashes of mere disenchantment. Traditional black leadership has turned inward to the nation's ghettos and, in a dire search for a meaningful existence, to the political arena for survival. From city to city, leadership has vied for the seats of mayors, city councilmen, and school boards. It is as if white flight has left for blacks a limitation of power, with elections to vacated white offices becoming an oasis in the desert of nothingness. Ironically, this silence has appeared at a time when loud shouts of protest should be heard. The roof of white institutional racism should be raised to reveal the agonizing portraits of old and young blacks who are devoid of security, loans, unemployment programs, who are experiencing welfare cutbacks and a deterioration of faith in a nation that ensures the pursuit of happiness.

With Martin gone, the black church once more returned to Jesus, while our cities are still prime for the burning. Old-time religion may have been good enough for my dear mother, but even she must begin to see—and she does—that it is not enough for me. It was Martin Luther King who taught me that, not out of disrespect for the black church but out of respect for its potential to unleash a powerful force for social change.

As the 1982 National Baptist Convention once more elects Joseph Harrison Jackson to be its president, history will remember him only as a footnote in the struggle for freedom.

From him emerged no new theology, no thrust for social change. I will long for the voice of Martin Luther King; but from the grave comes no sound. No reverberation of his passionate litanies, no replacement for the rapturous past. No trumpet to sound us to battle.

It was Martin Luther King whom historians have lauded and will laud as the author and initiator of the black theology of protest.

CHAPTER 12

The Black Theology of Protest

"Every man's work shall be made manifest, for the day shall declare it, because it shall be revealed by fire. . . ." (I Corinthians 3:13)

"Yea, he warmeth himself, and saith, 'Aha,
I am warm, I have seen the fire.' " (Isaiah 44:16)

*D*EEP WITHIN THE HEART OF THE SOUTH AND scattered throughout the North, a new emotion gripped black people. It was a new birth. This was the legacy of Martin Luther King.

At gatherings of civil rights groups the predominating theme of protest swept the country. The black youth of the nation demanded to be heard, seen, and recognized. In their meetings they presented a picture of the burning church of old. Even their songs were adaptations of a fiery church. To a large degree, many students were participants in the silent religious rebellion within established black churches; yet, in their struggle for freedom, they turned back the clock and used the spiritual fire that spurred them onward. The typical freedom rally contained all of the ingredients of the burning church. Songs were "lined" out, and the freedom seekers responded as their grandparents did. Prayers of old were heard, and the speakers dwelt on the hard times and tribulations of second-class citizenship. The charismatic protest service came into full sway.

The connective links that established the burning church with the protest movements were not incidental. The phenomena experienced in both of these areas were occasioned by a similar need: the need of escape. As in times of old, the religious atmosphere provided the emotional release necessary for self-esteem and respect. It was the growing black self-image that gave it impetus. The leaders of these groups appealed to this imagery in ecclesiastical tones:

"We're tired," they exclaimed.

"Tired," echoed the masses.

"We're tired of going to back doors," they went on, "tired of riding in the back, tired of standing up while the white man sits, tired of second-class citizenship."

"Tired," the agreeing response came with fervor.

"We're tired of being the last hired and the first fired. We're tired of discrimination and segregation."

"Speak up, that's right, speak tonight, we hear you."

"This is not Russia and we are not slaves," the leader reasoned. "This is the United States of America and we want freedom . . . now!" He took his seat in righteous indignation.

A shout went up from the freedom seekers. The speaker had electrified them into action. Some laughed, others wept. A song began, led by a well-dressed college student:

> Freedom, free-eedom, free-eedom, freedom, freedom
> A little louder now
> Free-eedom, free-eedom, free-eedom, freedom, freedom
> Gonna get some
> Freedom
> In the morning
> Freedom
> Right now-ow
> Freedom, freedom, freedom.

Around they marched. All present were caught up in the spirit of their movements. Mothers who were present and watching their children perform in such manner shouted out as if in the religious services of old. The children cried, filled with that unknown something that had put fire in their bones. On they marched, up and down the church aisles, singing one song after another, until finally, from sheer exhaustion, they stopped and waited for the black clergyman and laymen to direct them.

The clergyman approached the offering table. He spoke: "We need money. We need money for jail bonds. We need money for lawyers' fees. We need money." Black people marched up to the table with nickels and dimes from pinched groceries; students marched with dollars taken from tuition payments; wealthy blacks wrote out checks for hundreds. It was a new type of church service. From whence came this fire?

Any outlandish condition or indignity suffered by a black person would firmly establish a freedom rally. Whether it took the form of the lynching of Emmett Till in Mississippi, or Rosa Parks' refusal to take a back seat on the bus in Montgomery, the fire burned and was not consumed.

The widening areas of assimilation found the blacks there, throwing themselves bravely wherever there existed the slightest hint of rejection. Those who wondered at this boldness failed to recognize the 300 years of passivity, inherited from and taught by black forefathers. Blacks adopted the right of massive protest, and this right they would not relinquish. It became the new fire in their bosoms.

The black church bequeathed to black protest the fire of religious fervor. Without that religious orientation the spiritual form of the struggle for dignity would have been ultimately negated. Black religion informed us that our station in life was far short of the Christian concept. We were propelled by the "oughtness" that dared the "isness." The fire did not quit burning, and it fed upon the plentiful symbols that gave it spark.

Sit-ins, wade-ins, pray-ins, ride-ins were the symbols. To be sure, not all blacks participated; but those who did, did so with the prayers of millions of their black brothers. The extent of involvement in those movements of creative force can never be subjected to statistical inquiry, but the participating blacks were aware of mass black empathy. The sweeping reactions within the black community were religiously felt.

Later I was to develop a theological approach to the ministry which is best illustrated by an address I gave to an association of black pastors just two years after the assassination of Martin Luther King. During that period I formulated a philosophy of the mission of the black church that would preach more the necessity of social justice now than the ultimate hope of heaven in the by and by. Many black ministers were confused, particularly after a black militant group demanded that the white church pay reparations to blacks for past injustices. If, then, the liberal white church was to undertake this as a mission, what would be left for the black church to do?

BLACK POWER AND GOD

In the current crisis, the questions concerning the future of the black church and its mission are many. It appears to me that the times now require that the black church and its clergymen come to grips with the future, using the stony paths over which we have trod as our religious orientation. This message is not an appeal for a return to the fleshpots of Egypt, for indeed we must face the wilderness of urban crisis, and somehow attempt to reach the promised land of peace.

How is this to be done? Tonight, I will deal with where we came from and where we are; tomorrow, in the final presentation, I will present a suggested plan for the future.

What part did the black church and its clergy play in the early years of the Black Revolution? It was chiefly because of the religious orientation that black clergymen found themselves in a developing quandary. The black church was faced with a new force . . . and a new mission. Because it was the only massive physical structure in which the black community could gather, and because it was the one communication source where the events of the week could be reliably reported, it was a natural setting for protest gatherings and mass meetings. By virtue of long-standing traditions, between the worship hours, black clergymen reported to their flocks the occurrences and developments of protest, informing them that a meeting to deal with the issues would be held at the church. As a source of inspiration, they asked church choirs and singing groups to open the meetings with songs and prayer. The clergymen soon found themselves deep in the heart of protest, forced down there by both a demanding people and institutionalized imprisonment. Some sought vainly to identify only with the worship and the mechanics of arranging the meetings; but their voices were also needed. Leadership required those voices that boomed the loudest. Heaven could no longer be used as a sedative to rising expectations, and the youth of the land began to make that clear. The swift transition of the black church from an institution for worship to the gathering place for protestors found at least three classifications of clergymen: those who openly protested the tactics of passive resistance; those who applauded but would not become involved; and those who accepted the challenge of leading the movement.

The position that a black clergyman ultimately chose depended largely upon the kind of church that he pastored and the social stratification of his members. Large black churches, for example, with a demanding administrative ministry, were involved in the protest movement less than were churches whose ministers were freer from such demands. Thus black clergymen who provided the spark of leadership often came from smaller congregations.

Meanwhile, as black clergymen analyzed the conditions in their cities and the popular rising tide of black militancy, their thoughts and analyses were being reinterpreted by the black world as to their value for leadership. Comparisons were made, and jealousy entered the ranks. As we have seen, internal jealousy was not new within the black church ranks. Preaching styles and educational differences or attainments had already made their inroads for jealous comparisons. For years white society had chosen black spokesmen and often openly identified at least one as the voice of the black community. But now traditional black clergymen who had long been considered leaders found themselves supplanted and replaced within the black community by younger and more daring spokesmen who were prone to activism. These young black "turks" were viewed by their older conservative peers with alarm. The younger breed carried with them as part of their protest a disenchantment with the institutional black church that had sedated black people with emotions that had no outlets. Their style of preaching was an ambivalent mixture of old-time religion and creative social change.

This was the kind of black clergyman who was able to fit and operate in the transitional phase of the church. Black ministerial associations, which traditionally meet on Monday mornings, were often rent with the challenge of the "turks" who questioned the unused and untried power of massed black clergymen. The style of leadership was changing. Traditionally, conservative and older black clergymen had been elected by the group to head ministerial groups and associations. In that setting they dominated both the meetings and fundamental theological concepts. In such a setting, an announcement of pending mass meeting found little enthusiasm. In his traditional role as a black spokesman, the older clergyman seldom uttered words that were reported in the mass media—with the exception of announcements in the white press of his coming anniversary, his invocation at a white gathering, or his silent presence at white ministerial associations. The conservative black clergyman never achieved headlines.

Not so the young turks. With increasing courage, emboldened by the momentum of the rebellion in the South, they voiced intense verbal dissatisfaction with local conditions. And these voices were picked up by the press. Overnight, the black population had new spokesmen. The chill that set in the black religious world began to polarize the black community. Each clergyman became identified with his social position and concerns. "Uncle Toms" were discovered and discarded. Memberships in the various churches began to rise or diminish in relation to the progressive or conservative leadership. As to the issue of civil rights that was mounting in intensity, the black church swayed. Churches that went in the direction of progressive, evolutionary movements from the old worship patterns suddenly discovered that their minister found in the civil rights movement a stance that made him comfortable. The charismatic "old timer" was still yelling "give me Jesus," while his progressive counterpart was shouting "give us freedom."

Martin Luther King, Jr. had started it all. In addition to being responsible for the black revolution in America, he, more than any other, began it within the black church. From the day he was elected president of the Montgomery, Alabama, Improvement Association, and for that position left the Dexter Avenue Baptist Church and made the streets his worship center, the black and white world his congregation, he introduced a new black theology.

It was not a comfortable theology, for it included new directions for the total black church. Black leadership that could not adapt itself to its message of protest and mission of freedom was left stranded in its own confusion. Each demonstration produced new leaders; indeed, black clergymen were labeled "imitations" of King throughout the North and South. These clergymen wore that label with pride. Somehow they had caught the vision of the future, and they willingly suffered the derision of their peers and the white community.

From the local level to the state level of black clerical gatherings, the years 1956-1960 found intense debate and contemplation concerning the direction the black church and its leadership should take. The political forces within black organizations were either formed around or evaded the issue of King's philosophy of passive resistance. The state religious organizations in many instances attempted to shun the issue. After all, fellowship was the prime reason for the existence of these conventions and associations, and the national fights for black freedom were producing schisms within the clerical ranks. However, the progressive clergymen demanded that it be the *only* issue, and when elections were held for the first time, progressive and conservative black clergymen were identified by their selection of conventional and associational leadership.

The struggle for power and leadership in these areas where masses of black clergymen gathered was probably the best weather vane of the times. It is ironic that the institutional black church, historically noted from the time of its rise before and after slavery, became the battleground of the new black theology of protest. Within its ranks Martin Luther King brought the sharp knife that inflicted pain: the painful awareness that old-time religion had to make way for black people on the move. Civil rights had once more set the black church on fire. The fruits of those early years of protest were both to challenge and remove those who desired to extinguish the flames.

Now the flame has been extinguished. The black church is now clearly caught in the black-white swirls of crisis. Its traditional stabilizing role in the black world has not only of late been challenged . . . the black church is now threatened. It was the ancient practitioner of the Theology of Hope; that hope is now dissipating while momentum toward a separatist society gathers.

This momentum had its impact upon white denominations. In 1969, many accepted James Forman's advocacy of reparations, creating a strange present paradox. White racism is assuredly the cruel perpetrator of the black man's plight. The demand that the white church face up to setting in motion financial response to urban crisis is not debated. In fact, the Black Manifesto had put the white church in a posture of "uptightness"; it created an abrasive tension and struck with force and power into the bastion of white hypocrisy. It disturbed white status quo and took away the protective shield that sheltered its past, rendered its present meaningless, and threatened to dictate inaction in the future.

The responses of the white church to the Black Manifesto is by now a matter of record: it was checkered and spotty. However, what now concerns me is not so much how the white church responded but what is to become of the mission of the black church. I bring, therefore, a dimension beyond the Manifesto; for in the final analysis, a total white response to the Black Manifesto would leave the black church without a working theology or mission comparable to the earlier years of protest.

I submit to you that the church must theologize and stabilize the galloping dimensions of what we call black power. What is black power? I give to you the positive forms. After viewing white racism, I now define black power as watching white heads in Chicago being bloodied by policemen and understanding for the first time that the black man said, "We told you so." Black power is a white politician paying attention for the first time to welfare mothers, smiling at them, but refusing to come close enough to kiss their babies. Black power is a song, a rhythmic song, contagious and black, with a message that whites can never understand. Black power makes Roy Wilkins harden his voice to keep from sounding like Uncle Tom. Black power turns Whitney Young two shades darker when he argues for more money for the Urban League. Black power protests against a homemade Vietnam, against the ghettos that have always been like My-lai, where the old men, children, youth have always been slaughtered by hunger and joblessness and malnutrition. Black power recognizes this, rises up to condemn, defy, and—when pressed—to burn.

The burning in the ghetto is more than open fire and licking flames. It is a raging fever against the racist system, crying out to unlock the prisons and break down the bars. Black power is a fire of disgust too long absorbed by a white system. Yes, the ghetto burns because of black power. But it has always burned, three hundred years, smokeless and invisible.

If I were a white I would fear that smokeless, invisible sign of black power. In fact, I would have by now caught the spark of emotions of black burnings and yearnings by creating other fires—your own fires—within the racist system that ostracizes me as a black. Whites ought to catch the spark from the energy that black power creates. Black power is looking at white power and wondering why. Black power is flexing new muscles, writing new values, examining the constitution, and finishing up the loopholes.

Black power is decision making without compromise; it is pride without apology. Black power is loving oneself because no one else will. It is transplanting its heart into a newfound body, new life into dried-up bloodstreams. Black power is a cheerleader for the team that is down, a sniff of oxygen to stay in the game. It is the awakening insight. Black power is the moisture that turns buds into flowers, and black midgets into giants.

Black power is not going back to Africa. Black power suggests that we stay right here, in the land of our birth, until we are free. Whites have the choice to remain. Why not the same for blacks? I say to you, when all the English go back to England, all the Irish go back to Ireland, when all the Scots go back to Scotland, all the Germans go back to Germany, when all the Hungarians go back to Hungary, we blacks might then decide to go back to Africa. Until that time, this is our home, damnable as it may be. I say to black people, continue to build if you will have a new black society—economic, social, and educational. Argue if you will for black teachers, black schools, black businesses; contend if you will for Black Christmas and Black Santa Claus. But in the final analysis I see that a black country within a white country must soon come to grips with its own survival and the survival of its children. Separatism, in this age, for the sake of identity, pride, and manhood speaks well for itself—*until whitey wakes up*. No argument can or ever should be advanced to curtail this newfound spirit of unity and blackness together—*until whitey wakes up*.

Now it is this negative future that challenges the black church into a position of power and influence, to somehow tip the scales in the direction of ensuring the salvation of a race and the nation, while remaining true to the principles and need for black power. In this context the black church, I feel, should involve itself in a messianic mission: to surge forth out of its present-day quandary and to manifest the works of God. A realistic, hard look at the black church today finds black movements and theologies lying about in splintering disarray. Leadership exercised by the church and its clergymen at the height of the civil rights movement is gone. The heroes of the black church have externally suffered death—assassinated by bullets such as struck down Dr. King—and internally suffered the incursions of black extremists who picked up the gauntlet in another form of battle. The early cry "integration" has been replaced by "disintegration." "We shall overcome" has been replaced by voices shouting "We shall overthrow."

And so we drift, slowly but surely, toward the twin societies predicted by the Kerner Commission—one black, one white. We must assess, as the black church, who we are and where we are going. The decision-making process at this juncture of history will be painful, caught as we are between twin worlds of instability—one world racist by nature and the other fighting back with weapons that the true church cannot sanction. Separatism in any form denies the existence of God. Call it what you will, black pride or white racism, if any such condition becomes a permanent affliction of either race, indeed God can be proclaimed dead in us.

No attempt should be made to diminish the importance of the new thrust for black identity; but coupled with that thrust must be a firm theological base for the future. Within the framework of the black revolution, God must continue to exist, not as the God of vengeance, but the God of history—"The Rock of Ages, Cleft for Me"—that when the storms of life are raging, I want him to be there to beg of him, "Let me hide myself in Thee."

If this God, the God of history, is buried in the racial turmoil and upheavals of our times, no one dominantly black or white will be able to claim him. White racism is the generating flame that consumes our manhood; but if we allow it to consume our souls, there will be no God for us to claim.

Here, then, stands the black church and its clergy. The leadership required of us lies in the wasteland of black anger. Those who advocate the principle of love are laughed out of existence by the black world and subject to be overrun by the white world. The black clergyman, standing before his people, finds himself almost speechless, muttering irrelevancies or pulling out of the barrel stock messages of heaven. Untouched in the process are the lives of people now confronted with the prospect of genocide or, at best, doomed to remain in ghettos deprived of employment, food, and mobility.

CHAPTER 13

Leaving the Ministry

M Y DECISION TO LEAVE EVANSVILLE AND THE church was not an easy one. The Liberty Baptist Church, in its 100-year history of existence, had had only four pastors. I was the fourth. But my ten-year tenure had changed me from being a Negro to becoming a black man. I found it extremely difficult to conduct a ministry of healing my people rather than healing the nation. As a battered people sought equity and justice outside the church, I found that I was spending more time assisting them outside of the church than from within. I began to disdain the weak theological shorings of the traditionalists, and I sought for new religious meanings and a philosophy of religion that was both religiously sustaining and secularly fulfilling. There were no ways I could find that could meet those criteria. The change had seeped into me. Current events held me captive: the newspaper became my bible, the headlines my sermon. I agonized over various possibilities and settled for none. Whenever possible, I hurried south to join Martin Luther King and the SCLC in protest. But this in-and-out process wearied me. Others—men like C. T. Vivian, Wyatt T. Walker, Hosea Williams, and Andy Young—had long since discarded the trappings of the church, becoming lieutenants in the struggle, captains in the army of protest. I was a buck private. The protests that I was unable to attend, I documented. History, I knew, would not record the full flavor of those major moments, those heady feelings we had while joining hands and singing "We Shall Overcome." The life of the movement became a prayer, our marching feet a hymn.

The biting dogs, the cattle prods, the fire hoses, bit, stung, and probed into the flesh of black Americans—but they continued to march.

The 1960s were the years of elation, the high that comes from standing tall on the mountain of right, looking down into the deep valley of wrong. We were, in fact, superior to our white tormentors; for when blood did flow, it was our blood. Protestation became like oxygen in our air, a plasmatic secretion for those who had no blood. Our songs were sung as if written by angels, and our leader was Martin Luther King. On protest days, each day was Sunday, every marcher the congregation; but instead of sitting in pews, we sat in streets. Each symbol of segregation that fell produced a grand shout, swelling in a magnitude that vied with that of the "Hallelujah Chorus." It is no wonder, then, that the institutional church, with its stated mission of saving souls, shrank to minimal proportions as it vied with the saving of a race.

Each summer, on a Ford Foundation fellowship, I would return to Virginia Union Theological Seminary, and there with a score of black ministers, including Morris Synnes of Chicago, William Penn of Gary, Phale Hale of Michigan, and Dr. James Cheek (currently president of Howard University), I attempted to assess the theology of protest and the mission of the black church. The wide and varied opinions aired in such intellectual pursuits failed to nail down for me specific directions. Dr. Marcus Ellis, a former president of Virginia Union and my theological mentor, came closest of all. He advised me, "Do what you know you must." In essence, he informed me to heed and use the fire in my bones. Rev. C. T. Vivian, Martin Luther King's assistant, who, more than anyone else, developed King's Southern strategy, was even more compelling. He viewed the church only as a training vehicle to enter into battle, a "place to get your bullets to shoot the devil." He urged me to attend the Urban Training Center in Chicago, where he served as a staff member, developing black clergymen for a new mission to the nation's cities. Again, a Ford Foundation grant made that training possible. After eight weeks, Vivian, together with Dr. Archie Hargroves, had succeeded in moving me out of the institution of the church into opposing the urban institution of white racism.

It was a sad Sunday for me when I announced that I was resigning as pastor of the Liberty Baptist Church. For ten years they had sheltered me, loved me, and dealt forgivingly with both my excesses and other demands on my time. They too had felt the movement gradually pulling me away from my religious endeavors. They had shared me with the movement, and without malice or bitterness they now bade me adieu. For a few months, I accepted a position on the staff of the War on Poverty Program, and subsequently became the first executive director of the Human Relations Commission in Gary, Indiana. The fire was still burning.

PART III
Urban Crisis

CHAPTER 14
Gary, Indiana

WHEN I MOVED TO GARY, INDIANA, IT WAS MORE than the name of a song in the "Music Man." It was a youthful city trembling on the brink of the unknown. The majority of its citizens had withdrawn into a shell; or, like ostriches, they had buried their heads in the sand. No wonder! Gary, as it existed, defied comprehension or immediate solution.

Intelligent people were beginning to measure the strengths of a black power movement, and not without reason. No accurate census had been taken of Gary since 1960; however, the number of blacks in the city had been estimated at 55 percent of a total population that exceeded 180,000. If this was not an indicator of the present problem it certainly compounded the problems of the future. The city was running out of space. This would pose a problem for any ordinary city; but in Gary, because of its minority growth, it almost amounted to stacking up dynamite. Gary's slums vied with those of any large city in their nasty living conditions.

Seven thousand dwellings and buildings had been condemned and marked for demolition, while 34,000 out of the city's total of more than 52,000 housing units needed major and minor rehabilitation. This left only about 10,000 sound units in the entire city. As one would expect, the sound dwellings could be found exclusively in the suburbs, while those marked for demolition and major rehabilitation were identified, marked, and labeled in the ghetto. Three hundred and sixty-five families were on the waiting list for low-income housing—and no such housing had been built in twenty years. Over

395 families would be displaced by urban renewal in the year ahead (plus more than 400 individuals); and yet, even those affluent enough to live in housing other than low-income housing fought to find quarters out of the then existing vacancies—175 homes and fewer than 200 available rental apartments as of July 1966.

In 1966 Gary had one newspaper, three radio stations, and no local television outlet. This virtual communication blackout left most of the population apathetic to the living conditions, and all became silent observers of what was considered a prelude to disaster. Strangely enough, although Gary's minorities faced housing and employment discrimination, no aggressive action on the part of minorities had arisen to protest the conditions of the slums or other problems associated with ghetto living. Although 70 percent of the crime, juvenile delinquency, disease, and welfare were the exclusive domain of the ghetto, the local poverty program had not zeroed in on those problems. In fact, the main office of the poverty program was located in Hammond, with the Gary poverty operation merely handled by a Gary coordinator.

A national magazine featured a story on Gary as "Sin City, USA," which sent up protest howls in the city that were loud and vociferous. No wonder. Most of Gary's citizens were either unaware of or unattentive to the rolling momentum of the city's problems.

A parenthetical note on the publicized sins of the city is in order at this point. Our puritanical and vociferous objection to the existence of vice, crime, and prostitution was admittedly justified. Those subjects were the whipping boys of most upright citizens, and those discoveries were subject matter for headlines and front-page coverage. But the emotional disturbance generated by those activities did not carry over to form outcries against slum landlords who prostituted the future of black youth, or to the vice of discrimination in employment, or to the crime of segregated housing. Those subjects did not always make headlines upon discovery, but they were destined to become important discoveries in this "City of the Century." These were the walls that alienated its people; that was the threat of disaster! Unbalanced by the influences of disproportionate growth and outrage, the city spun crazily toward its unknown destiny.

One hope of social and economic survival in Gary was to become based on the political system. Whites and blacks alike contended for position and power; and this struggle not only alienated both races from dealing with the actual problems of the city, it threatened to alienate them from each other as well. Many white families who had retreated from the core of the city carried with them the fear of the growing power and presence of the minorities, while the minorities that remained, squeezed in the ghetto, stored up their hostility. Gary had few nonpolitical black leaders. Those who held promise of capturing and motivating the masses of blacks to act in concert had been successfully swallowed up by the political system or were captive to the spoils of political conquest.

For that reason, affluent and influential blacks were openly indicted by their grass-roots counterparts. The resentment and hostility toward them was on an equal plane with the resentment toward the white power structure. The latter segment of the community confined most of its human relations activities to asking questions of affluent black leaders, and they met occasionally to discuss rising problems. While both races deplored the rising white and black power plays, neither group was openly vocal on issues that confronted the city; nor were their observations made available to the city officials.

In 1964 the Gary Chamber of Commerce failed to support the Omnibus Civil Rights Ordinance. Consequently, all black members of the Chamber resigned from that body. None returned. The Gary Board of Realtors filed suit against the City of Gary for its passage of that ordinance. As a result, the white areas of the city contained few, if any, black families. White citizens in outlying areas angrily remonstrated against planned low-cost housing and the attendant potential of blacks living in those racially exclusive, untouched areas. The remonstrators were actively led by four white Council members, while three black Council members argued and voted in behalf of the much-needed housing. The remaining two sat perched on the fence of indecision, and when the time came for them to vote, they abstained. Tempers flared in Council meetings, as Council members accused each other of racism, no matter what issue was under discussion.

The anger of Gary's minorities was fierce, but contained; no violence had yet made its appearance. Gary's contained fury was its bright hope and its future's dark promise. Its struggle with the complex racial structure sapped the strength of those who were elected or committed to hold the city in firm check.

Gary's highest elected official, the mayor, was probably the most torn official of any city in the nation. The delicate balancing act necessary to assure his continuing in office called for the type of statesmanship that would inevitably prove to satisfy neither racial structure. He was forced to live with a combination of political hopes and daily crises, hoping for the best while fearing the worst. Considering the causes of the crises, one could see that his position was not enviable. His choices were limited and at times impossible; his decisions were critical. Few sought that office, and those who did sought it with the knowledge that to achieve it might spell political oblivion. If he were black, he would have to be aware that the economic and social power was white. If he were white, he would immediately have to recognize that he was lifted to that office by a majority that was black—but powerless.

Meanwhile, forgotten in the racial tug of war were the problems of other minorities. The city's Spanish-speaking and Puerto Rican citizens, constituting a sizable portion (12 percent) of the population, were virtually buried in the rush for power. The black and white thrust for power and position seldom included the forgotten minorities. Those people had no recognized, articulate spokesman for their cause, and the discriminatory damage inflicted upon them passed either unnoticed or unrecorded. Civil rights in Gary was the recognized area for blacks; other minorities were offered at best a free ride on the backs of their black fellow citizens. In spite of this obvious vacuum, Latins and Puerto Ricans had first choices in the midtown apartments that skirted the edge of the ghetto. In due time, some of them adopted a noticeable resentment toward blacks who entered their newly found havens. Thus the possible alliances that could have been formed between all minority groups were negated by the practices of the landlords and realtors. The latter discovered that it was the path of least resistance to offer the first housing crumbs to those whose social visibility was lower. The racial tempo increased.

As could be expected, the lack of attention to those minority groups would not last long. Knowledgeable political aspirants of both races, when squeezing votes out of their precincts, would be forced to make less than subtle overtures to a group of people who might unlock the racial standoff. The future of the city's racial progress was predictably in the hands of those who could control its political posture toward housing. It was this fact that would cause alarm. Continued housing discrimination would produce the disaster of two cities—the outer one white, the inner one black.

Like other cities whose black population was becoming a majority, Gary's black community developed political opportunists who tried to find the jugular vein of those who threatened their political future, whether such persons were black or white. Political guerilla warfare was being waged with relentless fury in the ghetto. Alliances would form and disband at will; deals and counterdeals would be honored and then discarded. Men of former integrity and ethical behavior would willingly become political chameleons. No opportunities would arise for a concerted black action for individuals, because the various opportunists preferred solo performances.

As a consequence of those factors, some of which had prevailed for some time, the professional class of blacks had retreated from the political arenas to find peace in their individual pursuits. Like the ostriches, they buried their heads from the sights and fears that were very much with them. By refusing to look, act, or condemn, they unwittingly added their notes to the discord of the prelude.

To the Human Relations Commission of Gary, every problem that I had outlined became a source of concern for programming and attention. Our Commission consisted of fifteen men; our staff, four persons. But had the Commission and staff consisted of fifty or one thousand people, we would still have fallen short of dealing with the problems of the city as they existed. Unless that city could deal with its racial imbalances from a creative position of mutual respect and understanding, the prelude would grow louder. It would continue to grow louder until the blacks of Gary found the courage to indict their political leeches, and the whites to indict their rising generators of racism. Unless solid citizens of both races created and encouraged untarnished political leadership that would not depend wholly on black or white power for support, the harmonious concert would never come.

Unless white suburbia opened the vault that contained the victims of past and present discriminatory practices, and ceased to take flight from the city, Gary would be prime for disorder. Ben Segal, liaison officer for the Equal Employment Opportunity Commission in Washington, D.C., spoke at a Human Relations Commission Employment seminar. He said that unless businessmen, industry, and merchants—banks, contractors, and unions—opened their doors to employable minorities, the worst might come. They would ignite the fires of resentment then smoldering. The Molotov cocktails should come as no surprise, for they would be actually manufactured not by the black hands that might hold them but by white businessmen who would not use those hands while they were still idle. I shared Mr. Segal's concern.

It was hard to speak of disaster, particularly when one was a man of peace. If predictions of disaster came true, the person who predicted it would be labeled a motivator of destruction; if it did not come, the person would be labeled a radical alarmist. This risk had to be taken, for it was far better to speak of disaster than to be silent and be forced to view it.

I saw myself, and all other Gary citizens, locked into a system to which others held the keys. We spoke without rancor, but with hope. Hope because the city was young, vibrant, and alive with promise. It contained dormant seed that, if cultivated, could bring forth good harvest. But the ground needed to be furrowed. Its weeds needed pulling and its stumps uprooting. The weeds could be pulled gently, but stumps needed to be blasted. Those of us who refused to do either had to accept Gary as it was and not for what it promised to be.

Unless human relations could be considered less as a "commission" and more as a way of life for all of Gary's citizens, the Commission itself could reflect nothing more than the puzzle of the city. Within the confines of the chamber where we met, we carried with us the burden of apathy, the hopes of the blacks, the fears of the whites, and the frustrating silence. We on the Commission were a confused composite of the whole population.

My concern at that moment was not the Human Relations Commission, for it could and would survive. My concern at that moment was how the burdens thrust on us could be shared by others. Unless Gary began to build more housing than it demolished and condemned, it would find its citizens, in concert, openly protesting their debasement. Unless city officials began dealing with issues alone and made their decisions based on total concern for all of the citizens, their chambers and offices would be mocking examples of lights that failed.

The future of the city was unpredictable. Unpredictable because of the varying problems that constituted its promise or disaster. Unpredictable because solid citizens had made it so. Most had an aversion to involvement; yet it was this lack of involvement that threatened to destroy the already weakened foundation. The battles that were necessary for fighting were in the minds of the uncommitted masses who allowed virtue to be scorned, vice admired, and truth silenced. It had to be fought in the white homes where children learned that the blacks were a *problem* and not a *people*. It had to be fought in black homes where children of the ghetto learned that black power was the answer while white was only a blank question. In some homes it was posed as a question that should have been erased from the blackboard. The discord grew louder.

In the basement of the Municipal Building was the Office of the Human Relations Commission. Perhaps this location was symbolic. Our effort to solidify the racial, economic, and social peace of that city was a burdensome task. The next year,

1967, the mayor had promised us space on the first floor. That was also symbolic. Who knows, if the people of Gary measured up to the challenges that faced them in coming years, perhaps we would lose that space and close up for lack of business.

CHAPTER 15

A Power Struggle for Gary

*I*T WAS BUT A FEW WEEKS AFTER I ACCEPTED THE
position of Executive Director of the Civil Rights Commission in Gary that troubles began. The slow, passive pace of
Evansville's political activities had not prepared me for "Sin
City." Prostitution, political corruption, and jailing of public
officials was the order of the day. As an advocate of integration
—and because it was my belief that Gary's 50-50 ratio of blacks
and whites was edging toward a "tipping point"—I selected a
staff that I felt could assist the Commission's efforts to enforce
Gary's open housing ordinance.

The Commission I headed had immense powers. Unlike
most city and state human rights commissions, Gary's, in the
year 1966, was backed by a strong municipal law—one of the
strongest in the nation. Application for the directorship had
been heavy; the names of the persons who had applied astounded me when I read them later in the files. They ranged
from cheap politicians to current *elected* officials. The search
had ended with my name. The Commission itself was loaded
with black militants, civil rights advocates, fiery white liberals,
and a sprinkling of moderates. They were, with few exceptions,
intense and forceful. Compromise was not in their blood. One
of the commissioners had also applied for my position, and it
was not long before I felt not only the forces of resentment but
also an attempt at clever manipulation to oust me.

I was first approached by a well-heeled black citizen with
what he considered an offer I could not refuse. Since I had been
searching for a house to buy, he offered to loan me the cash—
and I wouldn't have to worry about paying him back. I was

125

astonished. Why would he do this for me? He disclosed that I was in a very important position and could, from time to time, help some of his consultants. I showed him the door, and promptly reported the incident to several commissioners who I thought would be outraged. They were not! Was the incident a setup? I still do not know to this day.

Next came open complaint of my work at Commission meetings. This was testing time, and I fought back hard at the intimidating tactics. I knew I was doing my job well, and so did the blacks of Gary. Case after case of discrimination filed by blacks against white institutions—including the major banks and U.S. Steel—came flooding into the Commission office. I increased the staff for investigations, called for public hearings on U.S. Steel, challenged the police brutality incidents in public, and pursued a suit against Gary's white real estate association for denying blacks homes in white areas. I even filed a suit through the Commission on my own behalf after I was denied the right to buy a home. As the months went by, the people of Gary began attending the Commission meetings. The commissioners began to see that I was gathering community support, and my detractors slowly backed away.

Next came the threatening phone calls. By this time I knew the persons who were out to stop my activities: hired political assassinators of characters and careers, they searched for past or present weaknesses in order to publicize them. They made calls back to Evansville to find background dirt, but by this time people in Evansville and Gary were informing me of all my detractors' plans and caucuses. I managed to stay well ahead of them. Finally, I went to the editors of the *Gary Post Tribune*. I laid out for them all of the plots that had been conceived to entrap me. The editors printed the activities and the names of my detractors under the headlines "Moves to Oust King." As as a follow-up to that story, they printed a lead editorial entitled "Leave King Alone!" And they finally did.

I had been an admirer of Richard Gordon Hatcher as long as I had known him. After finishing law school, Dick had set up a practice in Gary, and was eventually elected to the Gary City

Council. His intellect, his quiet but persistent efforts to combat racism, and his outspokenness impressed me greatly. He was and remains a man of deep integrity. One day in a soul-food restaurant, Dick and his sidekick, Jesse Bell, approached me.

"We need your help," Dick said.

"To do what?" I asked.

"I'm going to run for Mayor of the City of Gary."

"You're out of your mind!" I told him.

"Why?" Jesse Bell asked me.

"Don't you think it's time for blacks to control their own destiny?" Hatcher challenged me.

"No," I told him, "Gary is not ready for a black mayor, and as much as I like you, I can't support you."

As I look back, I am surprised at my naiveté. I was a member of the city administration. I had been appointed to my position by the mayor, Marvin Katz, a white Jewish liberal. Mayor Katz, though never fully behind my Commission activities, had never interfered with them either. Some of the suits I had filed in Gary had been against some of his personal friends, and he had never intervened on their behalf, to my knowledge. (I did learn later that he was the major director of the character assassinators who were attempting to oust me. At this moment, however, I did not know that, and I considered Hatcher's pending venture as political suicide.) I honestly felt that Gary could become a model interracial city, and a black mayor would mess up my "tipping" philosophy. In the back of my mind I doubted the ability of a black man—even Hatcher—to rule a city with all of the complexities of Gary. Today, after Maynard Jackson of Atlanta, Tom Bradley of Los Angeles, Coleman Young of Detroit, and others, I kick myself for such a lame mentality, which even suggested black inferiority. On second thought, it could have been a simple case of jealousy. In two short years I had become Gary's best-known black; I was enjoying the fact that I was the city's highest-paid black and its most powerful figure.

Jesse Bell must have been thinking all of those things. An argument ensued. Bell called me a "house nigger," and our voices began attracting attention. Hatcher quieted us both. "I haven't fully made up my mind yet," he said, "but we thought we would sound you out."

I left that meeting promising Hatcher that I would not let the mayor know anything about our conversation. I did not know it then, but I had been exposed to a watershed in black history: the emergence of black cities and the development of the new black breed. I realized later that at that time I was still caught up tight with a white mentality, honestly believing that white liberalism was the key to black freedom. Implicit in that belief was the feeling that blacks had no power, could not obtain it, and would not be able to dispense it even if by some fluke they could obtain it.

Hatcher, whose vision of the city was greater than my own, publicly announced his intention to run for mayor soon after our conversation. In speech after speech, he outlined his vision for blacks. As Hatcher's campaign began, Mayor Katz called me into his office. It was a stern mayor who faced me.

"I hear you are helping Hatcher."

"That's not so," I answered truthfully.

"Then why are you not helping me get reelected?"

"I'm not helping anyone; I'm the executive director of the Human Relations Commission, not a politician."

"I appointed you to that position, and I can get rid of you."

There. For the first time I realized that I had been had. The mayor was not only putting the squeeze on me, but he was threatening me as well. The fire began to rise.

"Are you suggesting, Mr. Mayor, that if I don't help you, you are going to dismiss me?"

"That's right, and don't you forget it."

By this time I knew that his threat was meaningless. By law I could only be dismissed for cause, and the mayor's action had to be ratified by a two-thirds vote of the Human Relations Commission. I knew that most of the blacks were supporting Hatcher, and all the white liberals on the Commission were for Hatcher. The mayor could not fire me, and he knew it.

We stared at each other. Finally, he smiled and tried to ease the tension: "I'm only kidding," he lied. "What I really want you to do is to read over this speech and tell me what you think of it."

I sat down and read his speech. It was an unbelievably vicious document. It warned the people of Gary that if Hatcher would be elected, blood would run in the streets and that Gary would explode in racial warfare just as Watts had.

I handed Mayor Katz back his speech. My hands were trembling with rage. He was watching me.

"Well, what do you think?"

I tried to frame the right words, but there were no words to come. I felt the urge to slam my fist into his face, to scream out at him the grossest obscenities that had ever come from the lips of a Baptist preacher. Up to that moment I had been proud of the fact that Mayor Katz had worked hard to obtain a forceful ordinance against discrimination, and had personally insisted that a race-baiting provision be placed in the law. It said that any person who incited racial unrest, bigotry, or violence could be fined and punished under the Gary ordinance. And I had the power to implement those proceedings. Katz was a lawyer (later to become a judge), so I was dumbfounded that he would ever prepare such a speech as the one that I had read.

Riots predicted by a white man? What gall! Did he think that if Hatcher were elected, Hatcher would promote riots, as suggested, or would the blood that ran in the streets be black blood spilled by whites who would go to war? The utterly incendiary tone of Katz's speech would not only inflame the blacks of Gary, but the many blacks who already were backing Katz would desert him in droves. I went to the door and opened it. I had come through that door to talk to a man; I was leaving now, looking on him and thinking of him as merely a cheap white political animal.

"What do you think?" Katz barked at my insulting departure.

I came back to his desk. "I think," I said without fear, "that if you give that speech"—my eyes began to water—"I will take you into court under the law I took the oath to administer."

The umbilical cord that had tied us in the past was broken.

Katz informed me that not only was he going to give that speech but that he would also make damned sure that my tenure as a city official would come to an end. "By God, no son of a bitch can talk to me that way. . . ." I slammed his door, went to my office, and reread the law. I was on solid ground.

Katz, true to his word, gave his damnable speech, and it was carried on the front page of the *Gary Post Tribune*. Blacks, of course, were outraged. For the first time, I felt the kind of power that my office gave me. I called for a special meeting of the full Commission, and I announced the reason for that meeting at a press conference. The meeting was set for the next evening at the Gary Hotel because I did not think it proper to meet inside City Hall to discuss the activities of the mayor. The Commission met, accepted my charges, and issued a resolution denouncing the mayor and warning him that if he ever repeated such utterings, the law would be appropriately administered. As the commissioners left, I lingered behind to speak on behalf of the Commission to the media.

"The mayor wants to see you," one of his staff assistants informed me outside on the sidewalk.

"When and where?" I asked, wondering what to expect.

"Now," he said. "He's in the hotel, Room 503."

I went back into the hotel, up the elevator to the room where Mayor Katz was. It was the room immediately adjacent to the room where we had had our special meeting! Crafty Katz had evidently gained access to the room to eavesdrop on our proceedings.

He dismissed his assistant, and we were alone. He was not the same man: his face was distressfully pained. He had gambled and lost. At that moment I weakened.

"I'm sorry," I said, "but I had to do it."

"I know," he replied, "but damn, King, did you have to go all out like this? Did you have to have press conferences and get all the commissioners to gang up on me?"

"You threatened to fire me, remember? I had to get their support."

"I guess this means you're going to support Hatcher?"

"No sir, only the city ordinance."

"How do you think this whole thing is going to turn out?"
he inquired.

"You're going to lose," I informed him bluntly.

He lost. Richard Gordon Hatcher is currently serving his
fourth term as the mayor of Gary, Indiana.

CHAPTER 16

The Kerner Commission on Civil Disorders

ONE DAY I WAS SURPRISED TO RECEIVE A CALL from Washington, D.C., from an old friend of mine who had been selected to be a staff member on the President's Commission on Civil Disorders (later to become known as the Kerner Commission). He asked whether I knew of prominent blacks whom he could contact who could make recommendations to David Ginsberg about selecting blacks as investigators for the Commission. I asked him who had the power to appoint. He said that he did.

"What's wrong with me?" I asked.

"You're kidding," he said. "Would you come and work with us?"

"Sure," I replied. So I wasn't selected by Lyndon Johnson —just some lesser staff member. I was flabbergasted. All it took was one phone call. The ease with which I was appointed caused me to wonder mightily about the other appointments.

The Gary Human Relations Commission received the news of my appointment with mixed emotions. It was a hot summer, and disorders were prevalent in American cities. It was thought that Gary was primed for violence. After much debate, the Commission finally gave me a leave of absence to serve on the Kerner Commission.

The nation's blacks were, of course, expecting a whitewashed report, whited recommendations, and white-oriented solutions from the Kerner Commission. And, indeed, our first staff briefing gave every indication that the Commission's staff would desperately attempt to present the disorders in a way that would not indict the nation's white people or institutions. At the briefing, called by the deputy director, Victor Palmieri, I was shocked to observe that of the more than 100 persons assembled, including clerks and typists, only eighteen were black. Of the program analysts who were to travel to the cities, bring back the reports, analyze them, and make recommendations, ten of us were black. What was going on? Here we were, a nation engaged in violent disorder and bloodshed—and only ten black men were included on teams that were selected to determine probable cause. The fact that there were no black women at all escaped my then thoroughly male chauvinist sensibility.

"We need a balanced report," Victor Palmieri instructed us. "Our final report must deal with the wrongs both races have suffered; in other words, we should not indict one race at the expense of the other."

Here was the old "balance" game that I knew so well. In this first staff meeting, I knew nothing about the other analysts, nor did they know anything about me. I knew nothing of Victor Palmieri, and I am sure that he did not know me. But he soon found out. Something in me exploded, and the next thing that came out of my mouth escaped before I could exercise control.

"Bullshit!"

That expletive hung in the air for a full ten seconds. It was my calling card, my first venture into the role of shocking white people. Later I was to learn that I would be remembered by the staff members chiefly for that expression, and my participation on the Commission was to have minimum value from that point on. Looking at it in retrospect, I realized that it was not a strategic utterance: it drew for the other staff members a stereotypical picture of me as the bad "militant nigger." I would be accused of lacking sophistication, and worse yet, objectivity.

"How can you ask for balanced reports when you and everyone else in this room know that white racist attitudes, behavior, and practices are the fundamental cause of riots?" I angrily asked Palmieri. "And why are there not any more blacks on these investigating teams?"

The shock of my expletive, questions, and arrogant behavior did not settle quickly. Clearly, no one in that room had expected anyone to challenge the authorities and policy decisions from within—right from the outset! I had come to the Commission from a safe position of challenging whites—U.S. Steel, Bethlehem Steel, Sears, white banks, white realtors, etc. But no one in that room could deny either my experience or knowledge of how white institutions had harmed my people. I had already become addicted to the process of using the power of challenge, provocation, and shock—all intended to reduce white defenses.

Palmieri had been publicly challenged. His face turned red, angry red. But he collected himself. Then he did what most whites do when challenged by black militancy. He ignored me. I recognized it as the old "consider the source" evasion.

"Once again," he repeated softly, "I want balanced reports. Blame will be affixed, if at all, not by team members but by the Commission itself. Is that clear?"

It was clear to everyone. We were then assigned to go into the nation's cities.

The scope of our work clearly required the kind of discipline and insight that, without black input, would render most findings useless. Each report was to include a thorough analysis of each target area, plus a summary analysis of the city based on the area analyses. Each city analysis was to consist of a chronology of riot events, a historical summary of the city's strengths and weaknesses, an interpretation of the riot events in the context of this history, and a discussion of various pertinent themes, such as the status and role of the police in the city, the avenues of political access, the degree of distortion of fact perception, and the breakdown or success of grievance procedures. The themes, of course, varied from city to city, depending on the social, economic, and political factors involved. Also required for searching review was the part that the mass media played both before and after civil disorders, examples of the conduct of reporters, disk jockeys, and other mass media people, and examples of the *content* of mass media reports (radio, television, newspapers, magazines) which influenced positively or negatively the outbreak and course of the riot and the post-riot climate of opinion in the city.

As reams of material from the cities that had experienced riots poured in for analysis, it became evident that most of the teams were both inept and unaware of the importance of their function. It was distressing to read most of their reports, which were full of unnecessary and wordy inferences and short on hard facts. The white intellectual assumptions and "balanced" approach were dominant.

Perhaps the most scorching insight into team efforts was provided by Al Spivak, director of public relations for the Commission. After reviewing the rough drafts, he advised Victor Palmieri of his impressions of the team reports:

> You asked me to read the team reports that have come in thus far and to offer suggestions for improvements.
>
> My comments will deal with the written material I have seen. I will put some suggestions about the team's basic questionnaire in a separate memo.
>
> My initial reaction, from reading the material on Plainfield and Cambridge, is that while some of the material is good and contains adequate detail, there is an overabundance of superficiality in many of the interviews.
>
> The reports on the interviews are done in a stream-of-consciousness manner—perhaps because of the interviewers' inexperience in such matters—that runs up dangers of projecting what the staff man has to say rather than the interviewee. "So-and-so implied such-and-such and I thought he was sincere," is the tone of much of it. This should be replaced with direct, substantial quotation of the interviewees, when they have anything to offer . . . or at least with more specifics in the paraphrasings.
>
> The big problem is lack of detail. Too often, the interviewer states that his target wasn't on the scene at the time, didn't see things himself, etc. Why, then, bother? Find the people who were there, who did see things. Go back, if necessary, for another shot at it. Because there is so much vagueness now, that we run a real risk of being challenged if we accept some of the material as

gospel and base evaluations and scenarios on it. To be specific:

In the Cambridge interviews, a staff member says: "Yates said that it had been learned that Brown and Richardson were coming to Cambridge several weeks before July 24th." How had it been learned? Another interviewer said the militants themselves announced it. But how had this particular official heard about it? Through the announcement? Police intelligence?

In the scenario on Plainfield, mention is made that a unit of 100 National Guardsmen came in. What unit? Who ordered them in? How were they armed? Where did they come from?

In the interview with Mr. Cornish, Negro head of the Cambridge City Council—the only bit of background on him is that he holds the local school bus franchise. Does he have other economic interests that tie him to the city administration? (The city fathers like this particular Negro, the militants consider him a "Tom.")

In the Jones-Satterfield report on some Plainfield interviews, it is stated that not one of 35 local liquor licensees is a Negro. Has this been verified through other sources? It also is stated through a witness that Robert Lee, President of the Plainfield Bar Association, said that "no lawyer in Plainfield who is a member of the Bar Association would defend persons who were arrested and charged with participating in the riots, etc."? Did he really say it? Was he contacted and asked? (Not that I can see, though I may have missed it.) Did the lawyers actually refuse to defend those arrested?

The post-riot analysis is highly editorial, accepting as gospel various particular versions of events, characterizations of people and recommendations by the ACLU. All of these may be valid, but there is nothing in the scenario to back it up. There may be all kinds of material in the interviews or from other sources to back it up. But not in the scenario itself, which will be the basis for judging the credibility of the analysis.

On that basis, since the interviews are providing some problems and leaving some gaps—are we cross-checking those interviews with the on-the-spot news clips or with other data in preparing the scenarios?

In many cases, those news clips may form a better basis for portions of the scenarios than the interviews themselves.

To maintain credibility, we should label the chronology as coming "FROM INTERVIEWS AND OTHER MATERIAL ASSEMBLED BY THE COMMISSION STAFF AS WELL AS FROM NEWS COVERAGE OF THE EVENTS" or something along that line. This may seem like a superfluous thing to do, but I think in this kind of endeavor—where the slightest flaw will be picked at—we shouldn't pretend our scenarios or analyses come from the hand of God, but should make clear that we're operating on the basis of the best and the most information we could obtain under the difficult circumstances that matters of this sort arouse.

Under no circumstances should we—as is the case in the rough draft of the Plainfield scenario's post-riot analysis—leave in a line like: "The Conservative Republican Business Community fails to recognize what the problems really are and that the problems really do exist." One man's Capital C Conservative is another man's Capital L Liberal. Are they all registered Republicans? Etc. Etc. The scenario says, "The Business Community as a group basically fail to recognize the problem." Wouldn't this be better if it were along lines of "Representatives of the business community who were interviewed by the Commission staff indicated a lack of recognition of the problems underlying ghetto grievances"?

As the riot team analyzers hastened from city to city, it was evident to me from reading their summary reports that they were exactly that: reports, not findings. Many of them spent hours in hotel rooms documenting news reports. Since the majority of the analyzers were white, few if any of them ventured into the ghetto to receive firsthand reports of black grievances. Whenever opinions or conclusions were drawn, they were largely repetitious of white newspaper editorials. I became a gadfly. I requested permission to be assigned specifically to interview white policymakers—police chiefs, councilmen, chamber of commerce types. It was my idea to deal with the institutional mechanisms that I knew created black frustration. Permission was denied.

I asked to go to cities where no teams had been assigned, particularly to cities where riots were reported about to occur, or had recently occurred. Permission was denied.

Despite the fact that my official governmental status, GS-14, was a higher rank than that of most of the more than seventy-five white team members, I was never placed in the position of a team captain. The heads of all our five-man teams were white—with one exception, a black man named Tex. Since we were crisscrossing the nation, I seldom was able to communicate with the other black team members. Later I was to learn that my frustration of working with and under inept, ignorant, and insensitive whites was likewise their own. I began to feel that both my presence and my activities were window dressing for the Kerner Commission. Several times I thought of appearing unannounced before the Commission to articulate my disgust at the obviously racist orientation of the teams and their leadership.

I became so distraught with the "balance" concept that I began to editorialize my reports from a black perspective. I waited for the wrath of my superiors to descend. Nothing happened. To my chagrin—I found out later—they were not even being read! Why? All reports were distilled and congealed by an editorial team (which consisted of Antioch College graduate students) and issued to the officials as summary documents of all the reports. I became livid. The raw material and reports of our team, such as they were, were being buried, to be read later, made a part of the archives of history. I then requested that I be assigned as a distiller of reports. Permission was denied.

Sitting in hotel rooms, listening to my white counterparts' discussions of the disorders and the questions of race, prejudice, and attitudes, I heard "balance, balance, balance." Not one of them, as I can remember, brought up the specter of white racism. The "balance" became so unbalanced that it ended up with "blaming the victims." My unparticipating attitude further alienated me from them—and that was exactly what I wanted. I made a decision. I figured out how I could get my own reports to surface into the hands of the Commission without going through the distillery. It called for two reports: a white "balanced" report and a black perspective report that would indicate causative factors, analysis, and recommendations for change. In order to accomplish that, I requested permission to spend time in one city, to talk exclusively to blacks to check on their militancy, their ideas, and their possible planning for future disorders. Permission was granted.

The City of Milwaukee became my assignment for that task. Freed at last from my white leaders, I began my documentation. It was documentation out of the heart of my blackness—undistilled.

Milwaukee, a city of 770,000, had been warned in 1966—one year before its disorders—that its black population of 80,641 was primed to explode. Since 1960 the black population had experienced a 23 percent increase. Black grievances, on the whole, were in four specific areas: 1) police brutality and a lack of community relations; 2) de facto segregation of the public schools; 3) the lack of an open housing ordinance; and 4) lack of black and poor white representation on boards, commissions, and the Community Action Agency Governing Board.

It is ironic that all of those grievances were within the realm of immediate solution—and, in fact, without the expenditure of city money or special budgets. Yet white institutional attitudes, hardened over the years, would not yield on those issues. The mayor, police chief, and board of aldermen were the controlling causes of the social inaction. On July 30, 1967, Father Groppi and the Black Commandoes were arrested for leading marches and demonstrations. They were protesting the lack of passage of an open housing law. The police were unrestrained in their brutality. From a black perspective, the conditions that were to lead to thousands of arrests and millions of dollars in property damage could have been abated. Instead, the police served as midwives to the birth of a riot.

At 8:40 of that day, police waded into a black crowd that was gathering on the corner of North Third and West Brown streets. The police came in with their billy clubs swinging. In the time span between 9:00 p.m. and 5:30 a.m. the next morning, scores of fire runs were made (50 percent of them false alarms); buildings were burning, and snipers, reportedly, were keeping firemen from entering the area to put out the flames. At 2:27 a.m., Mayor Henry Maier declared a state of emergency and contacted the National Guard. At 3:40 a.m., a curfew was imposed on the city: streets were closed to all traffic, and all taverns, liquor stores, filling stations, and petroleum supply plants within the city were closed. Violation of the curfew brought a $100 fine or six months' imprisonment.

The cause of every major riot in our nation's cities stemmed primarily from the confrontation of law enforcement officers with citizens of the ghetto. The accumulation of frustration and contained hostility easily led to overreaction or simple miscalculation of the dynamics of ghetto anger and fear. To understand the tragic proportions of police overreaction, one must look at the massive number of blacks slain in the upheavals of Newark and Detroit, where the streets ran with black blood. At the time of those cities' riots, news reports highlighted the looting and burning—the thieves, robbers, and lawless. A *Life* magazine cover carried the unforgettable signs of the dominant public sentiment: a burly, cigar-chomping white National Guardsman, hostility in his eyes, straddled the body of a black boy, age eleven, whose life's blood was visibly draining from him and staining the sidewalk. It was as if white fears of black revolt gave license to white policemen and National Guardsmen to "shoot to kill" (which is actually the order Mayor Daley of Chicago gave his officers to stop looters). But how did the disorders begin? One can observe the record of the Detroit and Newark police for clues. Already in November of 1965, George Edwards, Judge of the United States Court of Appeals for the Sixth Circuit and Commissioner of the Detroit Police Department from 1961 to 1963, had written in the *Michigan Law Review:*

> It is clear that in 1965 no one will make excuses for any city's inability to foresee the possibility of racial trouble. . . . Although local police forces generally regard themselves as public servants with the responsibility of maintaining law and order, they tend to minimize this attitude when they are patrolling areas that are heavily populated with Negro citizens. There, they tend to view each person on the streets as a potential criminal or enemy, and all too often that attitude is reciprocated. Indeed, hostility between the Negro communities in our large cities and the police departments is the major problem in law enforcement in this decade. It has been a major cause of all recent race riots.

Whether or not the confronting officer was operating within the legal framework of his duties to uphold the law or outside of it, the very presence of that officer was considered to be—or was acted upon as if he were—representative of every oppressive institution that created, maintained, and condoned the ghetto. Law enforcement officers who did not recognize that fact failed miserably in interpreting appropriate responses in a tension-filled atmosphere. This is what the Kerner Commission discovered in Newark.

> At 3:30 p.m., the family of Mrs. D. J. was standing near the upstairs windows of their apartment, watching looters run in and out of a furniture store on Springfield Avenue. Three carloads of police rounded the corner. As the police yelled at the looters, the latter began running.
>
> The police officers opened fire. A bullet smashed the kitchen window in Mrs. D. J.'s apartment. A moment later she heard a cry from the bedroom. Her 3-year-old daughter, Debbie, came running into the room. Blood was streaming down the left side of her face: the bullet had entered her eye. The child spent the next two months in the hospital. She lost the sight of her left eye and the hearing in her left ear. (This and the following quotations are from the *Kerner Commission Report on Civil Disorders.*)

More was at stake in those situations than the arrest of the perpetrator of an alleged crime: what was at stake was the simultaneous arrest of the latent feelings that could mushroom into uncontrollable proportions throughout the Newark ghetto. Whatever act was taken on the spot, whatever method used to arrest, detain, or subdue a suspect, would invariably be witnessed by his friends or peers. Their reports later would likely be related out of proportion to the actual happening to prove that the officer was wrong or insensitive—or that the victim was right or innocent. The intensity of the exaggeration would, of course, increase if the law enforcement officers were white. The fact that they carried the badge of authority, weapons that could kill, and a historical burden of past police actions (whether the arresting officer was brutal or not in his dealings with blacks)—the baggage of those past realities was a necessary part of his profession.

Crime and criminal activities are a fact of life in the ghetto. Those who live in close proximity to hunger, joblessness, welfare, and hopelessness can easily rationalize criminal activity as a means of survival, a necessary tool to use in the vacuum developed by low esteem, the absence of social acceptance and concern, and the need to exercise some means of reaction to a life experience of oppression and inequality of opportunity. The disorders were born out of those dynamics.

Law enforcement officers, challenged on the spot, likewise heightened the self-esteem of potential rioters, who, in a sense, were protecting their turf from invading foreign forces. The disorders increased their momentum.

It was clear that most ghetto residents did not think that way, nor did they react that way toward law enforcement officers. But they were eventually to be swept into the vortex of the hurricane of emotions, particularly when the law enforcement officers' actions were brutal, observably insensitive beyond the point of need.

> Employed as a private guard, 55-year-old Julius L. Dorsey, a Negro, was standing in front of a market when accosted by two Negro men and a woman. They demanded he permit them to loot the market. He ignored their demands. They began to berate him. He asked a neighbor to call the police. As the argument grew more heated, Dorsey fired three shots from his pistol into the air. The police radio reported: "Looters, they have rifles." A patrol car driven by a police officer and carrying three National Guardsmen arrived. As the looters fled, the law enforcement personnel opened fire. When the firing ceased, one person lay dead.
> He was Julius L. Dorsey.

Police officers in these areas were highly vulnerable to overreaction:

> On Lycaste Street, between Charlevoix and Goethe, they saw a jeep sitting at the curb. Believing it to be another roadblock, they slowed down. Simultaneously a shot rang down. A National Guardsman fell, hit in the ankle.
> Other National Guardsmen at the scene thought the shot had come from the station wagon. Shot after shot was directed against the vehicle, at least 17 of them finding their mark. All five occupants were injured, John Leroy fatally.

When an officer works the ghetto on a sustained basis, he or she becomes hardened to the abnormalities of ghetto life. Permissive behavior is often allowed that would not be tolerated in more genteel settings. Misdemeanors are winked at, and a multitude of felonies, from murder to rape, are soon accepted as a fact of life. Some officers soon develop an attitude of "what's the use" or "that's the way they are." Unless actually witnessing a crime, or ordered to take action, they think mainly of the time left to end the shift of duty. Those are normal human reactions, but when exercised fully on a continuous basis, they will eventually overwhelm the "public servant" with a deep sense of guilt. That guilt, and a call to act to quell disorders, produced an emotional trauma. And even though the officers could not comprehend it, they eventually would overreact in the moments of stress and tension induced by their fear.

> At 11:00 p.m., on Sunday, July 16th, Mrs. Lucille Pugh looked out of the window to see if the streets were clear. She then asked her 11-year-old son, Michael, to take the garbage out. As he reached the street and was illuminated by a street light, a shot rang out. He died.

The overreaction and insensitivity were buttressed and fortified by the public's outcry and concern over the rising crime rates, highly publicized unsolved murders, armed robberies, rapes, and editorials that blamed the police. The national call for a crackdown on crime, low police pay and fringe benefits, and the increasing fear that any normal person would have walking the streets where crime is prevalent on a daily basis— all took their toll. Sensitivity diminished within those dynamics.

> On the tenth floor, Eloise Spellman, the mother of several children, fell, a bullet through her neck. Across the street a number of persons, standing in an apartment window, were watching the firing directed at the housing project. Suddenly several troopers whirled and began firing in the general direction of the spectators. Mrs. Hattie Gainer, a grandmother, sank to the floor.
> A block away Rebecca Brown's 2-year-old daughter was standing at the window. Mrs. Brown rushed to drag her to safety. As Mrs. Brown was, momentarily, framed in the window, a bullet spun into her back.
> All three women died.

What the Kerner Commission discovered in Newark held true in Milwaukee as well. Different city, same dynamics. Why? I was later to learn—after conducting awareness seminars with police officers in Springfield and Dayton, Ohio, Atlanta, Portland, and Washington, D.C.—that law enforcement officers everywhere consider themselves slaves of white institutions. The Kerner Commission's ultimate findings— that "white institutions created the ghetto"—carried with them the implicit need for police manpower to control its fury in order to establish control of the ghetto. But most police departments contain men and women whose weaker image and status is enhanced by the uniform, badge, and gun. They have been trained to deal with the worst elements of society—the lawless and untamed. That task, on a daily basis, creates a "them versus us" mentality. Human ties and sensitive nerves become hardened; it becomes a matter of survival for many policemen. Coupled with that progressive insensitivity was the increasing public clamor for "law and order" during the disorders. To many white policemen, those pressures created such frustration that blacks became the on-the-spot recipients of their hostility. They beat black heads and bruised black bodies with their nightsticks, their trigger fingers tightened, and blood flowed throughout the nation's ghettos. The officers who committed those acts, more often than not, considered themselves heroes. They were the protectors and enforcers, the judges and executioners. And white society condoned it.

During the disorders, black law enforcement officers, to a large degree, were not in evidence. One reason is the reluctance of blacks to become police officers (which seems self-explanatory). Another reason, perhaps less obvious, is that blacks were neither sought out nor desired by police departments. Older black officers of veteran status had lived through the period of not being able to arrest whites, being snubbed for promotion, and being held in disdain by the black community. Blacks of the ghetto viewed many black law enforcement officers with the same fear that they had for white officers. In fact, in some cities black officers were feared the most. On record are testimonials of ghetto residents who reported the reigns of terror exercised by black and white officers alike. Those officers who shunned violence and brutality were placed in the role of silent onlookers. They dared not speak out. Police peer pressure, like that of the medical profession, is very strong.

Regardless of the circumstance, they were prone to accept the thesis that it was "them versus us."

Witness verification of police violence, therefore, came mainly from black lips—lips that had been busted. The examples given, particularly in Milwaukee, of the police officers' lack of restraint were too minutely detailed to disbelieve and too horrible to dismiss. But, backed by a hard-boiled police chief, the Milwaukee police assured an escalation of that city's disorders.

In my search for realism and feeling, I walked the dark streets of Milwaukee at night, entering into the nightclubs, dives, and dens. I walked aimlessly, hoping to be stopped and questioned by Milwaukee's "finest." No such luck. It had been my intention to get arrested—for smarting off to questioning officers, or some such act—and then sent through the judicial process to jail. But reason won out. It was a foolish idea.

During the days I talked to city aldermen, black officers, and blacks who headed agencies. In two days I had a rough profile of the city—its feelings and its potential for future disorders. I dictated my thoughts and observations and flew the tapes back to Washington daily. They became a small book. I later learned that my work had indeed by-passed the distillers, even though the concept of white racism as a causative factor took away the "balance." I sought no balance. I began writing and recording from a completely nonobjective, black point of view. I named names and supported allegations that my emotions told me were true. I became drunk with the authority of my Commission credentials, flashing them bravely in the faces of white officials and reservedly to blacks. The blacks viewed me with suspicion: I was part of the bureaucracy that they knew had failed in the past and believed would be false to the present. White America had never been indicted for its crimes against black people. The nation had remained immune to the charge that it was racist by nature.

I questioned black teachers about the nature, hopes, and promise—or lack of it—displayed by the jailed blacks who had been accused of looting, burning, and even sniping. They were mainly teenagers who were school dropouts and unemployed. This was the typical profile of those in other cities whose reactions to police officers had spawned the disorders. It is important to note that the word "riot" was a misnomer; blacks were not rioting, *the police were*. Blacks were reacting to initial police disorder, creating retaliatory responses. Pawn shops, grocery stores, and furniture stores that capitalized on extended credit were the first to burn. As in Watts, whites who profited in the midst of black poverty paid dearly for the years of siphoning off the fat and leaving the lean. The media, the police, and city officials refused to look at their own practices and almost uniformly blamed the victims. Blaming the victim established more than the sought-after "balance"; it created a rationale for the continuance of the status quo, the same policies—keeping the cap on the dynamite.

I ceased to write as an analyzer of disorders and began writing as a black man, editorializing my fury. At night in my hotel room, each injustice uncovered added fire to my bones and, on occasions, tears to my eyes. I wanted to stay in Milwaukee and use that city and its ongoing problems as a strong indicator of white institutionalized racism. The daily marching of the Black Commandoes kept that city alert, apprehensive, and in the news. It was like a ticking time bomb. I requested permission to remain. Permission was granted.

CHAPTER 17

Father Groppi and the Black Commandoes

*F*ATHER GROPPI IS GOING TO BE LATE," A YOUNG white woman, a former nun who served as a receptionist, informed me. I assured her that I understood, and I waited.

St. Boniface Catholic Church, Milwaukee, is a large parish. As of October 27, 1967, fifty-eight consecutive marches had been conducted by Father James Groppi and the Black Commandoes from this church. These marches had been undertaken to pound home to that city its need for an open housing ordinance. In his appearance in Washington before the National Advisory Commission on Civil Disorders, the militant priest had expanded his arguments in an attempt to impress the Commission with the need for action in behalf of Milwaukee's black people.

The Milwaukee riot was over. The curfew had been lifted and the National Guardsmen were now disbanded and back with their families. That night the Commandoes would march again, with Father Groppi in the lead.

It was only 10 a.m., but at least twenty varieties of races and ages were already waiting at St. Boniface for nightfall. That evening at 7:30 the Black Commandoes would meet, chart out the course of the fifty-ninth march, announce it to the marchers, and they would be off under the eyes of the police.

Their marches had been ignored by the Milwaukee City Council, who refused to pass an open occupancy ordinance. Four times the Council had voted it down by a vote of 18-1. The lone vote for the ordinance had been always cast by Vel

Washington, the lone woman and lone black on the Council. "They don't get the message," Vel Washington had informed me earlier. The pert, vivacious woman attorney added, "It appears that some of them would rather see the town burn down than vote this ordinance in." In fact, the town *had* almost burned. Milwaukee's disorder had lasted three days.

In the autumn of 1967, Father Groppi, Youth Advisor to the Milwaukee Youth Council of the NAACP, had successfully culled out the Black Commandoes from that body and had begun marching. Today, I was to interview both Father Groppi and members of the Black Commandoes. I occupied my time watching the Commandoes enter and leave the hall leading to the rectory office quarters. On one wall was a crude picture of the Virgin Mary; her face was painted black. Innumerable signs hung about the place, all with the same message: "Black Is Beautiful." Father Groppi came in with a breezy greeting, wearing a tortoise sweatshirt, baggy pants, and white gym shoes. "For marching," he explained his attire with no apology. At the first sight of the priest, I was mildly surprised. Small of stature, with a small hawkish face, and horn-rimmed glasses perched securely on a dominant nose, he did not have the appearance of a militant advocate of black power.

"Remember me?" he exclaimed in surprise when I first introduced myself. I had to confess that I did not. "Selma, Alabama?"

Of course. Father Groppi had been one of the hundreds of priests who had responded to the Selma call. I did not remember him personally, but I accepted his recognition in behalf of the hundreds of indistinguishable priests who had blended with the blacks during those days of crisis.

In the huge room where he led me, he explained the setting. "Some of the commandoes will join us later. In case I have to run out once in a while, they will answer some of your questions." I thanked him. Did he think that the marches in Milwaukee were polarizing racial attitudes?

"Attitudes tend to remain the same as they did before our marches," he asserted. "Any fool can see the difference between our marches and the riots; if there is any polarization at all, it has gathered determined black citizens together to settle for nothing less than open housing.''

''Do you think that the entire black community supports your efforts?''

''I know they don't. I'm not fooling myself; Milwaukee still has its 'Uncle Toms.' However, I don't blame them; I blame the white population that made them that way. I would say that the majority of the black people understand our efforts and support the marches.''

A day earlier the press had reported a speech Father Groppi had made at a predominantly white college in Wisconsin. He was quoted as saying that blacks should not remain nonviolent. Was he quoted correctly?

''That's what I said all right,'' Father Groppi admitted. Weren't such expressions in conflict with the traditional teachings of the church?

Groppi laughed.

''No, it's not in conflict. I'm getting damned tired of people getting 'hung up' on scriptures that meet their fancy. Where did people ever get the idea that Christians were not supposed to defend themselves? When Jesus entered the temple, he knocked the hell out of the crooks . . . wouldn't you call that violence?'' He paused and laughed again.

''Then, don't forget, for many centuries popes swung swords in the name of religion. I don't think black people have any right to turn the other cheek just because they're black. Teaching them nonviolence has caused them to get the hell beat out of them for years. Look, I'm from the south side of Milwaukee, born and raised there. I know the hate out there. When we marched in that part of town, they came out by the thousands, swinging and hating. Bigoted whites. They attacked us. They were the ones that were violent. Now I ask you, how long do you think black people should take that kind of treatment? That's what I meant when I said, 'If a white man calls you a nigger, call him a honkie; if he hits you on the cheek, bust him in the damned jaw.' ''

"It's not because black people want to move out there where they live," he continued. "But, what the hell, why let hate live like that without challenging it?"

Was he interested in reconciliation with the white community? It would appear, according to his philosophy and actions, that he had lost all hope of achieving peace and brotherhood among the races. In fact, he himself had been accused of turning black.

"That's right, I have," he said proudly. "I consider myself black. It's not that I don't think that reconciliation should not be attempted, but that's not my 'bag' anymore. As far as I'm concerned, it's too late for that for me. Not any time left. In fact, I hate talking to white groups. They call here every day, want me to go to this place and that place to make speeches. I turn most of them down. How can I possibly explain what's happening to us?"

I could not help but note that each time Father Groppi referred to blacks he used the term "us." I asked him about that. When did he feel he had lost his identity as a white man?

"How do I know?" he answered. "I cannot recall when it happened; I imagine it happened so gradually that I never became aware."

Before the Milwaukee riots, Mayor Henry Maier had gone to the businessmen of the city to organize an interracial group of citizens called "We Milwaukeeans," formulated to work out a program of understanding and cooperation between the races. The mayor insisted that the blacks selected in the group would represent the "real leaders" of the black community, such as the "Barbers and Tavern Owners." The white businessmen objected, insisting that the "real leaders" were in the black affluent class. The mayor gave in to them. However, the black middle class that finally joined the group stated that they would join only if it were not connected with the mayor. They wanted no part of him.

"Do you think there is any hope working with other groups, such as the 'We Milwaukeeans'?" I asked Father Groppi.

"Hell, no," he answered emphatically. "Look, I work only with the Commandoes. These guys don't have time to be fooling around with groups such as that. They are in a hurry, and I don't blame them. We have no time to be sitting around talking. It slows things down and nothing is accomplished. Those days are gone . . . gone.''

Who, indeed, were the Commandoes? A few of them drifted in during my conversation with Father Groppi. Father Groppi explained: ''These are the men that will soon change the face of this city. Many are former prisoners and high school dropouts, yet they possess raw leadership and native ability to size up the problems of black people and move to bring about a change in the conditions of 'our' people.''

Jimmy Pierce (Commando Lieutenant Colonel) spoke up: ''The mayor calls us a bunch of hoodlums and thieves.'' He smiled. ''Yet, what the mayor and others don't realize is that before I became a Commando, I was a drunk in the alley. Now for the first time in my life, I feel like I'm somebody, really doing something.''

I looked at the huge, sweaty Pierce and saw that he meant it. Groppi smiled.

''That's right, and when you get to know the rest of the guys, you'll find the same thing. They have a purpose.''

In order to be a member of the Milwaukee Commandoes, one had to be eighteen years of age or older. The Commandoes were organized in military fashion, possessing rank from buck private to lieutenant general. Initially, qualifications for membership (imposed in order to counteract criticism of the group) called for each member to be fully employed. This qualification was dropped, however, when many of the Commandoes lost their jobs because of their militant activities.

''We discarded that qualification,'' Groppi explained, ''when one of the Commandoes who had been laid off insisted, 'What better job could we get than marching full time for black people!' ''

The other Commandoes nodded in agreement.

The Commandoes had a code of ethics, and this code was strictly adhered to; those violating it were drummed out of the organization. Leadership in the Commando ranks had changed three times in the last year. The leaders were chosen through democratic elections. I attended one of their elections for selecting new officers. Fifty-six of the seventy-five Commandoes were present for the election.

"Nominations are in order for the positions of corporal, sergeant, lieutenant, captain, and colonel," Lieutenant General Green informed the assembly, "five men to be nominated for each rank. The one receiving the highest vote for each rank will be promoted to that rank."

An orderly election followed: Each man nominated stood on his feet when his name was called. On each nominee's face was a look of pride, as hands were raised to cast votes. The losers took their seats magnanimously; those elected took their oaths solemnly. There was no gaiety or horseplay: to be an officer in the ranks of the Commandoes was serious business.

"The main function of the Commandoes is to protect the marchers," Groppi said, "and in order to instill discipline, they practice it themselves." Any time a Commando steps out of line, he appears before an executive board. I attended a discipline session of the executive board. The board consisted of all field officers and the sergeant major of the Commandoes.

Lieutenant General Green addressed the Commandoes standing at rigid attention before him. "You have been accused of shirking your duties during the marches. I warn you, and once only. When we march, your main duty is to protect the marchers; we cannot allow any Commando to. . . ."

"May I say something?" the sergeant asked.

"You may not," the sergeant major standing beside the accused one barked. "You will be silent until the General is finished speaking."

"My main point," General Green continued, "is that in light of your lack of appreciation for the rank that you hold, we are thinking of reducing you down to corporal . . . is that what you want?"

"No, sir."

"What about it, men?" General Green asked the other members of the Executive Board.

In the discussion among the officers that followed, it was finally decided: the offending sergeant would be given one final chance to straighten out. The sergeant major would, in the future, handle all offenses and mete out the appropriate punishment against noncommissioned officers. The Executive Committee would handle all cases of commissioned officers' infractions. The offending sergeant saluted smartly, visibly relieved that, at least for the moment, his rank would remain intact.

"Dismissed," barked General Green.

Several of the Commmandoes, including its initial leaders, had been drummed out of the ranks. Commandoes who had a leaning toward initiating violence, for example, were not tolerated.

"One part of our code deals with self-defense," Captain Lawrence Friend informed me. "We come to the defense of any marcher who is under attack by bystanders—beyond that, we practice non-violence."

Captain Friend is married, but his family lives in poverty. He is one of fourteen brothers. He successfully completed 1008 hours of Welding School. He has been unable to find a job— except the job of marching daily for open housing. Brigadier General Hank Waters was laid off when his employer discovered he was a Commando. Colonel Vernon Mallet was employed by the Harley Davidson Company in Milwaukee as a parts repairman. His pink slip dismissal cited "excess absenteeism."

"These guys see a hard way to go," explained Father Groppi. "The marches have caused a lot of problems."

The pictures of Captain Lawrence Friend and General Hank Waters were taken with Father Groppi and other Commandoes, and they appeared in a local newspaper. The two men were arrested by police and charged with "suspicion of being a lookout for burglary." The burglary had occurred two months prior to their arrests. They were arrested on the basis of the testimony of two white youths, ages fourteen and sixteen, who informed the police that they "looked like the Negroes who were on the scene at the time."

"How in the hell two white kids can identify two 'Negroes'

from a newspaper group picture is beyond me, especially since everyone knows that 'we all look alike,' " Father Groppi said in anger.

"Some of the fellows have profited from their Commando training," Groppi informed me. "Take for instance Prentice McKinney. Here was a guy who was a natural leader in his neighborhood. No one knew what this guy had on the ball until he became a Commando. When McKinney came to us, he had problems galore; he had been in prison for non-support. He came to us a hep guy with a 'process'; we had a helluva time getting him to cut it off."

"Why?" I asked.

"Have you ever read Malcolm X? Well, I read that part to the Commandoes about pride in race—you know, trying to ape white culture—man, I believe black is beautiful. You won't find any processes around here, not among the Commandoes."

"You know what the saying is," Corporal Rufus King injected, "when you ape the white man's hair you wind up with 'processed mind' and 'kinky brains'."

"Why should the white man's hair be the thing?" Captain Friend argued. "The only reason why black people do that is because they think the only thing to compare their hair with is long hair; so kinky hair becomes bad to them. Why not let our kinky hair become the thing; then all their hair will be bad."

Groppi laughed, "Get the point, man? Black is beautiful!"

"Right," chorused the Commandoes.

"Anyway," Groppi continued, "Prentice McKinney cut off his hair and is no longer with us."

"Where is he?" I asked.

"He's now working for the Industrial Commission, making over $150.00 per week."

At that point, Father Groppi's receptionist came in to inform him of a problem in the outer office. When he departed, I sought to find out more about his relationship to the Commandoes.

"He's the best thing that ever happened to me," Captain

154

Fortune Hunphrey confessed. "Without that guy we would have given up long ago. He keeps us going."

How is it that a white man can lead a black power movement? I wondered.

"To us he's black," Lieutenant Colonel Jimmy Pierce emphasized. "Besides, our kind of black power don't exclude white people; in fact, on weekends over half of the marchers are white."

"But what about your conversations when you talk about 'whitey'; isn't that insulting to the whites that are a part of your movement?"

"When we talk about 'whitey,' we talk only about white structure, you know, the power boys; that ain't no hate against white people."

Did they believe in the H. Rap Brown and Stokely Carmichael kind of militancy?

Lieutenant Colonel Pierce said:

"Listen, who the hell are those guys? What have they done for black people, I mean, except shoot off at the mouth. All those guys do is jump from state to state hollerin' 'fire.' I don't get it. Man, riots have only hurt black folks. Any fool can see that."

"Do you mean," I asked, "that all of the Commandoes reject Brown and Carmichael?"

"At first we didn't," Pierce confessed. "When a lot of us first started we were kinda drifting into that kind of thinking . . . but after you get involved in what to do to help solve problems, like we're doing now, you get hep to the jive that those guys are putting down. We're on to something bigger now, something we think is going to help people—so, where is Carmichael now? Somewhere over in China or Cuba shooting off his mouth. We're doing something about it."

"Another thing," Pierce added, "when you get to marching and discover things like a crippled boy with polio comes out every night to march with us, and a white man over seventy years old comes in from Chicago every night to march with us, it kinda changes your mind about a lot of things. Carmichael's

155

content to live off the fat of the land, or whoever is paying him. When those guys yell to blacks to get their guns, man, that barrel is pointed right at us."

"Does Father Groppi make the decisions?"

"He's our advisor, he is not our leader," Brigadier General Waters answered. "When we meet, we make the decisions and Father Groppi doesn't interfere. You know, like last night during the meeting, you were there . . . did you hear Father Groppi say anything to us?" I admitted I had not.

"Do you know why? Well, I'll tell you: before you came in, he started to say something on one of the things we were trying to decide. . . ." At that moment Father Groppi reentered the room, not knowing that he had been the topic of conversation. General Waters asked: "Father Groppi, remember last night when you spoke up in the meeting, what did we tell you?"

"Take a seat and be quiet."

"Right," Waters smiled at me. "Man, we run our own show, but lots of people think that Groppi gives us orders. That's not to say we don't listen to him; but on policy decisions, movements, problems, and so on—the Commandoes handle them."

Father Groppi broke in: "What we're trying to prove here is that black people must be their own decision makers. Particularly black men. This is what has been missing in the whole scheme of things: black men taking the leadership over the problems of blacks. No white man will ever be able to do this. A lot of people think I'm the leader, but they'd be shocked if they knew what was really going on."

"Are you saying that no white man can lead blacks?"

"Not today," Groppi asserted. "No matter what kind of leadership ability he has, he can't join the black power movement in a leadership position."

"Traditional concepts of black power," I informed him, "do not make it possible for any white people to join; how is it that whites take part in this movement and yet you call it black power?"

"Whites *can* join the black power movement providing they don't bring to the movement their own thinking," Groppi explained. "If they come in at all, they come in as the servants and not the masters, as students, not the teachers. In other words, they gotta lose whatever sophistication they have in their own culture and make it subservient to the decisions of black leaders."

"In that case, is it possible for a white man to be a member of the Black Commandoes?"

"Sure," General Waters acknowledged, "in fact, one of our Commandoes, Ed Thekan, is white. We accept anybody over eighteen."

"You can see, though, why very few whites could ever be a member of the Commandoes," Groppi elaborated. "There just aren't enough of that kind of white folks to accept this philosophy of black power. It means they have to give up being white."

I discovered the clue to Father Groppi's continual usage of the terms "we" and "us" when speaking of blacks, and "they" and "them" when speaking of whites. He had indeed become black—by his own definition.

One by one, and then in growing numbers, additional Commandoes began drifting in and speaking out. Certainly there were jobs available in Milwaukee, they said, but most of the jobs available were classified "nigger work," like "bustin' your balls" in the tannery.

"Most of us didn't finish high school; like I dropped out of school in the eighth grade," Colonel Pierce related. "And do you know why? I had a white teacher at Wells Junior High who said that Negroes were the dumbest people in the world. I heard him, and I ain't never forgot."

Colonel Vernon Mallet was an exception: he had finished high school. He got through as a wrestling champion. However, when he went to take an entrance examination for college, he suddenly discovered that he hadn't been taught a thing that would get him into college. "They gave me a test at MIT, and nothing on that test was anything I had ever seen before."

"I liked history," said Corporal Rufus King, "but the only history they taught me was bleached history—Washington, Lincoln, those guys. Why didn't they teach me about black folks' history? I would have liked that and would have passed it too. The other history I flunked, so I quit."

"Do you know what I got kicked out of school for?" Sergeant Howard Thomas asked. "Well, in school they said I desecrated the flag. They took me before the magistrate, and he gave me a lecture on the flag. He started explaining what the red and white stripes stood for, you know, like for blood and purity, and I popped up and asked him, 'Why ain't there no black stripes in the flag to represent me?' "

All the Commandoes laughed at that one.

"All these training programs they claim they got for black people," Lieutenant Shakespeare Lewis complained. "Me, I finished welding school over a year ago. I got me 1085 hours and a certificate saying I'm a welder . . . got applications all over town . . . for a year. I still ain't got no job welding."

The Commandoes marched daily for open housing. They charged that in the early marches the police were quite free with their nightsticks. Sergeant Marion Glass displayed a three-inch scar on the top of his head.

"I saw the blow," Father Groppi said. "It made me sick."

"All of us got it that night," General Green stated. "Man, those guys were flailing away."

"Man, I was bleeding so much when they put me in jail, I wrote on the wall 'Black Power' in one-inch letters from the blood that came out of my head," Glass told me.

"During the days of the riot," Father Groppi said bitterly, "Mayor Maier called out the National Guard and slapped a curfew on the town. Yet, when we marched into the white part of town in the South Side, and received rocks, bottles, curses from whites, we could not get protection. I called upon him to impose a curfew against the whites and call out the National Guard like he did against us, to protect the marchers. You know what he said? He said that the whites were 'hardworking' citizens and he saw no need to call out the Guard or impose a curfew against them."

What about violence?

"I don't like it," Father Groppi explained. "Whereas I have no problem in it being used in self-defense, as a tactician I have enough sense to see that it won't work."

The Commandoes were a hungry lot. Their hunger was not only confined to the cause for which they march; but there was simply little income, little food.

"We have very little financial support," Father Groppi revealed. "These guys, many of them, have families and no jobs. Most have holes in their shoes. The only money we have is the money that was first raised when we all went to jail—the bail bond money. The guys are faced with rent payments, groceries, light bills. Somehow, we help out where we can, but there's really no money."

"Does the public at large know this?"

"Very few people know it; in fact, most of these men haven't eaten today, and we're trying to figure out a way to get food."

"How many of you fellows haven't eaten today?" I asked some twenty Commandoes present. Twelve men raised their hands. It was three o'clock in the afternoon. Ironic, these Milwaukee Commandoes, ushers of the dream for Milwaukee open housing, were marching for that which none of them could buy, on empty stomachs.

We figured out a way. A ten-dollar bill from my wallet and four dollars from Father Groppi's thinning purse ensured food for all. We dined sumptuously on hamburgers and soft drinks.

Watching the Commandoes eat, I was constantly nagged by a troubling question I had not dared to ask. I finally posed that question to Father Groppi. "Father," I said quietly, "the Commandoes are now in the eyes of the nation. What happens when the headlines are gone, when the marches have ended? What will these men do then? What cause or project will enable them to hold on to their discipline and philosophy without splitting at the seams?"

I asked the question in private, away from the men in question. For the first time, Father Groppi became silent. He looked at me with a defeated look. He pondered the question, then confessed: "I don't know; damn it, though, there must be something for them to do. I blame myself partly for not thinking ahead, but we just haven't had time to live but one day at a time.''

Strange—strange indeed. The steady marches in all kinds of weather, the beatings, the punishment, the deprivation experienced by the Commandoes. If their march purposes were successfully concluded, it would destroy the foundation beneath them. Or would it? I asked Lieutenant Colonel Pierce.

''There's a lot of things we can do,'' he spoke challengingly. ''We don't have to stop. We can go on to slum housing, cleanup, job placement bureaus . . . things like that.''

I reminded him that there was no glamour in that kind of work, only a long, hard uphill pull against almost insurmountable odds.

''We can do it,'' he insisted. I wanted to believe him.

After the meal, the Commandoes and Father Groppi discussed the future. Projections poured out of the group like fire. They established the priorities for future action as follows:

1. To keep marching until open occupancy was achieved.
2. To begin a program to correct bad housing by instituting protests against slum landlords.
3. To press for rat control legislation.
4. To ensure that North, King, Lincoln, and Roosevelt High Schools would teach black history.
5. To compel the government to make Briggs and Stratton (which had a governmental contract for making parts), located in the ghetto, move their employment offices from beyond the bus stop out of town, and bring that office into the ghetto so more blacks could be employed in a practically lily-white factory.
6. Force three shoe factories, all located in the ghetto (namely 5th and Chambers, 6th and Ray, and 11th and McKinley), to change hiring practices.
7. They debated with Father Groppi the expedience of requesting that the federal government fund the Commandoes' organization for continued operation. The funding idea was discarded after appraisal of the fact that they would be forced to limit their activities to those things that met with the approval of the political forces that were involved in granting the funds. However, it was stressed that whatever programs or funding coming to the ghetto had to be run and administered by black people.

Finally, the Commandoes left.

Father Groppi and I were left alone. I looked at him with apprehension. He was obviously tired, weary with the strain of the thought session. The ideas had all come from the Commandoes; yet he was riding with every decision, making mental notes of the positive and negative factors of the future. In a few hours he would begin the fifty-ninth consecutive march. I apologized for the time I had consumed with him. He looked up at me from his deep thoughts, the cross of the Commandoes now obviously heavy upon him.

"I'm tired," he said simply. "I don't think I'll be able to make it tonight with the guys."

"You'll make it," I assured him, "they depend on you."

Three young priests wandered into the room. Seeing Father Groppi, they immediately left.

"Your helpers?" I asked.

"No, I don't know who they are. Priests come and go here."

"Who is the pastor of St. Boniface? I notice you are always listed as the assistant."

Groppi laughed. "No one now. Absolutely, positively, no one is in charge. The last three pastors couldn't take it; the Commandoes and the marchers ran them off. In fact, you can hardly call this a parish anymore. It's total confusion."

"What about the Bishop, is he disturbed about what is happening?"

"Who knows. I never see him—and he leaves me alone. I guess you might say I am in charge by default."

"Who conducts the mass?"

At the mention of mass, Father Groppi became alive. It was time for afternoon mass for the children who were now out of school. They would be waiting for him in the church. Would I join them?

Moments later, Father Groppi was adorned in his priestly vestments. The sight of him in the traditional robes of a religious order was incongruous. Somehow, I thought, the man will be lost in the garments that gather him up. He was a symbol of a rebel, a prophet, a voice crying in the wilderness, but now he was returning to the trappings of organized religion.

At the altar stood the children. At least thirty of them surrounded him. Black children, beautifully black. Their eyes
were fastened upon the man of God who now was about to say
mass. Opening the scriptures, Father Groppi read:

"He that is not against us . . ." "Who is against us?" he
asked the children.

"The Devil," the children chorused.

"Who is the Devil?"

"White people who hate us," chimed in a young sweet
thing.

"That's right," Father Groppi said. "Who else?"

"Policemen who call us little dirty bastards."

"That's right."

"Are we all those things they call us?"

"No. We are black children of God."

"Tell me something about black," Groppi's eyes were now
on mine.

"It's beautiful," the children chorused.

Suddenly, Jackie Williams, age fourteen, began to sing a
chant:

Mama, Mama, please tell me, why was a darky born?
He was born to hoe the cotton, born to pick the corn.
Mama, Mama, please tell me, why was Groppi born?
To keep us from hoeing cotton, keep us from picking corn.

As the young black voices rang out the chant with the
rhythm of rock and roll, Father Groppi, behind his horn-
rimmed glasses, closed his eyes and swayed with the beat.

"Name me a saint," he requested at the conclusion of the
song.

"Harriet Tubman," came the response from Doris
Harold, age thirteen.

"That's right, she was a saint. Who here can tell me what
Harriet Tubman did for black people?"

He looked once more at me with pride as Deborah Grey,
age fifteen, recited the history of Harriet Tubman, the "Moses
of her people."

"Do you know any more saints?"

The saints were named.

162

Medgar Evers. Frederick Douglass. Emmett Till.

"Why was Emmett Till killed?"

"He was killed for whistling at a white girl."

"Is that all he did?"

"That was all."

"Who killed him?"

"White bigots."

> Were you there when they crucified my Lord?
> Were you there?
> Were you there when they crucified my Lord?
> Were you there?
> Oh, Ohhhhh, sometimes, it causes me to tremble,
> tremble, tremble,
> Were you there when they crucified my Lord?

Turning back to the scriptures, Father Groppi read hastily:

Now, oh Lord, who taketh away the sins of the world. . . .

Concluding, he asked: "In what form does the Lord come to us today?"

"Through civil rights marches and the Commandoes," they answered in rote.

"How do the marches help?"

"They help to gain equal rights, good education, votes, and give us dignity when we walk."

"Was Jesus a civil rights worker?"

"Yes."

"Paulett, tell us how the devil treats us sometimes."

Paulett Blackman, age fifteen, related how a policeman, the year before, had yanked her out of the line while she was part of a group picketing the home of a judge who belonged to the Eagles Club (a white organization that practiced racial exclusion).

"What did he do to you when he picked you out of the line?" Father Groppi asked softly.

"He kicked me in the stomach," Paulett remembered.

"What did he say?" Father Groppi spurred her onward.

"He called me a dirty little mother f_____."

"How do we show our love and forgiveness toward those who misuse us?"

163

"I know," Paulett Blackman responded, "I know."

"Give us an example, Paulett."

"Well, there was the time last year when that white lady wouldn't rent a house to Ronald Briton who was just back from Viet Nam."

"What did you do about that?"

"A bunch of us went out into the area where she lived and sang Christmas carols in front of her house."

"What did she do?"

"She turned all her lights off."

Hail, Mary, full of Grace . . .

Chalice in hand, Father Groppi made his way around the altar. To each upturned black face of a child he deposited the sacrament on the tongue. Looking him full in the face, I accepted the element from his hands. As a Baptist minister, I welcomed the sacrament from the hands of a Catholic priest. Somehow, it seemed right this time.

Outside, the darkness began to fall. Black children stood on the pavement waiting for the Black Commandoes to come out of their meeting and begin the march. I waited. Before long, they came: tough, husky, changers of the city, ushers of the dream.

"Forward, march," Lieutenant Colonel Pierce spat out the command.

Black is indeed beautiful. This in spite of the fact that as they tramped off into unknown parts of the city, a white priest was out in front. He had earned that spot. It was the only place where he could follow, for the Black Commandoes had led him there.

CHAPTER 18

Leaving the Commission

A FTER SPENDING THE TIME I HAD WITH THE Black Commandoes, I knew that I could not continue my role in the Kerner Commission's "whitewash" and "balancing act" of the racial situation in America. On November 6, 1967, I submitted my letter of resignation to David Ginsburg, executive director of the Commission.

November 6, 1967

Dr. David Ginsburg
Executive Director
National Advisory Commission
on Civil Disorders
Washington, D.C. 20036

Dear Mr. Ginsburg:
   Submitted herewith is my resignation from the National Advisory Commission on Civil Disorders. I have tried in good conscience to abide by the policy decision that our staff should not analyze developing crises in cities, and find such policy totally inconsistent with the hopes and aspirations that concerned citizens have placed in this Commission. The failure of this Commission not to make this policy publicly clear is regrettable.
   In the hope that my resignation will serve some measure of reappraising the current policy, I enclose suggestions and recommendations for your consideration. It is my fervent hope that those recommendations that are applicable will be seriously considered.

Sincerely,

Charles H. King, Jr.
Program Analyst

165

The day I resigned from the Kerner Commission was the day before Richard Hatcher was elected mayor of Gary, Indiana. After my fallout with Mayor Katz, who lost, I was unsure of my future. I had made a foolish statement to the Gary Commission when I was granted a leave of absence to work on the Commission on Civil Disorders.

"How do we know that after you go to Washington you won't accept a permanent position in the Johnson Administration?" a commissioner had asked.

"I might do that," I answered honestly but foolishly. Any person likes to move up, and I am no different than most people who desire to further their careers.

I walked the streets of Washington that night. I had more than a month left of my leave from Gary and was now without a job. I was angry at the Commission on Civil Disorders and the Gary Commission—but more so, at myself. I had, by my actions, precipitated a crisis for my professional survival. What should I do?

I still had the information I had compiled in my reports and my notes on riots and disorders. I convinced myself that they and my findings would be ignored by the Commission since I had resigned. I convinced myself that the final report would be a "whitewash," a "balanced" report. So I decided to make an angry blast, via the media, which would force the Commission on Civil Disorders to change its policy of nonintervention during riots and disorders. Up to that point, it had been working in silence. The media had no inkling of its behind-the-scene activities. The public, I rationalized, should know of its failings, its refusal to indict police officers who killed, political figures who refused to cooperate, and most of all, cities that I knew or felt were about to explode and in which no remedial steps were being taken to alleviate that potential.

Looking back at my naiveté, I can see that what happened to me next I fully deserved. I called the Washington bureau of *Life* magazine. Would they be interested in an exposé? I asked. They certainly would. The next morning I found myself facing one of their news editors in his office. I explained to him what I wanted to do and why. He took all of my documents, leafed through them briefly, and handed them back to me.

"Let me think about this," he said. "That's pretty hot stuff. We have a man covering that area, so give me the number where you can be reached and he'll get in touch. Meanwhile, if I were you, I would think hard before releasing that stuff."

I promised him I would, but I was disappointed. I then went to the *Washington Post*, gave the night editor a copy of my letter of resignation, and told him I would be available to talk to a reporter. He said that a reporter would call me later at my hotel.

The next morning I picked up a copy of the *Post*. I had been betrayed. A two-inch column that made note of my resignation quoted my reasons and then went on to quote a Commission spokesman who belittled my former position as a mere "program analyst," a "lesser staff member." End of story.

Aside from my belittlement (I was a GS-14, which was equivalent at that time to a colonel in the Armed Forces), the news report gave more space to the spokesman's response than it did to my resignation. Then came a call from NBC. It was Richard Valariani; he was interested in getting more details. I agreed to meet with him in a Greek restaurant. He arrived at the appointed time, trench coat and all. After we had sat down and I was dumping my story on him, I could tell that he was losing interest. Another black man complaining. Another black man accusing whites of being racist. An unknown black, not even a leader. A single voice crying out against Washington's bureaucracy. No story here, not big enough for the morning news. Those must have been his thoughts as he thanked me for my time, shook my hand, and left.

It had been always my assumption that newsmen would never squeal on their sources. But *Life* magazine did. A black team member with the Commission notified me.

"King," he said over the phone, "a few of us want to meet with you. It's very important." So I met with them—four blacks and one white. They informed me that *Life* magazine had notified Commission officials that I tried to unload "hot" Commission papers on them.

"Turn that stuff in," they pleaded. "You can go to prison for this"—and indeed I could have. They reminded me that I had sworn to keep all information confidential because all files, including FBI reports, had been made accessible to me. The material I had was explosive: it could both stall and undermine the Commission's work. Not only that, but it would cast a damaging reflection on all blacks on the Commission staff. They reminded me that I had a career to think of, that I could be ruined as a professional.

I did not argue with them, because, as I regained my senses, I knew that all they told me was true. I had operated so long as a loner, as one voice crying out for justice, that I had lost touch with the meaning of teamwork and trust of and in systems. The fire in my bones had consumed my brain. In essence, I had been a thief. To this day I tremble at the thought of what might have happened to me if I had been taken up by the media.

I was told by my friends that the reason they came to see me was that my resignation had attracted the attention of the Commission directors. They had immediately gone to the files, had dug out my reports, and had been amazed at the volume and clarity of my investigatory findings, and of my analysis of the cities I had been to.

"Don't blow it, they are impressed," they said.

I told them of my frustrations. For two months I had attempted to arouse my superiors into discarding the philosophy of "balance." I had tried to make them aware of white racism, to interpret and make known the cause and necessity of black militancy. Only by resigning did my work and my reports emerge from the reams of meaningless submissions that sang the old tunes of "balance." My letter of resignation, I was now told, had impressed the director. It was being considered.

"Don't blow it, you've been heard. Trust us," they urged.

So I did. When they finally left, they had my material with them. I gave it all back. They took back with them the mistakes of the FBI, the miscalculation of governors, the murderous conduct of National Guardsmen, racist remarks and observations of their commanders, the jailing of non-rioting blacks, the deaths of innocent children, etc. *Life* magazine would not print it; newsmen considered the source and ignored it. I gave it all back. True, much of it had been culled from the FBI files, but much of that came from my own assessments and investigations. I had compiled all of that raw data into documentary form with an unmistakable conclusion: white racism.

The President's Commission on Civil Disorders ultimately issued its findings some months later. I am not foolish enough to believe that my reports and conclusions alone influenced their findings. There were too many people involved to believe that. I would rather think that after Commission officials examined my analyses, they began to see the mountains of evidence that pointed more toward white racism and less toward a "balance" of the blame.

Change also took place, I discovered later, among many of the white staff members who in the initial phases were looking at the cities with eyes blinded by their own ignorance of blacks, and by their own racism and reluctance to affix blame. Those changes produced a final report that made me proud that I had played a part in the incisive conclusion. President Johnson had instructed the Commission to find out once and for all the causes that led to racial disorders and what had to be done to stop them. The conclusion:

> What most white Americans have never understood, and what most black Americans can never forget, is that white institutions created the ghetto, white institutions maintain the ghetto, and white society condones it.

CHAPTER 19
A Test Tube of Urban Crisis

*A*FTER LEAVING THE KERNER COMMISSION, I RE-turned to Gary to resume my position as director of the Human Relations Commission. It was immediately obvious to me that, once Gary had a black mayor, the dynamics at City Hall underwent a drastic change. Two cities, Cleveland and Gary, which had elected the nation's first black mayors, became test tubes for black political activity. The disorders had brought forth a national fear that cities once turned black were potential kegs of dynamite. These two cities, then, would serve as indicators of what all cities could expect when power changed hands.

In a well-appointed office in the Municipal Building, Gary, Indiana, behind a walnut desk, seated in and surrounded by deep, luxurious chairs, sat the mayor of 180,000 people. Mayor Richard Gordon Hatcher had walked the tightrope of local and national apprehension. The uphill fight that he waged to gain that administrative post and the ultimate success of that venture rightfully posed a significant question about the present and future urban crisis: What happens when power changes hands?

Prior to Dick Hatcher's election, the white population had followed Marvin Katz in predicting that the election of a black mayor in Gary would destroy the city. That destruction would come to pass as a result of a mass exodus of whites from the city; school boards and appointed administrative offices would be stacked with blacks; business would leave town; crime in the streets would increase; and welfare recipients would be given handouts. (Some even predicted that pigs' feet would become compulsory fare on the menus of downtown restaurants.)

These were, of course, grossly exaggerated fears—some of them honestly believed but most of them used as white threats to retard the day now upon us. The black population explosion was occurring nationally with great rapidity. It was predicted that the black population outside of the South would double in cities by 1980. And by the year 2000, nearly three blacks out of four would be living in the North and the West. Those who doubt those statistical projections would do well to remember that in urban areas the black population is considerably younger and the birth rate hence higher. Coupled with this is the fact that in twenty-four metropolitan areas of a half million or more residents, the "inner cities" lost 2,392,000 white residents between 1950 and 1960, a drop of 7.3 percent. Those same areas gained 2,641,000 new black residents during the same period, a rise of over 50 percent. The mass white exodus and black in-migration had established (by white default) a new political black power base.

Those engaged in the human and civil rights movement began adopting new interpretive insights for the future. It had been my observation that many whites, even the most liberal, tended to view those statistical imbalances with alarm. The less than subtle inference was that all black cities would be catastrophic occurrences. I preferred to think of those cities as the coming challenges and opportunities. To say less would imply that hundreds of cities dominated by whites were likewise catastrophic phenomena—and in large measure, some were. In short, I never asserted that the problem of power changing hands necessarily spelled disaster. It was not the color of the hands holding the power that would ultimately save our cities as much as it would be the integrity of those hands and the honest commitment of that power to *all* people.

Gary, Indiana, therefore, stood as a test tube, an urban marker that eventually would give its political power into the hands of black people. Prior white administrations had been correctly identified as corrupt fish bowls. The difference had to be made clear: no fear or apprehension was ever associated with fishbowl political power as long as such power was in white hands. No matter how corrupt, how inefficient, or how inept such administrations had been, they were accepted by both blacks and whites as part of the necessary evil of political structure. These administrations were tolerated and even alibied away as inevitable outgrowths of political power. In fact, Hatcher was only one mayor away from a white chief administrator who served a term in the federal penitentiary, was paroled, and returned as a strong political force accepted and honored by his party. That honor was certified by a massive celebration sponsored by the past administration to raise funds that would enable the former mayor to pay off back income taxes. In the traditional posture of the ostrich, no one bothered to mention that the income tax the former mayor failed to pay was on kickbacks to the tune of $250,000. And the city had not been reimbursed.

Tolerance of acts such as these shows that often, when power was in the hands of whites, its abuse was granted liberal interpretation and forbearance. This was the fish bowl within which we viewed white fish. They swam at their leisure, and the citizenry felt no danger as long as they were confined in the bowl of political action, however murky the water.

Now witness the change. Power changed hands. The black administration was not given—not should it have been—the latitude of the fish bowl. Instead, it was scrutinized in the narrow confines of the test tube. The nation stood by with bated breath, for these test tubes had been known to explode. Not so in Gary; Gary would not explode.

In fact, I was convinced that the one remaining hope of saving such cities from corruption, blight, and disaster was to quickly thrust power into the hands of those who had traditionally been denied the true power of their numerical presence and the potential of their untapped creativity.

History may well record that the black mayors of urban America were its eventual saviors, and that the challenge of urban rejuvenation and restoration of the lost spirits of men was both motivated by and acted upon with the religious fervor of self-determination. In cities that were fast becoming black, the white political structure had to realize (as a result of riots and disorders) that it had failed—and failed dismally. The crumbs traditionally handed to black masses from the master's table had the ultimate effect of turning victims of ghettos into raging balls of fire. White political structure in urban areas, where teeming blacks had been traditionally denied their place in the bowl, whether the water was murky with corruption or clear with faint hope, was now being dissected by the razor's edge of history.

When power changed hands, it had the effect of pumping a new blood into an anemic democracy, and democracy then assumed a new dimension. That dimension took the shape of pragmatic action rather than romantic idealism. However, I will make no assertion that this change of power did not have some adverse effects. Polarization between the races had a tendency to increase. White racism, as it always seems to in our society, surged to the front in an unabashed display of a last-ditch effort to return power to its original base.

It was not to Gary's credit that, when Dick Hatcher won his party's open primary, the white political machinery, which normally supported the winner of the primary, switched its power and money to the opposite party, where the white hope remained. Thus, when power changed hands, white structure had a tendency to form weird alliances and seek strange bed-fellows.

Party labels became lost or discarded. Traditional white political opposites suddenly became equally concerned about the "creeping influence of communism"; "crime in the streets"; "riots and violence"; "every man's home is his castle"; "takeover of the federal government"; "liberal Supreme Court." Then topping off this obvious racial menu with dessert, they cleverly connected the names of Stokely Carmichael and H. Rap Brown by innuendo with black candidates. Those blatant or subtle implications had a direct emotional effect upon the diminishing white population. The de facto segregation of schools had already instilled an isolationist view of the black population, and white politicians further compounded the fears and heightened the emotions, successfully creating a climate of hostility and fear. The damnable results of this remained with cities for years, and in some cases the scars never did heal.

A victory was achieved when power changed hands. But the black population was not to escape a critical analysis of its own shortcomings. Cheap black politicians and traditional political hacks surged out of the basements of their own political lives and attempted to mount the platform of political stability and responsibility. Change of power to them meant only a bid "to find an equal opportunity to gather in the withered fruits of past white corruption." When responsible black leadership failed to appoint them to political plums, they formed colorful alliances with strong white political figures, who successfully encouraged each one to run for all available offices. In an obviously futile effort to exercise their new-found "equality," these men fell all over each other to file their candidacies. It was not unusual to see five or six black men running for the same office, hoping they would be endorsed by the mayor on the qualification of mere blackness.

The ghetto also had a rude awakening when power changed hands. Hopes for the magic wand to descend upon the slums and eradicate the evils fell quickly. A black mayor was faced with the hard reality that the power residing in his hands was limited by a dominant white system that still controlled the major institutions. Banks, real estate, business, and industry fretfully retained their powers.

*   *   *   *   *

One night the city that had elected its first black mayor joined Newark, Cleveland, Detroit, and Watts by experiencing its first civil disorder. I felt a personal hurt unlike any other in my life. During the long, hot summers, because of the dark mood of the nation's ghettos, Commission staff members were asked not to take leaves or vacations until fall, winter, or spring. Blacks in the nation's cities were responding in the form of riots and disorders not only to the injustices, but to the media hype as well. It was as if any city that had young, unemployed blacks felt embarrassed that they were keeping the peace while others were looting and burning. Since most disorders occurred from three prime causes—insensitivity, unanswered grievances, and police brutality—I insisted that the Gary Human Relations Commission give priority to two programs that would minimize the possibility of disorders.

A mobile roving Human Relations unit was established to obtain ghetto grievances. I asked for and received total support from Chief of Police Hilton (white) to monitor all police calls, and to have our specially trained staff summoned to all calls that required help or to situations that could lead to a potential eruption. Our Police Community Relations unit worked twenty-four hours a day. I had selected a former teacher of Spanish, Gloria Bernal, to direct that special unit. Ms. Bernal, who had originally formulated the concept while still a member of the Gary Public School System, was hired away from that system to implement the program. Her dual language abilities gave her a wider scope of inner city contacts. Rev. Floyd Dumas, a prominent minister, volunteered to man the evening patrol, and other special field workers were scattered throughout areas of poverty and high crime. From the police and our special units, I was able to monitor the mood of the city. Response to grievances was immediate. We distributed leaflets and brochures to emphasize our availability to respond to human needs and injustices.

But one night I was awakened by the police, who came to rush me to the inner city—Broadway, where it had been reported that a fireman was shot by a sniper. Apparently, firemen were at the location to extinguish a building fire that had allegedly been set by black youths. My heart sank as the police car screamed through the streets of Gary. Was this city going to go up in flames like the other cities had? Was looting and burning going to take over despite the fact that the city was now governed by a black mayor? The specter defied my concept of logic. After reporting and analyzing the disorders of other cities, I had contended that institutionalized white racism and the powerlessness of blacks created the climate for racial disorders.

175

But at the scene I could see that the city was not burning. One building was. In the flash of the police squad cars' blue lights, I saw a lone black man in the middle of the street, gun in hand, firing wildly. Both onlookers and police had scattered in the face of the shots. The police officers' hesitation to do something did not surprise me, because they had been warned that shooting anyone who was involved in property damage alone would be considered an insensitive act. As I emerged from the car, my only thoughts were, Gary must remain a city without violence and free from disorders. It was as if I had a personal stake. "Keep the peace, baby" had been the Commission's motto and appeal to the black community. Where this lone gunman had come from I did not know and did not care; he had to be stopped. In retrospect, I can now understand what I did next as a personal act to save the work that I had done.

There were no heroics involved in my next move, but unlike the firemen and policemen who had ducked for cover, I moved toward the gunman. His back was toward me. His posture, as I can recall, was one of defiance, as if he were claiming the street as his own. My eyes were cloudy from the mist of gathering tears, not for the fireman who had been reported as wounded, but for a city, now controlled by a black mayor, now to be added to the long list of urban disasters. I had staked my belief in a new hope that the elimination of white racism, or at least a concerted, recognized government response to black protestation, would silence the guns, curtail the burning, and stay the fury of youths prone to violence. Yet here, standing in the middle of the city, was a young black who no longer gave a damn about the city, the mayor, or even his own life. Ordinarily snipers snipe, run, and hide. They do not stand still, out in the open, gun in hand, and defy. The brief flames that had erupted from the structures in the block sealed off had been quickly extinguished, but the burning in the gunman's guts had not gone out. He was searching for targets, human targets, and nine were in sight.

Perhaps I should have left him there. Eventually, I am sure, he would have been legitimately cut down by a hail of police fire, once they had postured themselves behind the barricades of buildings and cars. I did not hear the warning shouts for me to move back, to "look out, he has a gun." I saw the gun, saw the man—and he was black. I had fooled myself into believing that the ghetto youth, particularly the members of the "Sin City Disciples," would not resort to violence. As the director of the Human Relations Commission, I had openly supported the obtaining of federal funds to finance recreational equipment, a skating rink enterprise, and a job skill bank for those whom the media had described as hoodlums. Out there in the street was a member, contaminating both the laboriously built-up image of the Disciples and the hope that begged-for programs for young blacks would not dry up, as had been predicted by whites if the Disciples would lead civil disorders. Those were my thoughts as I moved toward the gunman. I was attempting to appeal to my open and honest—up to that point —concern for their welfare. He turned as I approached. He recognized me; I recognized his face but not his name. To my amazement, he slowly raised his gun to my head. We were no more than two feet apart. I froze, the words I had planned to speak sticking in my throat.

"Get out of here, Mr. King," he mumbled, almost incoherently. It was at that moment, looking into his eyes split by the barrel of his gun, that I knew the source of his defiance. He was drunk. (I later learned that it was drugs, not alcohol, that had spurred him out into the street.)

"Give me the gun," I told him quietly. My voice trembled with a mixture of fear, anger, and disgust—mostly fear. "You really want it?" he asked, holding it in my face. We glared at each other, and his reply created a buckling in my knees. I was no hero, and I knew it. So did the gunman; in fact, he knew that what I represented was the source of his disdain: the educated, suit-wearing blacks, placed in positions of power, yet remaining powerless to change the plight of the ghetto. A disdain for the grand pretension that black politicians and black elected and selected officials would clean up the slums, obtain jobs for the unemployed, give hope to the hopeless. Our efforts, up to that moment, had been to appease them with funded programs that were designed to fail. To monitor those programs as if they were children, bent on careless, spendthrift activities, and to watch them like hawks, lest they be tempted to steal. Black school systems pumped them out for antisocial behavior before the twelfth grade; policemen dogged their every move, picked them up constantly for suspicious conduct, and searched their homes without warrants. They were the misfits, the outcasts, reviled on radio talk shows, condemned by editorials, debated in city council, and lied to by politicians. Defiantly, these men, denied the dignity of opportunity, banded together as a society of outlaws. They stood, when funded, one step inside of the law—when not funded, outside of its boundaries. Sonny McGee was their leader and they rode their motorcycles hard, like bats out of hell they came, the Sin City Disciples. The barrel of that gun was pointing at more than *my* forehead.

Whether or not he knew that his gun was empty I will never know, but when the hammer fell, and I heard that welcome click, the strength in my arms and legs returned. One swift, massive fist in his face felled him. I swept up his gun from the concrete and ran as fast as I could to a restaurant across the street. The door was locked from the inside. I yelled and screamed to enter, because behind me were three Sin City Disciples, emerging from God knows where to retrieve the gun. That gun, in the hands of the authorities, would send the drugged one to jail for murder if the wounded fireman would die. I knew that, and so did the Disciples. I was finally let in, and the door was locked behind me as I collapsed on the floor, completely emotionally spent by the experience. There was pounding on the window pane, pleas, entreaties from the Disciples to the proprietor. They wanted that gun.

The police? Why they never intruded on the scene I have just described has never been explained to my satisfaction. In fact, I later learned that what seemed to be happening in minutes actually took place—from the beginning to the pounding on the door—in no more than forty seconds. The proprietor begged me to give him the gun; he wanted to throw it out to them, like a bone to hungry dogs. I gave it up, and he threw it out.

Chief Hilton, a white chief appointed by a black mayor, entered the restaurant and personally escorted me back to the station, where Richard Hatcher had set up a riot command post. The streets outside were quiet; the disorder had been almost as quiet. The tally: one wounded fireman (in the knee) and one bruised black official (on the fist). I quietly informed Dick Hatcher what had occurred and why I had done what I did. His response to me I'll never forget: "Damn King, that was foolish . . . but I understand, and thanks." I was soon surrounded by newsmen, hungry for the story. But I broke down like a baby and refused to answer questions. The incident to me was like a family affair. It was a heartbreaking experience: my black brothers had turned on me. I was not proud of that night, the night I almost died. In retrospect, the night that a black turned on a black, both of whom were victims of social injustice and institutionalized racism, was the night that Gary as a city began to die. Later, warfare was transferred from the street into the black political arena. Dick Hatcher's best friends, in each succeeding election, attempted to politically shoot him down. And thus, though Hatcher remains, a city has died.

PART IV
Encountering Racism

CHAPTER 20

Encounter with Extremists

O N THE AFTERNOON OF MY RESIGNATION FROM
the Kerner Commission on Civil Disorders, Richard
Gordon Hatcher was fighting for his political life at the polls in
Gary, Indiana. That night I heard the news in my Washington
hotel quarters: black power had come to Gary.

The Commission's failure to go and analyze that city had
left me feeling empty—and alone. But no riot had occurred; in
fact, not one arrest had been made on the day of the election.

Chief executives in cities like Gary must walk a tightrope of
apprehension. A mayor must possess the capacity to execute a
delicate balancing act of racial concern when his black population is over 55 percent. This calls for the kind of statesmanship
from which he derives no personal benefits, applause, or acclaim. He must live with his political hopes endangered by the
daily crises that he faces. As a black, Hatcher was destined to
make choices that were agonizing, severely limited, and at
times seemingly impossible. As the first two black mayors of
major cities, Carl Stokes and Richard Hatcher would soon become aware that, because of the delicate balancing act and the
requirements for statesmanship, the office that they had sought
might spell political oblivion for both of them. It is no easy task
to satisfy a multiracial electorate.

If the mayor is black, he cannot help being aware that the
economic power is white. If the mayor is white, he cannot ignore the fact that he can only be lifted to office by votes that are
black. To successfully weld together a community of power and

color in an effort to achieve peace and equality is a task of herculean proportions.

The elections in Gary and Cleveland signified a black power movement that I could feel for and identify with. I thank God for this kind of black power, developed through the democratic process. And my association with Father Groppi and his Black Commandoes in Milwaukee was another expression of black power that had meaning.

Not so in Washington. In the nation's capital I confronted black power in all of its cruel dimensions. It was not the first time, nor the last.

My first experience with the cruel side of black power was in the form of a SNCC newsletter, June-July edition, 1967. This publication contained distorted views and flagrant misrepresentations of the facts of that summer's Middle East crisis between the Jewish and Arabic nations. It contained a violently anti-Semitic cartoon showing Cassius Clay and General Nasser (both presumably popular heroes of the black masses of the third world) about to cut the rope around their necks. The rope was held in a hand marked with a Star of David and a dollar sign. Obviously the sole purpose of the cartoon was to vilify the state of Israel and thereby induce black anti-Semitism.

It was the old insidious trick: divide and conquer, the historical theme played over and over to each generation. Black power movements that have engaged in this trick have attempted to create for our times a new kind of discrimination—shifting the blame for the black man's plight on a people who themselves had to fight, and still fight, this nation's blight of racism.

Because of the diversity of the black power movement, the civil rights movement had taken so many diverse turns and had been spread over so many areas that it became difficult to take a position on any one aspect of black power without running the risk of being condemned by those whose philosophies and tactics in the racial struggle covered the full spectrum from votes to violence. But those who shouted "black power" can find no place in their souls for people of other races and religions did a great disservice to the cause of civil rights—and to black people themselves. Black power has had many legitimate positions; however, racism is not one of them.

In that regard, the vocal vacuum resulting from the silence of the concerned created the atmosphere for the cruel side of black power to flourish, thus setting the stage for future racial conflict. Black people must never forget that just as they have had their Klans, the Jews have had their Nazis. How dare any of us ever forget that bitter lesson of history! The march toward freedom is a march of all people, and shouts from the lips of babbling fools should never change that basic truth.

These thoughts were in my mind as I prepared to respond to an invitation to speak to a group of Howard University students on the creative aspects of black power. The political victories of Hatcher and others had given me positive illustrations of black power, and the SNCC cartoon (I thought) would emphasize the negative and extreme form of black power that youth should avoid.

I never had the opportunity to use either, for what I found in Washington among students of Howard University and militant black power advocates was a chilling benediction to the fire I felt in my bones.

It was with an empty feeling that I entered the Prescott Methodist Church, Washington, D.C. Resigning from the Commission had left me with an empty feeling. I was continually attempting to convince myself that I had done the right thing in resigning. However, there were moments when I felt that I had mistakenly identified the ideal of courage and integrity, and had really acted the fool. Perhaps, from within the structure, I would have finally been heard, and changes would have been made that I knew had to be made. Too late—it was done.

I was met at the door of the church by the Reverend Don Hallard, Director of Wesley Foundation, Howard University, and student advisor. Standing beside him were three black students. I was then introduced to Dr. Nathan Hare. Dr. Hare had the appearance of a student: small features, "natural" hair, and a slight build. We shook hands, and I softly reminded him that I had met him in the pages of *Negro Digest* a few years before. He had written an article entitled "Negro Ministers Have Failed." In a subsequent article in the *Digest* I had taken him to task. He remembered.

In the sanctuary of the church the students from Howard University had gathered. In his opening remarks, Rev. Hallard (a white man) reminded the sixty students that the discussion was to be limited to the aspects of black power and what they as students could do to help other black people in the ghetto through concerted effort. Earlier, when he had extended an invitation to me to debate the subject with Dr. Hare, he had warned: "A few of the students have very strong views on black power, so prepare to answer some pretty rough questions." I had prepared, but not for what followed.

I did not know it at the time, but the majority of the students present were disciples of Nathan Hare. Dr. Hare had been dismissed by Howard University in the summer of 1966 because of his attempt to challenge the administration, its program, and leadership. He had organized a black power faction at the university whose primary purpose was to create a black power base for university and community action. Previous to this meeting, he had been on the campus with the students protesting the administration's policy of requiring freshmen and sophomores to take military training.

He began his remarks at 8:20 and concluded them at 9:30. I was astounded when he sat down to thunderous applause. I was astounded because in that period of time Dr. Hare, in a low, mumbling voice, had advocated overthrow: overthrow of "whitey, Howard University, the District of Columbia, and eventually the nation." He continually emphasized that black power was the only way, "black bullets" if necessary.

"I am not interested in politics, nor political action, and any black man who thinks he's going to win through voting power is a fool." From that point on he spewed out his hatred of whites, not all whites, but "nine out of ten." He included President Nabrit of Howard in his denunciation of white structure. The late President Kennedy, Hare stated, is now considered a hero and a martyr; but he hoped they would believe him when he said that "Kennedy was no good, and I know he was no good." Black preachers were next. As the son of a Baptist minister, he knew that "bag," and wasn't going to be "hung up" on "religion or Jesus." To him black power was living in a black world with no room at all for whitey. He wanted no part of "polka dot power"; it had to be black. Somehow he wanted to find a way to destroy the white man, even if it meant marrying his daughter. He was out to get even.

Dr. Hare then berated the students for stopping short of violence in their march the day before. "How many times have I told you, we don't want to do any more talking; as far as I'm concerned, we ought to burn down the whole damn hill." Occasionally skipping away from his hatred of whitey, he lambasted the university as another "plantation" belonging to Uncle Sam. Its President, Dr. Nabrit, was worse than a "Tom." With eyes still flashing from left to right, he was reluctantly reminded by the moderator that his time had expired. Five minutes later he sat down, and the applause was virtually deafening.

I was sick. And in my opening remarks I told them so. I ignored the notes I had prepared for the occasion, those notes recounting the glory of protest and the opportunities for young people to use creative black power—working out theories of black power in political and economic forums that I thought would challenge their attention and interest. I had entered a den of black lions, and there was no way out. I decided to challenge Dr. Hare, and challenge him hard. Sheer logic, I thought, would meet his devastating display of hatred.

"Hate destroys," I began. "Not only does it destroy the one hated but the hater as well. I came prepared to intelligently discuss the virtues of black power; instead, I have been exposed to one hour of idiotic ramblings that prove nothing more than to make me fear that most of you are sick."

The low murmurs became louder, and students stood up as if to carry me out. I shouted over their protests.

"You must show something besides hate and anger as a goal of black power. The danger in what Dr. Hare proposes is that it destroys, and no man has the right to destroy black peo-

ple by leading them down the path to bloodshed.'' I was temporarily able to command their attention by sheer lung power.
I informed them of the tragedy of the wasted potential they represented. That the racism expressed by white men had virtually
broken the backs of black people. That students in the twen-
tieth century, with an inverse twist, were about to break their
own backs. What logic informed them that they could live
in a multiracial world as black men without coming to terms
with reality? How could they survive in a black world? What
would they eat and where would they get the bullets that they
were going to shoot the white man with? What fool among
them thought that stones and Molotov cocktails could stand up
against the United States Army, Navy, and Air Force, while all
they held in their hands were weapons no longer than matches?
Was this the answer to the dilemma of this nation and the
future of black power?

It was Dr. Nathan Hare's turn for rebuttal.

"Mr. King," he stated sarcastically, "is a bitter man."

Applause.

"He is bitter because by his own admission he has fought
for integration and admits that it has been a complete failure."
His eyes blazed as he spat out, "Move the hell out of the way,
it's time for us to take over now." A Malcolm X-bearded student then leaped to the floor.

"Man," he addressed me, "you're out of touch. For instance, you keep saying 'Negro, Negro'; don't you know the
word is *black folks?* I mean, baby, you don't even talk right, I
mean, from nowhere, baby. And what the hell do you mean
when you say violence destroys black people? Violence is the
thing . . . what's wrong with black folks getting them like they
got us?''

I found myself shouting: "What has violence produced so
far other than black blood flowing in the streets? How many of
you are there? How can you survive? What's the nature of your
army, your supplies? . . . and where in the hell do you think
they must come from? I'll tell you where—from the *very white
structure you declare you must destroy.* Again, by what right do you
people, representing a handful of blacks, dare chart the course

for a mass holocaust of whites whose only alternative will be to seek retaliation against all blacks, blacks who are pursuing a way of life within the structure. No matter how damnable that structure might be, you've got to face the fact that millions of black people belong to it and will never survive without it!''

"Revolutions," Dr. Hare reminded me quietly, "do not seek mass acceptance; it is up to those committed to overthrow to pursue that course, and be damned who follows."

My mind returned to history.

Frederick Douglass met with John Brown in Chambersburg, Pennsylvania three months before Brown's raid on Harpers Ferry. Brown was attempting to persuade his friend Douglass to accompany him on the raid. He informed Douglass that with his band of raiders, they would swoop down from the mountains, liberating slaves, retreat back to the mountains, and continue this maneuver until he had gathered an army . . . then they would strike. Douglass pleaded with Brown not to go. He reminded Brown that the only weapons he had were his passion and poles with knives lashed to the end of the poles. It was not enough.

"Come, go with us," Brown pleaded. "I shall protect you with my life."

Douglass whirled hard on Brown. "I do not ask you to protect me with your life," he shouted, "I will lay down my life when I choose." Then, in a moment of anguish, he looked deeply into the eyes of Brown and pleaded: "I beg of you, don't go."

"I must go," Brown reminded him.

"Then you will hang," Douglass predicted. With tears streaming down his cheeks, Frederick Douglass, black, embraced his white fanatic friend, and departed into the night.

"Say, baby," a student shouted at me, "you know what you are? You ain't nothing but a 'Tom'."

Well, there it was. At last I had achieved the public announcement of the utter futility of my life. The sword of black rejection had descended. I had been committed to the twilight zone of the struggle.

As the students laughed, I squirmed in my seat. The beatings, the insults, the jailings, the hardships I had sustained during my years in the Civil Rights movement flashed across

my mind. Where had they led me except to this public proc-
lamation of the utter futility of my efforts?

No words can express the feelings I experienced at this moment. I suddenly wanted the entire nation to share the moment
with me. A nation that brags about its accomplishments in the
fields of space and education but needs to be exposed to these
young people bent on destruction . . . products of the
American system.

I made no attempt to defend myself from the accusation
that I was a "Tom," so turning again to their leader, the
students besieged him with questions of strategy.

"Dr. Hare," an attractive young girl asked, "I believe in
violence and riots, but where do we go from there? Will we
eventually have to move to another country?"

"No," Hare replied, "we can live right here. We can build
our own society with our own stores, banks, police . . ."

"But are there enough of us to survive without help from
the white structure? It appears to me that . . ."

Hare, knowing that he had been trapped by logic, retreated
into an easy compromise. "Don't misunderstand me, I'm not
saying that *all* whites must go—only those that are in the way.
With some, we can strike up a mutual agreement. For instance, we'll give them our chitterlings if they give us their
corn."

"Oh," said the young girl in response to this explanation,
"I see." I looked at her closely and was encouraged. The expression on her face as she sat down indicated that she did not
see. The question she wanted to ask didn't come: Where did he
think the chitterlings were coming from? The same place as the
corn.

"Listen," a tall, fair-skinned student exploded, "All we've
been talking about is how we're going to survive. Man, all I
want to do is go up in the mountains with a high-powered rifle
and shoot every damn 'Whitey' that comes close." His fists
were clenched in anger. "Am I right?" he asked Dr. Hare. "Is
this the thing to do?"

"Let me return for a moment to the young lady's question.
I want to amplify what I said about chitterlings and corn ex-

change. I didn't mean that if we can't get a fair exchange, we won't blast them down."

Cheers and applause.

The girl who had asked the question didn't join in the cheers and applause but looked up at me in a silent appeal that seemed to say: continue to challenge.

"As to your question about going up into the hills with a rifle," Hare now continued, "you have the right idea. But you must kill selectively. If a white man is bringing you corn, wait to see what side he's on. It might be he is that one white man out of ten who is all right."

"Dr. Hare," said another student who was obviously upset, "I just don't follow you. In essence, you are saying the very same thing Mr. King has said: that ultimately we will be forced to compromise and live peacefully with white structure."

"I never said that," Hare retorted angrily. "If I have been misunderstood . . ."

"No sir, you haven't been misunderstood." The student was now shouting at Hare. "Let's face facts. I believe in black power, but I'm sick and tired of all this talk about retreating into the mountains or exchanging corn and chitterlings. Where is the great plan, the grand design? I want to get on with the show, to produce a revolution with less lip and more action."

"We have strategy and plans," said Dr. Hare, "but it would be foolish for me to reveal them here. What we have to do is meet in secret; then we'll be in business."

It is hard to believe that in Washington, D.C., in November of 1967, in a semi-open meeting, such a call for anarchy could be boldly issued and discussed. Yet, the day before this meeting, I had resigned from the President's Commission on Civil Disorders because of its failure to come to grips with just such developments. It was evident to me that no investigation of past disorders would throw light on the full dimensions of the peril we now face: a restless breed of young Negroes ready to erupt in civil disorders that will not be spontaneous riots but carefully planned guerilla actions. The hostility expressed at the meeting in Washington was, to me, symptomatic of a mood that grips young blacks all over our country. Granted, much of what was said might be just talk. *But it was being said.*

I stood up again. Turning my back on Dr. Hare, I made one last attempt.

"What has been proposed here is mass suicide. Your commitment not only flies in the face of reason but threatens to erase the memory and efforts of every black man who has sought to achieve peace and progress within the American structure. If you must kill and destroy, what targets can you find that have meaning for black folks? Is it to be slaughter for the sake of slaughter?"

Catcalls.

Turning then to Dr. Nathan Hare, I reminded him that he had not dealt adequately with the problem of survival. Whatever strategy he might develop based on violence was doomed to failure. Like Nat Turner before him, he would wind up only a bloody footnote in history.

By this time, the moderator was pounding for order. Some students were shouting me down, others were urging that I be given a chance to speak. I took a quick glance at the young lady who believed in both violence and survival and saw that I had won her. I sat down.

"Several students have raised the question of plans for action," said the moderator. "These plans will be developed tomorrow, in another session. All those who want to know what they can do and how to do it—don't forget, tomorrow is the day." Though not invited, I decided to attend the second session anyway. Perhaps there were other students like the young girl who would listen to me.

When I arrived the next day, a new black militant was holding forth. Julius Hobson, chairman of the Washington chapter of ACT, was berating black-power leaders who shout slogans from the housetops. He reminded his listeners that any fool could stand on a corner and shout about burning the town down. In the final analysis, none of them ever do. He said that what he himself had formerly done—such as marching, picketing, and being jailed—would not accomplish anything either.

No. What was needed now was a new type of strategy that would take advantage of the existing structure and utilize it for the black man's benefit.

As an example, he cited a suit he had filed against the Washington, D.C., school board. He knew he had a case. He took it to Negro lawyers, businessmen, fraternities, and to Howard Law School. They all turned it down. Suddenly, out of nowhere, a white lawyer took the case, fought it for Hobson, and won it (the Judge Skelly Wright Decision that forced the Washington school system to integrate). "That's what I mean by using the white man," Hobson explained. "As black-power advocates, you don't have to love him—just use him." Hobson then revealed *his* plan.

"I am not against starting riots," Hobson explained. "I'm only against losing riots. You students have an opportunity to do what I am unable to do. You've got to plot, plan, lay the ground work. Stokely Carmichael found that out; that's why he's running around trying to establish an international movement. When he was in Red China, ranting and raving, an old Chinese took him aside and told him that revolutions aren't established by shooting off at the mouth. They are organized slowly and quietly. You don't go around exposing your plans; you meet secretly, build a hard cadre of revolutionists, *then you erupt*.

"All you students that have been following me around on street corners," Hobson continued, "are not helping to bring about revolution at all. It distresses me to see you content yourselves with supporting my rantings—you can do much better."

"What do you think we ought to do?" came a question.

"First of all, you must remember that just because a man's face is black doesn't mean he's with you. Some of the knives that have been thrust between my ribs have been thrust there by black men. Remember when they arrested those guys that were going to blow up the Washington Monument? Well, I'll tell you this, so you can learn a lesson from it. That was the RAM organization. It might surprise you, but I was in on every meeting they had when they were planning, and there wasn't a white man within a hundred miles of these meetings. How do you think the FBI broke up that gang? I'm telling you, the fact that a man's face is black ain't nothing."

One of the young students sitting beside me was visibly excited by Hobson's words. "Sir," he asked, "when do you think the time will be ripe for a revolution in this country?"

"When you start a revolution, you must go in it to win," Hobson answered. "Perhaps in your day this will be possible. But you've got to start with a handful of people, perhaps no more than six men in a dark room."

Suddenly I noticed that the young girl I had won away from Dr. Hare was now listening enthralled to Julius Hobson. "Is it possible to have a revolution without violence?" she asked. Hobson laughed.

"Of course not; the revolution I speak of will have to be violent."

With that, I knew I had lost her; in fact, at that moment I knew I had to get out of that room. She did not notice my departure. Julius Hobson had completed the pattern for which she had been searching by linking violence and survival. I probably will never see her again, but I know where she can be found. When and wherever those six men gather in a dark room to plot their revolution, she will be knocking at the door of that room, demanding to be let in.

CHAPTER 21
Encounter with a Black Panther

*W*HILE I COULD UNDERSTAND THE FEELING OF rebellion among the young militants, I found it necessary to do battle with those blacks over the concept of violence. But the events that took place at Attica Prison and the rebellions that led to bloodshed were part of the continuing developments that produced massive resentment on the part of young black Americans, who began to adopt an attitude that it was better to die as men fighting racism than to live under its oppression.

I met such a young black man. His viewpoint and the events of the times traumatized me further. In our battle over the direction that black people should take, he shouted that violence was the only direction of survival for blacks in America. It was not a pleasant, fulfilling, or resolving experience; I am still upset from the shock of that confrontation. He made so much sense, and yet he was destined to die early or go back to prison.

Even after Attica, which highlighted the badly needed look at prison reform, few thoughtful citizens would take time to analyze the demands that the prisoners made as legitimate: what was always emphasized in the public's mind was the lawlessness of the prisoners. Yet their sole concern was to live like men, and to be treated as men who still possess the right to protest subhuman treatment.

During the past several years I have personally conducted research and many interviews among prisoners accused of capital crimes within the Georgia penal system. This work has convinced me not only of the inhumanity within this country's prisons but also of the corrupt nature of its law enforcement and judicial systems that condemn blacks and poor whites to inordinate punishment, often for crimes they did not commit.

Prison reform, however meaningfully implemented, still does not touch the cornerstone issue involved. Beyond the treatment of the prisoners themselves are the causes behind why they are behind bars to begin with. The fact that 75 percent of the 1,142 inmates at New Jersey's Rahway Prison were black was no accident. These men were sent to prison to receive an education they did not receive in the public schools: to learn crafts and trades they were not permitted to learn while free men, and to be employed at meaningless tasks to keep them busy, a procedure frowned on by the outside labor market.

Slowly but surely, as exhibited by New York City's welfare plan, society was beginning to recognize that the social disorganization created by systems that freely discriminate inevitably creates too costly an expenditure. This cost can be calculated by wasted black potential and taxes that society must pay to imprison those whose dignity and lives have been destroyed in the process. Obviously, even if every demand set forth by the prisoners at Rahway were to be met, neither the courts, nor the system of justice, nor the fact that men will always steal if they are unable to work, would be changed. The Atticas and Rahways will continue to be the future junkpiles for the children of the men who now resort to "unlawful behavior" at the very place that was designed to curtail such behavior. It is also utterly ridiculous to expect rehabilitation behind those walls until schools, employers, labor unions, courts, and law enforcement officers rehabilitate their own attitudes and practices toward blacks and other minorities. Unfortunately, the national outrage poured out against prisoners, most of them black, is rarely directed against those systems that send men into prisons. It is one thing to be "too soft on prisoners" and another to be too soft on those who make prisons the catchall for their failures. You cannot break a man's leg and then blame him for limping.

"Don't you believe that changes will be made?" I asked the young Panther. He met my question with scorn and laughter. At age twenty, he had been jailed three times in three cities; he was handsome, black, and convinced.

"The white man and his system will never change." The way that he said it unnerved me.

"If no change comes, then by the way you feel, eventually, you will die," I told him.

"That's right," he conceded, "and I'm ready."

The Black Muslims still remain a positive influence among blacks, though their vocal social gospel diminished with the death of Elijah Mohammed. However, in the middle of the black revolt years, when "passive resistance" was a byword among blacks, the Muslims startled both white and black Americans with one of their demands: set all black prisoners held in state penitentiaries free. The Black Panthers, after shifting their emphasis from "off the pig" rhetoric to a concern for imprisoned blacks, have faded as a force for revolution. It is not by accident that the most radical black leadership came from those released from prisons. These were the men who formulated a black base for the philosophy of revolution: Elijah Mohammed, Malcolm X, Huey Newton, Eldridge Cleaver, Bobby Seals, and others. The chemistry at work within black men behind walls was explosively, actively bitter. The time for thinking and planning did not pass unused. No longer caring about survival, or fearing death, they reentered society bringing the shock waves of their pent-up fury directly into the black community, alarming it to the deep-rooted dimensions of racism that exists behind prison walls as a microcosm of the racism outside the walls. The killing of George Jackson at San Quentin, after he had spent seven of his ten years of confinement in solitary, electrified every prison black into a thoughtful analysis of his future.

I gazed into his eyes and observed the determined set of his lips. He gave a lengthy recital on how the brothers were being "ripped off." "Attica, San Quentin's George Jackson.

. . . They say he was shot trying to escape. . . ,'' he laughed bitterly. "We all know better than that, don't we?"

Jackson himself had predicted he would never leave prison alive. Tom Wicker, noted writer for the *New York Times,* in his hotly debated eulogy to George Jackson, shocked most white Americans with a searing, soul-searching exposure of his feelings about a society that condemns a disproportionate percentage of blacks to prisons. Blacks in prison constitute a potential collective army of men who, once released, could and would form an activism with an "I don't care if I do die" operational base. Attica and Rahway, in that sense, appear as only a prelude to the unreleased tension now building up in the nation's prisons and its cities. Only the naive would dare suggest that the disorders and riots will now cease. On the contrary, desperate men, fed daily rations of spoiled food and white racism, cease to be rational. Guards who have been relegated to the role of their keepers will fan the sparks of hostility that are already at the combustion point. Prison guards will become pawns to community sentiment, freed to become more racist, more repressive. These guards are poorly paid and hold a thankless job. But public attention focused on the prisons has suddenly propelled them into the spotlight as heroes. They will become increasingly conscious of the spotlight and the massive expectation for them to hold back the black waves of anger that now come surging out from behind those walls. State legislatures, politically mindful of their constituencies' chagrin with a "soft on prisoners" mentality, will be reluctant to vote tax dollars into prison reform. Predictably, they will balk and form time-consuming investigatory committees. Unheeded in these political by-plays has been the answerable and legitimate demands made by the prisoners at the Atticas and Rahways; in fact, the petition signed by the prisoners and given to Governor Cahill at Rahway states simply: "To be treated as human beings is all we ask of this administration." The cost for a major overhauling of our prisons will be extremely high and time-consuming. Meanwhile, how long and how much is needed *now* to treat men as human beings?

Why did the Panthers emphasize "off the pig" statements, I asked him. "Isn't that one reason for many of the problems you now have with the police?" Even before I had finished the question, I had to agree with his response. The slaying of Fred Hampton in Chicago, as proven by a later grand jury report, was a brutal response to unproven, unfulfilled ghetto rhetoric.

Those who contend that the only hope for prison reform is the outlay of millions of dollars may be correct. However, I make no such claim, nor expect such massive outlay or reform. Indeed, if such monies were made available, like the sums given cities for crime prevention, much of it would wind up in the form of new repressive instruments, programs, and controls designed to curtail riots and not to prevent them. Cities that were handed millions after the riots immediately invested those funds in tanks, stoner rifles, mace, helicopters, and finely trained riot squads. It would be folly to expect anything less from those who are now faced with the problem of curtailing prison revolts.

"Have we ever conducted a raid on any police department?" he asked. "If 'off the pig' was our goal, how do you account for the fact that only seven officers, but forty Black Panthers, have been offed?" He added that most of those killings took place in *cross fire action* at raided Panther headquarters. "We call that year, 1969, 'the year of the Panthers.'"

I began to feel tired, depressed. The anger, his feelings of futility, I knew, would ultimately find him back in prison. Outside those walls now, his return would ignite the fuses already burning behind those walls. Why?

The built-in weakness of any reform movement will be based on the inability of the public to care or become concerned about treatment given prisoners. The man who screams about increased taxation is completely oblivious to the fact that he will soon be taxed for the negative attitude and behavior patterns of prison guards. The clue to what's bugging prisoners is not hard to find, identify, or to change overnight. For example, look at the demands that came from Rahway: better medical care, adequate food, lower prices in the commissary, less confused parole practices, more and better vocational training, better mail delivery, and the curtailment of racism by the guards. None of the above requires huge financial outlays; yet all of those demands reflect the need for dignity, care, and respect for the sanctity of life. Animal shelters provide that much. Attica's demands were just as common: soap to wash the body, change of clothing and underwear, food free of flies and other insects, and release from brutality and racism. Strange that these commodities and services are considered by John Q. Public to be natural rights and privileges, expected and obtained at no cost or very low cost; yet for prisoners their absence becomes the explosiveness that burns down the prison. Those demands should give some insights (without the costly investigations) into the barbaric practices that now take place behind prison walls. Officials who condone or allow themselves to be blinded to the irrefutable evidence that prisoners are, more often than not, treated like animals should now be called into question by the same public who will soon be asked to put up taxes for major reform.

What is needed first, it appears, are governors who will demand an accounting of the attitude of wardens, guards, and commissioners who have the gall to blame the public's lack of interest as the raison d'être of inside violent activities. This shocking excuse was given by the warden of the Ohio State Prison on the Phil Donahue television show: "I admit that there is some brutality and racism," he responded in answer to a question. He then went on to explain that the only way to stop it was for the public to become outraged. What was missing in his summation of the solution *was his own outrage*. We may concede that it is difficult to hire black guards or educated white ones; but not one penny need be spent to insist that all men behind bars be treated as men by their current guards. A prisoner's confinement is legally mandated by courts that reason that lawbreakers should be removed from society at large. But who or what grants an extension of punishment that also strips a man of the protection of his body and manhood?

The easy answer will be for officials to demand more tax dollars for the proliferation of cell spaces and television monitors to assist in guarding the restive prison army. These will be necessary unless the massive sums needed for reform can be directed toward more legitimate targets: the relief of loaded court dockets that cause men to become bitter while waiting for justice; the hiring of additional prosecutors and defense attorneys; the quickening of grand jury meetings; the establishment of halfway houses for released prisoners. Without these changes, men are destined to return to all the new prisons that must be built to contain their legitimately developed wrath and bitterness. Behind those newly erected bars the next lawless generation will inherit the same bitterness.

Skills learned in a prison laundry cannot be applied outside; no industry will cry out for a labor force that only makes license plates for automobiles. If one couples the problems of the ill-prepared released prisoner in the future with the color of his skin, one can see that a double whammy is placed on his rehabilitative potential. The increasing dope traffic will further jeopardize the ex-prisoner's adjustment. The quickest money will be found in that marketplace, and whether the person is a user or a pusher, crime rates will soar to keep both the market and the addict painless. One need not be a prophet to predict that local jails will soon become—and are now—the breeding grounds for prison inmates, the sowing of municipal seeds for eventual state penal harvest. What else can be expected when on any day of the week the courts of the land can be found empty while men languish in overcrowded jails—waiting for justice?

Once again we were back to the subject of his survival. I found myself unable to make headway. Each time I presented the argument of potential death if one resorts to armed struggle, I was called foolish—and too late. "It's arm or harm yourself," he told me. I could not dislodge him from that premise because *he had no fear of death.* "Better to die fighting like men," he exploded.

In the light of that dismal backdrop, prison riots of the past seem small compared to the holocaust that is sure to come. The silent past and insensitive present will ignite the awesome future. Add to that mixture the racial isolation of the ghetto, the poor education that is a by-product of segregated education, the escaping white population from the inner city, the weary judges, the overworked police, and the day will soon come that if a week passes in which there has not been a prison revolt it will be a week of mystery. Prison reform should begin not only from behind the walls, *but outside of the walls before the prisoner becomes a prisoner*. That is where the vast sums need to be expended. It is long past time that we stop labeling such appeals to the conscience of the nation as appeals coming from bleeding hearts. The issue is one that should now be raised by every taxpayer, every mother and father. For it will be their sons and daughters who will inevitably be caught in the web of the developing patterns. They will be caught as either the lawless or those victimized by the lawless who are spawned in the hell holes euphemistically labeled as prisons.

I too exploded. "But I don't want to die, neither do twenty-five million blacks; please give me some other alternative than death." He fell silent—a telling silence. This young man of twenty years had no faith left in any system other than the suicidal one dictated by his own despair. He was artful of speech, precisely articulate. I saluted his manhood in my mind, silently, and continually expressed openly my fear for his life. It too would be snuffed out, consumed by the fury of his hate. He could have been my son. I suddenly felt ancient. The protest years came to my memory. Were they so long ago before the year of the Panther?

George Jackson was considered the most violent of all prisoners in the nation. Jackson, whose death catapulted the problem of prisons into national focus, uttered the one sentence before his death that no penologist can match in scope or wisdom. In a letter to his lawyer from Soledad Prison he wrote:

Criminals and crime arise from material, economic, sociopolitical causes. We can, then, burn all of the criminology and penology libraries and direct our attention where it will do some good.

He could have been my son, this young Panther. I found myself wishing he had been—before the fateful year of 1969. I thought then of my own son. Fourteen so far . . . so near to arming or harming himself. Would he wind up at twenty without meaning, without hope? I had given him his identity, his blackness, his pride. Would his eventual discovery of his manhood be his decline, his demise?

"Two state groups, a five-man panel to review 14 inmate grievances at Rahway State Prison, and lawyers from the Office of the Public Defender are looking into the causes of the 24-hour rebellion." Thus reported the *New York Times*. That news item, of course, would satisfy the public: Rahway, just like Attica, would soon fade from the public view. What is there left to study that has not already been reported and studied? In fact, what study need be made of any penal institution, unless it is to determine why *no* riots have occurred? Any intelligent citizen, viewing from a distance, can ascertain what's wrong with prisons by observing the facts. In the Ohio State Prison at that time, for example, blacks made up 50 percent of the inmate population and less than 5 percent of its guards. The qualification for guard duty was an 8th-grade education, and fewer than one-half of those guards had finished high school. The guards came from the same economic-social stratification as did the majority of the prisoners. There were over 10,000 prisoners in the state, and none of those prisoners had overcoats to wear outside in the winter; they wore blue denim jackets without linings. A new prison, at a cost of 44.5 million dollars, was to be erected far from any major city—Lucasville, Ohio. This secluded location would prevent lawyers and families of prisoners from visiting without extreme inconvenience and costly travel arrangements.

Such facts need no additional investigation or analysis. The conclusions are clear. This gradual dehumanization of men who happen to be prisoners loudly proclaims that our penal institutions are becoming increasingly insensitive in practice and uncivilized by design. The consequence of all this is summed up in one of the last letters that George Jackson wrote to his lawyer from Soledad Prison:

> If I leave here alive, I leave nothing behind. They'll never count me among the broken men, but I can't say that I'm normal either. I've been hungry too long. I've gotten angry too often. I've been lied to and insulted too many times. They've pushed me over the line from which there can be no retreat. I know they will not be satisfied until they have pushed me out of this existence altogether. I've been the victim of so many racist attacks that I could never relax again. . . . I can still smile now, after ten years of blocking knife thrusts and the pick handles of faceless sadistic pigs, of anticipating and reacting for ten years, seven of them in solitary. I can still smile sometimes, but by the time this thing is over I may not be a nice person. And I just lit my 77th cigarette of this 21 hour day. I'm going to lie down for two or three hours, perhaps I'll sleep. . . .

Multiply those feelings by thousands of other prisoners, and it is easy to project the day when the animal turns on the hunter —to kill before he is killed.

"Anything else you want to ask me," the young Panther interrupted my thoughts.

"No, that's about it," I replied, and it was.

Attica and Rahway, in that sense, might well be the last warning signals of an immediate need for penal sanity. Much can be learned, and one thing for sure: there appears to be a spark of hope and decency left in men condemned to prison. Secondly, more violence was committed by the lawmen than by prisoners. To date, no sufficient evidence has been uncovered to indict any inmate of those institutions as acting less than a man, with the attendant lack of respect for human life.

This warped and confusing state of affairs should be honestly portrayed for what it represents, rather than the repetitions of public outcry for retaliatory measures against rebellious prisoners. It portrays, at least to me, the last appeal of the damned for release from brutal treatment. Yet, all that now appears is the gradual increase of cell spaces, with no change or reform in sight.

I watched the young Panther strut away with the ease possessed by the confident. I envied that beautiful walk. I fought back the impulse to cry out to him, to plead for his return—that he find another way. I could not bring myself to do it, for at that moment I was not as strong as he. All I have left now is the painful truth that there, but for the grace of God, I too would go.

CHAPTER 22
Encounter with Fools

HEAR, O ISRAEL

*I*T CAME AS A SHOCK TO ME, A FEW YEARS AGO, that the National Grand Wizard of the Ku Klux Klan had consented to appear with me on a one-hour special of the nationally syndicated television program ''Black Perspectives on the News.'' Appearing along with the Grand Wizard, lending him ''moral'' support, was National Socialist Party of America (or American Nazi Party) national coordinator Frank Collin. I fully intended to demolish them with the precision of right, the weapon I had long kept for the day when the white schoolteachers of my youth, the Navy officers, the Mr. Emorys, the Bull Conners, and other blatant white racists would cross my path. The fact that a few of those people are still around and willing to be exposed to the national spotlight not only boggles my mind and starts the adrenaline flowing, but also offers the hope that, at last, my soul will be freed. But I was sadly mistaken.

David Duke was a personable and handsome man. Alone before the program was to be taped, we shook hands and exchanged pleasantries. It was difficult to feel hostility toward this prime candidate for all-American boy awards. Instead, I experienced a sense of bewilderment. There was a softness to his voice; the harsh, abrasive, fiercely commanding tone and eyes glaring hatred that one would associate with the KKK were not there. Rather, Duke evoked the feeling of a relaxed debate, a philosophical rather than racial appeal to white fears.

He made a concerted effort to divorce himself from the sheet-wearing, cross-burning image of Klansmen, and he abstained from and deplored violence. His speaking, of course, was laced with white-oriented logic. And throughout the program he made a naked, unabashed effort to get viewers to subscribe to his newsletter. His "it's in the book" approach was crude but effective in stirring up interest in what he could not verbally accomplish in the time allotted to him on the "Black Perspectives" program.

Collin, on the other hand, arrived amid a flurry of ostentatious activity. He entered the waiting room dressed in a snappy brown uniform, swastika, boots, and brown belt—just as if he had been resurrected from the battlefield of World War II. Standing at his side were two large storm troopers, weak-faced men, eyes darting left and right, as if danger lurked in every corner for their leader. They never spoke.

Introductions were short and snappy. The other two blacks were Harvard historian Lawrence Reddick and the host of the show, Reginald Bryant. It was an incongruous sight: three blacks, a Nazi, and a KKK leader socially conversing prior to engaging in verbal racial combat on a nationwide television program. I leafed briefly through the biographical data of both Duke and Collin, including newspaper clippings of their activities and statements. I was not impressed by Duke's; but the brevity of my insights was to later distress me during the debate.

My appearance on that program was a horrendous mistake. The format, from what I knew of "Black Perspectives on the News," was a program that featured prominent blacks who were questioned by experienced black journalists on their reflections on current events. This particular program defied that traditional theme. Too late—and far into the program—it was obvious that the moderator, without an experienced black journalist, had chosen two black intellectuals who had not done their homework on extremist groups such as the Nazis and the new Klan. The program opened with a ten-minute film of the activities of the Klan and five-minute excerpts from W. D. Griffith's film "Birth of a Nation." After that, the moderator, eager to involve himself personally in the setting, deliberately decided to question both Collin and Duke in a ping-pong fashion, while they blurted out their perspectives on race.

I felt like a fool—indeed, I thought I was one, for by the time Duke and Collin had dealt with the moderator, a total of eighteen minutes had elapsed. During those eighteen minutes I sat dumbfounded. Twice I angrily interrupted the moderator on the method of his proceedings, only to be told that we would be given a chance for rebuttal. When we were finally called upon to respond, too much, far too much, of Nazi and KKK philosophy had been mouthed. "Black Perspectives" had, in essence, become a forum for white extremism: blacks and Jews had been placed on the defensive. Duke and Collin had successfully written the script as the moderator aimlessly asked them question after question. The answers he received, without successful rebuttal, were enough to incite a riot:

> Collin: Hitler was right. The Jews should be exterminated. Blacks should be sent back to Africa. America must once again become an all-white nation. Blood flowing, war declared on race seems to be the only viable alternative to the present. The swastika stands for truth . . . like a bullet, the message of Hitler will pierce this nation.

> Duke: The problem? The Jews! They are the ones who control the nation, the press, the banks, all media! White people get all of the benefits, welfare, jobs.

Duke was not for violence, as Collin was, but he thought Collin had a right to his opinion and ultimate solution. He was not there to disagree with Collin but to warn the nation about the Jews. He had been to Israel (a lie) and discovered that Israel was the most totalitarian nation in existence.

The unusual aspect about the "Black Perspectives" program was that I was totally unprepared for both the format and the intense concentration and attack upon Jews. I had always considered Jews to be whites, separated from other whites only by their parallel to the black experience of suffering through historic oppression. Judaism as a religion was the foundational stem of my own Christian faith. The biblical theme of the slaves in Egypt had rung true as a precursor of the enslavement of blacks in America. My exposure to the anti-Semitics on that program taught me that my insights into ongoing anti-Semitic activities had been shut off by the personal hurts of the black experience. I had seen oppression and discrimination only in the black condition. The traditional black alliances with liberal Jews had not created for me a backdrop of empathetic concern about anti-Semitism. Indeed, I had calmly accepted the fact that their whiteness excluded the need for empathetic concern. I had bought into the old stereotypes that they had money, were successful, and were white.

The rage that I should have felt did not come, and later I wondered why. It struck me that that lack of rage is what allowed the holocaust to take place. I had personalized the holocaust into my own experiences. Later, the NBC production of "Holocaust" left me numb and painfully aware that the black experience is not uniquely black. There are many parallels to the Jewish experience, not only during the days of the holocaust, but from the days of their very beginnings, when they were torn from Jerusalem and taken into Egyptian slavery. Jerusalem has been reestablished for them. Yet one can now better understand the Menachem Begin stance of "never again."

HEAR, O ISRAEL.

The Nazi degradation of the Jews had been forgotten by many Americans, most of whom, when reports of the holocaust first reached their ears during World War II, refused to believe that such atrocities were possible in a civilized Germany. Worse yet, those who knew, including the political and military leaders of our nation, did little or nothing to stop it. In fact, this was the greatest crime of the century: not the holocaust itself, but the silence on the part of Christian people that accompanied the holocaust. Once again, the black experience has its parallels. In this nation, and in other nations that have espoused humanitarian ideals, the rape of an entire race took place under their very eyes. The cries of anguish and the smell of burning flesh fell on deaf ears and pinched nostrils. It is out of this past suffering that today's Jews fought and climbed to restore their dignity, homeland, and lives. Were it not for the airing of "Holocaust," many of us would retain the damnable stereotypes and lack of sensitivity for those who paid for their existence in blood. Few peoples' heritage takes them back to such massive dehumanizing and hate-filled epochs. During those years, the majority's final solution, as it was called, was to exterminate a race. And this extermination plan did not involve just letting them die naturally as a result of hunger or disease, but hastening the death process through gasing and burning.

In today's increasingly polarized world, we must recall, we must remember: the Jewish experience demonstrates the tragic three-cord scourge of the human condition—those who suffer, those who cause it, and those who ignore it. We are inextricably bound by those three cords. And as long as people suffer racism, sexism, anti-Semitism, or any "ism" that destroys, those cords are intact. If we are to survive as a nation or as a world, they must be broken.

HEAR, O ISRAEL.

It is unwise and unfair to compare the suffering of one race with that of another. But it must be added for emphasis that if six million blacks had been exterminated in America, one-third of our black population would have been wiped out. "Holocaust" underscored the parallels. We share much, the Jews and blacks: the selling into slavery, the pharaohs that knew not Joseph, the rising up of a Moses as a leader, the use of religion as the eraser of pain, and the hope of a promised land. So much in common, yet so far apart today. The strong and bitter pill we all had to swallow will create new meaning and a new future.

HEAR, O ISRAEL, THE LORD OUR GOD IS ONE.

The tendency of most minority groups to ignore the plight of other minorities, on a feeling level, I was already aware of. What I was not aware of was that I had prepared no argumentation for or refutation of anti-Semitic activities and utterances. My first thought was that no Jew had been asked to participate on the panel. In reverse, I knew how I would feel if I were viewing a program replete with racial slurs against blacks, while the moderator and white liberals could only sputter back weak and mumbling responses to such attacks. I knew that my responses to the attack on Jews were inadequate, and it sickened me. Neither the moderator nor Professor Reddick was any better prepared. "Black Perspectives on the News" should have been renamed, during that hour, "Nazi and KKK Perspectives on the Jews." The emotional drain on my intellect and emotions almost left me speechless—but not quite. I was at least able to pose a question similar to the "Sir, have you no decency left?" posed by Senator Welch to Senator Joseph McCarthy. However, my own question lacked the fire of my blackness.

"Do you realize, as we sit here exposed to millions of viewers, the awesome hurt and trauma you are creating by your anti-Semitism? Or, do you care?"

"Certainly I care," Duke answered suavely. "Let's talk for a while about hurt." He then moved on to the subject of how whites were hurting because of civil rights, etc.

The program, as I feared, created a national uproar. The following news article and editorial on the subject appeared in *Variety* magazine.

'BLACK NEWS' CUES A PHILLY UPROAR

NAZI PARTY, KKK REPS INFURIATE VIEWERS
By Harry Harris

Philadelphia, Oct. 4.

After only three months as president and general manager of Philadelphia-Wilmington public station WHYY, Jim Karayn has reaped a whirlwind.

His decision to air on Friday (30) a controversial edition of the station's only origination for the PBS feed, "Black Perspective on the News," in which Ku Klux Klan and American Nazi Party spokesmen engage in hatemongering, has polarized the community and triggered demonstrations, legal action and threats of reprisals against the station, its management and its board of directors.

A suit filed in Common Pleas Court filed on behalf of three concentration camp survivors sought a restraining order to prevent showing of the hour-long program on the grounds that it contains incitement to criminal and unlawful acts. Judge Stanley Greenberg on Thursday requested a tape of the program for the guidance of court and counsel.

When the station declined, arguing that prior restraint would be contrary to the First Amendment, Greenberg ruled that the program could not be telecast before being made available as "evidence."

The station promptly appealed to the Superior Court of Pennsylvania. Judge Edmund B. Spaeth Jr. overruled Greenberg, and the program went on as scheduled (see review page).

Last Thursday (29), more than 1,500 demonstrators assembled outside the station's Philadelphia studios to parade, display placards and applaud representatives of Jewish, black and labor groups speaking from a floodlit flatbed truck. The protest was spearheaded by a coalition of community groups led by the Jewish Community Relations Council (JCRC).

Also on Thursday, City Council President George X. Schwartz urged the station to cancel the program, charging that it was "pointless" and "not newsworthy in any way." He said it contained "remarks that were grossly offensive to Jews and blacks," adding that two black panelists who appeared with KKK grand wizard David Duke and National Socialist Party of America national coordinator Frank Collin "apparently were ineffective in countering most of the anti-Semitic canards."

Instead of black journalists, who usually question the guests in what is essentially a black-oriented version of "Meet The Press," the panel consisted of Lawrence D. Reddick, Harvard historian, and Charles King, of the Urban Crisis Center in Atlanta. Moderator was Reginald Bryant, who coproduces the program with Pulitzer Prize-winning *Inquirer* reporter Acel Moore.

Lots Of Support, Too

Karayn's insistence on airing the program was supported by the station's board of directors, headed by banker John R. Bunting. His stand was also endorsed by WCAU g.m. Bob Sherman in an on-air editorial and by Spencer Coxe, exec director of the Philadelphia chapter of the American Civil Liberties Union in a letter to Karayn.

"Public enlightenment is furthered," Coxe wrote, "by the tradition of media to resist any pressure from interested parties to suppress materials which these parties find objectionable or harmful.

"ACLU is not naive enough to believe that the professional judgment of editors and producers is never in error; we do conclude that the danger of prior censorship-by-pressure is greater than the danger of irresponsibility by the press . . . The answer to 'unfair' speech is more speech, not suppression. . . .

"It would be dangerous to establish the precedent of permitting interested parties to 'screen' materials before publication; such a precedent would put the media at the mercy of a horde of special interests, each with its ax to grind, and would quickly vitiate the professional responsibility of the press."

Additional support came from the *Philadelphia Inquirer,* which volunteered to institute "friend of the court" proceedings on the station's behalf, and from the First Amendment Coalition, comprised of various Pennsylvania journalistic organizations, which promised similar action.

Among threats by protesters were discontinuance of the city's $250,000 annual grant to the station, withholding of contributions, closing of accounts at Bunting's bank and personal reprisals against other board members. . . .

PROGRAM REVIEW
BLACK PERSPECTIVE ON THE NEWS
With David Duke, Ku Klux Klan grand wizard; Frank Collin, national American Nazi Party coordinator; Lawrence Reddick, Harvard historian; Dr. Charles King, head of the Urban Crisis Center, Atlanta; Reginald Bryant, moderator
Exec Producer: Richard Crew
Producers: Reginald Bryant, Acel Moore
Director: Russell Kneeland
60 Mins., Fri. (30), 9 p.m.
WHYY-TV Philadelphia

As Theodore R. Mann, chairman of the National Jewish Community Relations Advisory Council, notes in a 30-minute "equal time" follow-up taped Friday (30), more than two months after completion of this double-length "Black Perspective On The News," the crux of contention is not WHYY-TV's right to air the controversial program, but its wisdom and judgment.

The program is appalling on several counts. If the intent was to permit hatemongers to demonstrate that they merit public contempt, it fails. The sum effect is a propaganda coup for anti-Semitic bigots and white racists.

The Ku Klux Klan and American Nazi Party spokesmen dominate the proceedings. Their black interrogators seem ill-prepared and are ineffectual. It is a grievous mismatch. Duke, in mufti, is glib. Collin, in uniform, is bristlingly hostile. Dr. King blusters, Reddick is virtually mute. Bryant makes futile attempts to keep the discussion on course.

Duke and Collin win on points, because "Black Perspective" this time inexplicably doesn't call, as usual, on astute, trained black journalists. Despite the moderator's efforts to bar them, anti-Semitic slurs abound, and no Jew is present to rebut them.

Scenes from "Birth Of A Nation," man-in-the-street interviews about the degree of threat seen in a Nazi or KKK resurgence, and voice-over statements by more knowledgeable black leaders fail to provide a sense of balance. Neither does a 10-minute coda to the program, in which the two panelists try to assess what Bryant terms "whatever we just did with Mr. Duke and Mr. Collin."

Reddick, with reason, expresses concern about "the extent to which the average listener will be able to make a distinction between what is reasonably accurate and what is inaccurate." Dr. King calls what has just transpired "theater of the absurd" and, incredibly, notes that Duke and Collin are "personable and congenial" offcamera and suggests they said things they didn't necessarily believe—for dramatic effect.

The postscript, moderated by former Bulletin editor George Packard, has as participants Bertram Gold, exec veep of the American Jewish Committee; Homer Floyd, exec director of the Pennsylvania Human Relations Commission; James Karayn, president and general manager of WHYY, Mann and Bryant.

Gold labels the program "a kind of primitive, obscene political pornography." Floyd deplores "the very low level of debate." Mann, endorsing the First Amendment right of Nazis and KKKers to speak on the street, questions the propriety of providing them with a larger audience.

Bryant and Karayn claim "educative" motivations—and shake their heads when Mann predicts that because of the program, "some sickies will join the Nazis and the three K's."

That headshaking comes two months too late.—*Hari*.

That experience taught me a lesson that I shall never forget. From that time on I have turned down every invitation I have received to debate with a bigot. The lesson, too late learned, was given by an anonymous wise man: "Never argue with a fool, for in that debate one can never discern which one is the fool."

CHAPTER 23
Wittenberg University

THE EARLY FEELING I HAD OF COMING OUT OF
the urban setting of Gary into the quiet academic setting
of Wittenberg University was one of shocking contrast. There,
on a sprawling campus, I was greeted by a sea of white faces,
peppered only occasionally with black ones. Three thousand
students, ninety of them black. My duties in this white setting
pleased me immensely. I was to serve half time teaching at
Hamma School of Theology, the other half conducting a race
relations program throughout the state in white Lutheran
churches. Wittenberg University is located in Springfield,
Ohio, on the same campus as Hamma School of Theology.
Since Wittenberg had only one black faculty member, I was
asked if I minded teaching a course in black history as well as
black theology at Hamma. After I had consented to undertake
all of those tasks, it slowly dawned on me that I was being used
by all three white institutions. I became the visible "Negro"
for the white church, the white university, and the white
seminary. What a wide arena I had in which to pursue white
racism! The hours I spent to battle racism in those three arenas
are, even today, uncounted. The intellectual and emotional
drain—never to be measured. The hurt, the pain, the disillusionment, and frustration—unrecorded. The friendships
gained, lost, and eventually recovered—a mystery.

I became a workaholic, standing before classes, answering
questions about blackness, and traversing the state on weekends, conducting racial awareness seminars in white churches.
Analyzing the relevance of white theological thoughts as contrasted to the black experience was a continual and exhausting

process. Exhausting only for that day, for the challenge of the next day, the next class, the next church encounter, energized me continually. I thought initially that I had a thorough understanding of white people. I had been exposed to the hard-core racist practices of segregation, police brutality, employment discrimination, and KKK mentalities; but I had always accepted passive white nothingness as being separate and apart from white racism. The smiles, handshakes, conversation, and styles of communication, hypocritical as they might have been, never aroused me. I had always accepted white liberal association with a liberality of my own. Rarely if ever had I released the fire of anger into white Christian passivity. The memory of the riot-torn cities of Detroit, Gary, Newark, Chicago, and Los Angeles had not left me. The churning anger against law enforcement officers, their dogs, fire hoses, and nightsticks remained as the seed of disenchantment with the white American way. Those remained as the symbols of racism. The white church remained, at least to me, the best that was left of white America. It was—and remains—my feeling that white clergymen represented untapped potential to jolt the whites out of the sham of religiosity and unite the full bloom of the gospel fulfilled.

Upon accepting the challenge of entering into the white church world, I researched the history of the Lutheran Church of America, searching for links that tied them to the black experience. I found a few links.

The Kerner Commission report on white racism had to be translated into the intellectualism of white theology. I attempted to find out how to translate the cries of the ghetto into a gospel message, to translate slum housing, dehumanizing welfare systems, and police brutality into a language that did not smell of rot and decay. I spent long hours digesting white theological thoughts into a black theology so that they would both mean the same thing—justice and equality under God. It was a challenging pursuit. I wanted to prove to my white seminary students that I had a mind and a brain, a creative process unknown to them or to their white professors. I dared not use the old Missionary Baptist concepts. I was not ashamed

216

of my fundamentalist roots, but I had a necessary mission to blend my blackness, my past, into the white present.

Once I had become established on the Wittenberg campus, I became for the first time in my life a part of a white institution. This is where I was to earn my living; I had chosen to separate myself from blackness completely and orient myself into whiteness. I became very conscious, as are all institutional blacks, of my clothes, my hair, my speech. I was a showcase "Negro," one to be introduced and socialized at faculty teas and receptions. I had to exude every charm imaginable to prove to them and to myself that I belonged. My reception on the campus was warm, welcomey. I became a dinner guest in many homes, cocktailed to the point of dizziness, and questioned until weary.

The classroom was the easiest, for there I was in charge. My lectures at the university were the typical recountings of familiar events in black history from slavery to the Black Renaissance of the 1920s. Whites had signed up in large numbers, precluding some blacks from taking this black history course. Ironically, the black students had demonstrated the year before for a black history course taught by a black professor. The university gave them both, but did not offer priorities in who could take the course to black students. Most of them felt cheated. I became aware of their silent anger, their frustration, and their questioning of my blackness. Inside of me, I knew I was black, but external social endeavors and my proclivity toward white administration types queered my black identity.

The blacks had a Black House—a place demanded by and given to them, where they would gather to escape from the white surroundings. It was a mixture of an opportunity to talk black and to search for the African past. It was a place to plan a social and to act a fool. There blacks talked about whites, and about themselves. Accusations of turning white were flung in the faces of those black students who did not join the Black House or attend its functions. The hurts were plentiful, the frustrations numerous. I went there sometimes to escape, sometimes to be energized back into my blackness. My presence, however, created a problem for the black blacks. I was a member of the administration: I worked for whitey, had sold out to him. I did not take part in their plans for protestation; my advice to them was a tortured mixture of advice to rebel against the racism they felt, and at the same time to get all the education they could while they were there.

My flip-flopping soon became evident, when what they had wanted was a black leader. My reputation in the field of civil rights had preceded me, but my academic life quickly erased my past, and all they could see or understand about me was the present. I had been purchased and paid for by their last year's anger. It is no wonder that they thought that their emotions had been spent in vain. From a white perspective, it was the good life: the sharing of ideas, the matching of wits, the respect given to intelligence. But it was a bland, colorless existence, devoid of the trauma of the urban stress and strains. Clean classrooms filled with innocent white youth, destined to become great leaders of society. It just oozed the highest expression of white church-oriented morality.

*   *   *   *   *

A question that plagues most blacks contemplating higher education has risen now more than 20 percent over the last decade or so. That figure indicates a rising and potentially explosive impact for good within the black community. The rising expectation of black Americans and their gradual shift into middle-class status suggest that white educational facilities will be hard pressed for space to accommodate the blacks seeking education there. And the question still remains: which institution, white or black, offers the most and best for young black Americans?

What most white educators cannot understand is that the traditional scope of white-oriented education creates psychological barriers to those who have waded through the black experience. And what most black educators do not face is the fact that beyond the black educational process is a white world—a world where opportunity for success and survival is more pronounced among whites than it is among blacks.

But the need and thrust of white businesses and corporations for more black presence has grown beyond the use of
"showcase niggers," and recruiters roam the halls of ivy seeking ebony brains, if for no other reason than to secure government contracts and fulfill Equal Employment Opportunity
Commission mandates. Almost overnight, blacks have become
relevant to white educational processes and exposure. White
colleges and universities, exposed to the eyes and threats of the
Department of Health, Education and Welfare, and shaken to
the core by the militancy of the late 1960s and early 1970s, are
honestly seeking to checkerboard their campuses. Yet, while
this was taking place, blacks were experiencing a new identity,
a new self-concept. Blackness had become not negative in its
implications, but a motivating, exhilarating surge of energy.
The political scene in the inner cities produced leaders with
power and charisma, and black men and women projected the
new day. Thus, while whites began seeking blacks, blacks were
correspondingly finding themselves. Blacks have found their
elusive roots and are now digging in.

The positive need for this new black identity cannot be
denied. Yet when a black attends a white university, one must
expect him or her to undergo traumatic reversals of image and
identity. The reason for these reversals is obvious. While the
extent and range of a lost or diminished identity will differ
among blacks, whenever whites are in the majority, blacks out
of necessity must adjust themselves to whites. White majorities
rarely, if ever, adjust themselves to the unique nature or problems of the black experience. Whenever whites adjust to black
needs, it is mainly on a temporary basis and usually after experiencing the shock of black protestation.

White institutions are inherently racist—*not by design, but in
practice*. Whites cannot perceive their racism because racism is
by definition "the normal practices, customs, and habits of a
majority group that tend to disadvantage a minority group."
Thus, if blacks are to survive in white institutions, they must
curtail their feelings, hurts, and anguish by boxing themselves
in and accommodating themselves to whiteness.

The problem of identity and image is the key to why more
blacks are seeking black institutions for their educational

growth. During my tenure as a professor at Wittenberg, most white students could not understand why blacks demanded and received such things as black history week, black culture week, a black social hall, a black house, and mandatory black history as part of the total curriculum. Those black students (92 out of a total enrollment of 3,300) were fighting for survival—personal, social, psychological, and spiritual. Insensitive, ignorant, and unteachable whites, by their normal customs, traditions, and habits—if those go forward unchecked—can rape the black experience. This raping of the black experience produces a dullness in people as their potential for self-esteem and worth is stifled.

Paranoia becomes a way of life as black personalities become dichotomous. Living in a white world is like skating on thin ice. A hypocritical posture of well-being and adjustment must be projected lest the full dimension of inner black thoughts and feelings disrupt white illusions and perspectives. The only other alternative is to release one's blackness completely to the white environment, close off all emotions, and enslave one's blackness to the system. Blacks who choose the latter course are well accepted and well liked, and they encourage the absurd conclusion among whites that color makes no difference.

The university atmosphere becomes the training and testing ground for the shaping of black personalities. Educational goals are made more complex for blacks than for whites because they must twist their inner beings into monstrous contortions as blackness becomes a cross and not a crown. It is no wonder that what currently appears to be black educational progress has contributed heavily to increased black suicide rates. It is tragic that those two facts are parallel. And, in the face of that, it is the height of stupidity for white institutions to resist putting into effect changes that will at least ensure priceless black identity.

If white institutions gear up to become more sensitive to this dilemma in black education, that problem will not be solved. But at least it will be diminished. What blacks now face are the questions, Is it worth it? Can I sustain four years of whiteness and remain black?

Fortunately, many do. But that large and unmeasured number who are now banging on the doors of black institutions are echoing a new song to whites who now are attempting to integrate them into their settings: "When you could, you wouldn't; now you want to, but you can't." It is, in essence, a farewell to the white plantation.

In the years between my Wittenberg experience and now, I have been invited to over sixty dominantly white universities for lectures and seminars. What I found on those campuses is what I found at Wittenberg: black faces popping up in an ocean of white milk. Black students, submerged in both numbers and potential, living two lives. The retreat from white customs and traditions into the solidarity of blackness was occasioned by establishing a black house on campus. This separate world within the white world was the only means of escaping the trauma induced by racism. The insensitivity of white professors still prevails to this day. Invoking color blindness as their rationale for teaching, they completely ignore the contrasts of the black experience with that of whites. They do not know or deal with the nuances of stress produced by social visibility, adding to the eternal black paranoia. The subtle insults in casual comments made by whites are like claps of thunder in the ears of blacks. But blacks must hold their peace, resist angry replies, and pretend that all is well.

*   *   *   *   *

At Wittenberg, the college president, Dr. Andeen, portrayed both his ignorance and insensitivity one day after he had asked to speak with me in his office.

"Dr. King," he began, after a few moments of exchanging false pleasantries, "I think you can help us solve a problem here at Wittenberg." He went on to say that he wanted to see more blacks mix with the whites. He could understand the establishment of the Black House, but could I encourage more blacks to sit with whites during the meal hours? The separation of the races bothered him, gave a false impression that Wittenberg was segregated, and I knew as well as he that that was not so.

I was dumbfounded. Ninety black students versus 3,000 whites. Two black professors, 190 white ones. I had another urge to jump to my feet and become obscene. I wanted to tell him how I felt when I was laughing and smiling in the white faculty lounge, pretending I was at ease, ignoring racist remarks made more out of white ignorance than intent. There was no way to let him know of the eerie feeling blacks have when diving into the oceans of whiteness—struggling to maintain identity, yet daring not to expose it completely lest they be destroyed in the process. Whites never have been able to comprehend that their bland existence, sameness, and lack of emotional substance has denied them the gift of difference. The fact that blacks were dichotomous out of the need for psychic and emotional survival was a truth that, either known or unknown, was denied by whites.

"I will not do that, Dr. Andeen," I replied after suppressing my fire.

He, of course, wondered why.

I took the risk of explaining to him all of the reasons referred to above. The more I explained each one, the more defensive he became. He accepted none of my explanations and, worse yet, understood none. I was talking to an institutional robot, a man trained in, geared for, and controlled by a white racist society. I tired of the exercise in futility.

"Did you ever stop to think that the black students are not sitting together, but that really the white students are," I finally said. "I strongly suggest that instead of you asking me to have the blacks integrate with the whites, why don't you ask the whites to sit with the blacks . . . that will achieve integration."

The manner I used to get across that point was a disrespectful one. And I meant it to be. I stood up as I said it, informing him by that act that this was my last word. I did not wait for his reply, nor did I want one. I knew I had blown my relationship with him, but I didn't give a damn. I felt free of the pressure of giving him my smiles. From that date on, we never exchanged pleasanties. The fire was in my bones and was becoming blacker. It felt good.

It was the "put down" mechanism that I began using continuously. Whenever I had the occasion, socially or in the classroom, to exercise my blackness, I began doing so without fear or favor. I had decided that there was no nice way to challenge racism. As white students continued to inquire into the meaning of racism, I began to utilize campus incidents and faculty member statements and writings to illustrate my points. As a result of that, I received this letter:

Dear Mr. King:

I received today two reports from students of references to me made by you in a Black History course last night. One student, on the word of another, reported that you labeled my letter in the Wittenberg *Torch* as "racist" and criticized me for not doing anything myself toward the establishment of Black Studies at Wittenberg. Sometime later I was told that you wished me to contact you with regard to Black Studies. Somehow the two reports seem to me to be in contradiction of each other.

With regard to the first report I received, if it is accurate, I wondered from what source you had obtained your facts. From Dean Dahl? From ex-President Bransom of Central State University? From the Dayton-Miami Valley Consortium? From the American Studies faculty committee? I do not feel that accusations or name-calling (allowing the person the courtesy of reply notwithstanding) serves any productive purpose whatsoever in what I see as a Herculean task in the present situation at the present time and so am totally abstaining from replying in kind.

As to the second report, I again have no knowledge of its accuracy. Since most people rely on the standard communications media (mail service, telephone, etc.) to forward messages, not trusting the accuracy of second-hand reporting, I felt somehow that if you wished to contact me you would find a means of doing so yourself.

I have been looking forward to meeting you, having heard and read so much about your effect on Wittenberg last year while I was gone. I do hope we can work together toward what I somehow feel is a common goal of both of us.

Sincerely yours,
Harvey Damaser

I responded to Professor Damaser in an open letter.

AN OPEN LETTER TO PROFESSOR DAMASER:

Pardon me, sir, but your racism is showing.

I was amazed at your letter to the editor last week. The impact of that missive upon blacks and their problems on this campus was devastating. Undoubtedly you write under the banner of a Liberal, but your attitudes and actions (or the absence of action) portray you as a racist.

The source of your complaint seems to stem from the fact that blacks did not come to hear your learned dissertation on black studies. Having labeled you as racist, allow me to explain the reasoning behind that title. Any person who is of a dominant race, who knowingly or unknowingly perpetuates the cycle of oppression against a minority race, condones such practices and thus is a part of the system that oppresses (check Webster for a more exacting and precise definition).

So you spent a year at Yale devoted to African American Studies. Great. Yet you plead inability to speak "authoritatively on the black experience." What in the name of Heaven were you learning during that year? Does not the study of the black man include your knowing of his experiences? The best that you now have to offer to the problems of black people appears to be "an academic analysis of existing black studies." If you have studied studies, and not the black condition itself that necessitates such studies, then we have been dehumanized and now exist only as tools for your intellectual appraisals. Need you experience starvation before you are able to speak authoritatively against poverty? Or go to Vietnam before you can speak authoritatively against the horrors of war, or become a drug addict before you can speak out against pushers? Sir, you mock us when you become angry, because your subject was misposted as "Mr. Damaser Speaks Of The Black Man in America." To address yourself to such a topic as that appears reprehensible to you, regardless of your preference for the weak, anemic Black Study emphasis.

So you take blacks to task for failing to show up for your intellectual gymnastics about them, and to date you have not lifted a finger to implement your studies at this university *for* them. That fact is obvious through your own admission that "for months you have eagerly awaited the opportunity to present an academic analysis." Why wait? Why not present them to the President, the Deans and the Faculty? It's perfectly obvious that most of them are completely oblivious to the need and thus express another form of white racism—blindness to black needs and obliviousness to black presence on this campus.

I back up that statement by calling your attention to the black demands now buried in the archives of Wittenberg's fears. Search for them, Professor, and you will find pragmatic and creative direction for the implementation of your newly found studies at Yale. Can't you see, it is the whites who should be the recipients of your anger, not the blacks. You should be angry at them, if for no other reason than that they caused you to take a year out of your life to study a subject that, if racism were not so prevalent, would not need such crutches as black studies.

Pardon me, sir, but your racism is showing.

Have you no power or will to influence those that you expect CBS to influence? Blacks have historically attempted to move the monstrous racism within white institutions, thus suffering the pain that accrues to those who have no power. Enlightened white students who challenge and press for change only invite themselves to repeat the suffering of the black experience. So I ask, what "hard work" have you exercised as a white man against white racism? Who are you, sir, and what have you done? The courtesy you expect from blacks while you have diligently, "eagerly waited" to give an "academic analysis" will be long in coming from us. As blacks, we refuse to save you from the pain that should be yours if you claim to be armed with the knowledge of what should, could, or must be done.

Pardon me, sir, but your racism is showing.

In your letter you take to task the extent of our commitment. Let's look at your own. Because you discovered that no room "had been reserved" for your lecture, you state that you "had rather forgotten the entire thing." You also state that the only reason you went through with your lecture was that you had "invited a few friends." In fact, it appears that the only reason why you "demanded a room" was for *that* reason. My, what a commitment you have!

Believe me, I do not blame you as much as I blame the cold institutional rigidity that allows you to be blinded by the idea that an "academic analysis" as it relates to black conditions is a substitute for action. Until you prove that your subject is worth fighting for, afflict us no longer with your lectures until the ivy on Wittenberg's buildings shake with the wrath of your newly found knowledge. I too have been invited by the Union Board and CBS to give a lecture. I shall give it. And just in case Mr. Shields doesn't place on the bulletin board the correct title, let me announce it here and now: "Wittenberg is a White Plantation." My subject matter was not studied at Yale, so rest assured it will not be an academic analysis. At that time, I will be presumptuous enough to speak authoritatively on the white experience, even though I am black. If by that time no room is available, I will shout about that experience from the steps of the Union. I am extending no special invitation to either my friends or CBS, for my subject is already known by them, felt by them, understood by them, and daily experienced by them. You see, sir, it is not for them; it's obviously for "y'all."

When that date is announced, will you then afford me the "courtesy of your presence," and "take the responsibility" of encouraging your President, Vice Presidents, and faculty to attend? I shall present at that time all that I have learned on a 35-year fellowship from the university of the ghetto.

Answer me! Answer me! . . . you have just been encountered.

Yet, even after I had reasserted my own blackness and forged the beginnings of a bond with black students on the Wittenberg campus, I realized that I was still not getting my message through to white students: that the reality of the black experience was a product of white racism.

CHAPTER 24

To Chart a Course for Blackness

*F*IFTEEN MILES FROM WITTENBERG'S CAMPUS WAS Wilberforce University, a historically black institution. As my intensity increased in my fight against white institutional racism, I became known to the blacks there and was invited to speak. Students in such institutions tended to view white society as a hopeless obstacle to freedom. This sense of despair perpetuated attitudes of either apathy or inevitable separatism. The theology of hope was beyond their concept of change, and so my message to them had to be an honest look at what the future held once hope died.

I had addressed myself to blacks on a predominantly white campus, but now I had to make sense to those matriculating in a predominantly black atmosphere. My purpose was not to *arouse* these black students but to make them think how best to survive in a racist world. I wanted to help them maintain *identity* and *hope*—both essential to survival—one for the perpetuation of dignity, the other a nonviolent methodology for survival. After the death of Martin Luther King, nonviolence had become an unpopular posture. But I was convinced that it was the only posture of sanity for blacks in the white world. So I delivered the following speech to the black students at Wilberforce.

I accepted this engagement with mixed emotions. My first inclination was to reject the invitation, not because I did not desire to be with you, but because of the psychological problem posed by the dilemma of our times. The problem is this: What can a black man say to 550 black students entering a virtually all-black institution for the first time?

The prospect frightened me. I have been a witness to the gradual transition from the early days of the Negro Revolt to the dawn of Black Separatism. I know that your generation stands at that crossroad. I shall never forget those early days when our youth, fired up with the determination to be free, assaulted white structures with bodies and spirits, offering up their blood, and at times their lives, to achieve the American dream. Those were the glory days of the black revolution. The passive resistance movement somehow struck a spark of hope, which later leaped into flames of destruction. There was a dream in those days that the fight could be won.

It was not won. Filling the jails with our bodies, we suddenly discovered that all we had gained was a right to eat a hamburger. It was not won, for the very leader who led us with peace on his lips was butchered on the mountaintop of his expectations. It was not won, for in spite of the laws that came to us like crumbs from the master's table, the dignity of the black man was never affirmed by this nation. It was not won, because the very laws that we achieved affected only middle-class Negroes, while the black man in the street still hungers and thirsts for both food and freedom. It was not won, because the ghetto still remains, and the police have not changed their habits. The employers have not opened wide their doors; they merely slit them to receive the token Negro. It was not won, in spite of the Supreme Court decision of 1954 that outlawed segregation in the public schools. Today there is more segregation in the school systems of our country than when the Supreme Court first issued its edict. It was not won, for after the march on Washington, George Wallace almost became President of these United States. It was not won, because the welfare system still remains the same; black people are still intimidated to keep them from voting; black babies still die at a ratio of three to one to white babies; school boards are uptight about busing, and black Americans are dropping out of school almost as fast as black graduating classes are presented false hopes.

In virtually every major city, whites have left the heart of those cities and established in suburbia little white Americas. Meanwhile, the core of the city has been left to the blacks—to rot and to burn.

I now find the need to report to you the chaotic consequences of the failure of our country to live up to our early dreams. The mood of the black man has changed, and you are a part of that mood and that change. It has changed from begging in the courts, pounding the streets in protest, filling up jails with black bodies, to Molotov cocktails and rifles. It has changed from the hope of deliverance by the colored NAACP to that of the Black Panthers. The prediction by the Kerner Commission on Civil Disorders that our nation is slowly drifting into twin societies, one white and one black, is now at our very doorstep. The faces that I see before me visually reinforce that prediction.

It is for these reasons that I have mixed emotions, I have seen the attempts of the past, predicated upon our false hope that this nation would hear and change, fail dismally. Our faith in nonviolence was shattered, and what we once considered sweet legal victories are now recognized to be bitter fruit rotting on the ground of Eden.

That's why I did not want to talk to you—to dare expose those failures of white America to give to you a better world.

> The fathers have eaten the sour grapes,
> and the children's teeth have been set on edge.

But I am here and am forced once again to attempt to chart out, to strain after a course of action that might be the way.

First of all, the course of action that you take must not be in the direction of separatism or violence. Black people own less than 1.3 percent of this nation's wealth, and they constitute less than 15 percent of its total population. Make no mistake, a revolt against the white system based on violence will not free us from our chains; it will threaten to usher in genocide. Whereas we may understand violence and separatism psychologically, we must reject them with cold, hard, pragmatic facts. What are those facts? They should be evident. Blacks own no army, navy, air force, planes, police departments, national guards, Wall Streets—nor do I expect that either in my lifetime or yours the White House in Washington will turn black.

But even if such power were in our hands, somehow the prospect of inflicting upon another race of people the same crimes of dehumanization, poverty, and death flies in the face of our conviction and theological belief that "all men are brothers," that "no man is an island, and each man's death diminishes me." When black people adapt the strategy that physical violence and separatism are the keys to freedom, it will open up the other doors that lead to our ultimate demise as a race. We know from history that the fall of every great civilization was occasioned by its moral and ethical decline, and its insensitivity to the dignity and worth of the individual.

Between the twin choices of meaningless separatism and meaningless violence is *encounter*. Encounter means this: to refuse to turn white in a white world, to refuse to turn our blackness away and separate from the white world, but to deliberately and unequivocally remain black within the white world. We must say what we think, mean what we say, and say it loud: I'm black and I'm proud. White does not make right, and black does not mean wrong. Black is a fact—a cold, hard fact of life. I cannot change that and would not change if I could.

Refuse to be made white in your minds while wearing blackness, yet take that blackness out of isolation and dare press it into every corner of this nation and all of its institutions, and demand every right that is possessed by whites as your own. Retain the need temporarily to withdraw into a totally black world. Support black institutions, begin black businesses and black banks—which is your right. But make no mistake: you must still contend for white institutions to change, and seek to work in white stores and white banks—which is also your right.

Integration still remains the only hope for national and black survival. True love for this country's flag will only be achieved when its institutions remove the white racism that denies us the stars. When white people say to us, "We don't know what to call you," as blacks we must inform white America: "Call us arrogant, colored, Negro, Nigra, black, ignorant, stupid, call us 'nigger'—we don't care, just don't call us black racists."

You see, white world, racism is a system that has power and inflicts pain. We have no power, and the pain is inflicted upon us. We have never refused to serve whites hamburgers, we have never lynched them from trees, burned their bodies, and kept them out of our schools, forced them to live on welfare, denied them their dignity. We have never dehumanized their sons, castrated their men and their culture, broken up their homes, sicced them with dogs, mutilated their bodies with razors. We have never hosed them down with fire hoses, shocked them with cattle prods, bombed their churches, killed their children, forced them to work as slaves, starved them into submission, and leveled their colleges with machine guns. We have never taken away their heavyweight crowns, elected their Wallaces, Maddoxes, and Nixons, and have never crammed a black Spiro Agnew down their throats. Don't call us racists, because that title is reserved for those with power.

Finally, my black brothers and sisters, keep the faith and the hope. Determine within yourself that your blackness is both the badge of your honor and the messianic hope that will redeem our nation. For without that faith, without that hope, we are doomed.

CHAPTER 25

A Miraculous Discovery

*T*O MIX BLACK REALITY INTO WHITE CHRISTIAN concepts—and to seek the emergence of a pragmatic marriage—was a mind-boggling venture at Wittenberg. My initial writings and lectures, I am sure, were puzzling not only to my students but to me as well. I kept reading, redefining, working hard to introduce new thoughts into each class. But it was muddled. I felt myself losing grip of my own self-concept, drowning in the swamp of the white theological world, which was fast developing into quicksand.

In teaching my black history course I relied heavily on established black historians and writers. I made a foolish decision to begin the class on the issue of slavery. I had to bone up on black history. With the exception of Carter G. Woodson's *Negro History*, I had never studied or been exposed to black history. I used Lerone Bennett's *Before the Mayflower* as the standard text. I lectured from notes, and spiced up the class by using student reports of various readings, assigned to them out of my frustration of not knowing how to teach black history in a way that would make white students understand the shame of their own racism. What hurt me the most in those initial months was that the few black students in my classes were silent. The reliving of the history of slavery evoked only silence. Whenever they raised their voices, it was in vehement protest to stupid white questions or to whites who disdainfully discounted the agony of slavery. These white students would contrast the life of American black slaves with the slavery of the Jews in Egypt, with the horrors of the Holocaust, with the plight of those forced to live under Communism. I patiently attempted to explain the difference; however, all explanations were met with debate, denial, or plain silence.

I knew I was not teaching the class to the satisfaction of the blacks: far too few of the already few would talk to me after class. Not so with the whites. They followed me out of the classroom and around the campus with a deluge of questions, observations, and argumentations. The first two months were miserable. I ached to return to the tensions of urban life, to challenge the discriminating systems, to file complaints against corrupt employers, to hold public hearings. Instead of sweltering in a racial fiery furnace, I was a black man losing his breath in the funereal airlessness of racism's denials, intellectual evasions, and white religious hypocrisy. My blackness began to ooze from me. I began to cave in to intellectualism. I longed to be accepted by blacks and respected by the whites—when, in fact, I was losing both races. The fire in my bones was slowly being quenched. I walked the campus like a shadow, evading blacks, evading whites, locking myself in my office to ponder, to curse, to wonder why I had ever left the noises of urban life and its challenges to hear chirping birds on a velvet green campus. I tried to dream up methods of breaking through the intellectual process. I could find none. I buried my head in books, in Lutheran history, thought, religion, and philosophy in a vain attempt to out-intellectualize the intellectuals.

One day, by strange accident, I stumbled upon the key to the dilemma, and that key was to serve to unlock the door to the mysteries of white racism. The key was simple, and it demanded no additional study. The reaction from whites was instantaneous, and from blacks awe-inspiringly fulfilling. It was a matter of openly and unashamedly releasing the fire in my bones.

It happened in my class on black history. What happened in that one class period changed not only my method of conducting racial awareness classes, but it profoundly affected my life and career in racial activism. I was standing before my roomful of white faces, explaining the horrors of slavery and how, even after Emancipation, blacks still felt enslaved to whites.

"That's not so," came a male voice from the back of the classroom. I kept my cool in spite of the arrogant tone and the questioning of the validity of my statement.

"Why not?" I asked him. "Why do you question that. . . ?"

"Because I don't feel that way. Some of my best . . ."

"Shut up!" I screamed at him. "And don't you ever dare use your experience with black friends to refute my explanation of the black condition."

The classroom was in shock after that outburst. The electricity of rage surged into my body. The adrenaline was flowing, and my eyes began to water as I felt ready to purge myself of what had been restrained and contained for many years. The roar of my voice brought a smile of recognition to the faces of the few blacks in the room. But fear spread across the faces of the whites, racially innocent whites who were being exposed to black rage for the first time in their lives. Waves of anger, shock, and resentment swept into that classroom. All this I felt during that ten-second silence.

"You can't tell me to shut up," came the voice of the white student. It was a racial showdown—a shoot-out . . . black vs. white . . . the struggle for power and control. I realized at that moment that, if I did not continue, I would compromise not only my blackness but my humanity as well.

> Once to every man and nation
> Comes the moment to decide. . . .

I was back in Emory's barbershop. The blacks were waiting, the water was shark-filled, but I plunged in.

Right then and there I released the torrent of my inner feelings. By this time I was not speaking specifically to my antagonist of the moment. My words were addressed to the entire class—to white society in general. I deplored the arrogance, the insensitivity, the legacy of racist attitudes that emboldened them to dispute black feelings and experiences with unfeeling stupidity. I shouted that they would never understand black history until they could understand the feelings of me and the other blacks in the class. I said that I didn't give a damn how they felt about me but that they were going to listen if I had to lock the door.

How dare any of them refute my experience or tell me what I said was untrue? What was the source of their rebuttal? Their parents, who had given them their racist arguments and defenses? The university, which was itself racist? Every question they had asked me in class was racist, for the questions were asked out of ignorance—willing ignorance—of the black condition. I was tired, I told them, tired of explaining over and over again the same things and answering the same questions. There would be no more questions. They were to listen and take notes and remember. No longer would this be an academic pursuit of black history; it would pursue an understanding of the black experience. They would no longer obtain a grade based on what they remembered of events, I said, but on how they felt and how sensitive they could become to the subject of blackness.

The full impact of what I said there did not hit me until after I had stalked out of the classroom and secluded myself in my office. My anger and disgust at whites was now permeating my inner self. I was sweating in spite of the cool fall weather, my head was pounding from a sharp rise in my blood pressure, and my eyes could not focus through the tears. It was the first time in my life that I had given full vent, with uncompromising intensity, to my hostility before a group of white people on a sustained basis. I had sought not to impress them but to make an impact on them by emptying myself of the venom stored up over decades as a misfit in their society.

Within the confines of that office I made a decision to stop trying to teach white people. I realized that I had made a mistake in abandoning the urban setting of crisis for the still world of white intellectualism. These children, young and naive— even if they could understand—could not change institutions, could not help blacks.

How wrong I was!

What I did not know was that a white colleague of mine had been monitoring at the rear of the classroom and had witnessed my entire outpouring and the chaos I had created. In my absence he had spoken to the students and asked them to remain until he could bring me back. He was the chairman of the department, my boss, and he came to my office, put his hand on my shoulder, and suggested that I should return to my class. The walk back to that class was that of a man walking to the bench to be sentenced. I took that walk against my will and my better judgment. Strangely, I was no longer angry or hostile toward that class. What I felt was a fear for the consequences of my action on my future.

The students were watching for me to enter the classroom, and as I did, all forty stood up and gave me a five-minute ovation. The young man whom I had told to "shut up" came forward, tears in his eyes, and unabashedly hugged me.

God in heaven, what a moment!

My blackness had penetrated those white sensibilities. Their tears were real, and so were mine. Somehow my rage had produced a miraculous event. It seemed that God was alive and working through my black anger to produce a harvest of manna. Whites could change! What a revelation!

In that moment I knew that I had done something that I did not understand, or had not understood before. I had discovered the vulnerability of individual white racism. It was the discovery that few, if any, whites can hold fast to their veneer of racism once it is exposed to an inescapable black anger and truth.

*   *   *   *   *

The members of my black history class became missionaries on the Wittenberg campus. And the word began to spread. White students entered my classes in droves, hoping to feel what the others had told them about. I decided then to hold seminars for students. Instead of employing the rational and dispassionate manner I had assimilated in the academic setting, I began to use the bluntness of my feelings to shout, to correct, to rebut statements, and to intensify my reactions to white questions and ignorance. I used the full power not only of my ideas but of my voice to challenge them into facing reality.

Before that year had ended, hundreds of white students had been through the program. I continued to teach black history in an academically acceptable form, but at the end of the course my self-styled encounter program became the final examination.

CHAPTER 26

The Evolution of the Encounter Methodology

*I*T HAD BECOME INCREASINGLY CLEAR TO ME THAT the Lutheran Church of America, and its Priority Program, like most white institutions, had responded to the problems of race out of fear. White America had a tremendous investment in urban stability. Stability was the umbilical cord that tied them to the urban body politic. The looting, burning upheavals in the 1960s called attention to the weak and faulty sharing of a proclaimed morality that never existed. Strangely enough, it was the white Christian churches that were the first white institutions to feel the pangs of guilt. Ever since Martin Luther King wrote to them in his famous "Letter from Birmingham Jail," white ministers and their congregations began reexamining their official postures by posing the question, "What can we do?" Many white denominations had looked at themselves, repented for past inactions, and sought some means of quelling racial hostility and strife. The priority program of "Justice and Social Change" was the frontispiece for the LCA. I had taken the Hamma position out of my personal conviction (at that time) that if change were to take place, it could and should start at the house of God. These were the people who would be the agents of transformation. (Years later, in a continuous pursuit of white racism, I was to learn that racism centered in the context of a religious organization would prove to be the most agonizingly difficult kind of any white institution in existence.)

It became one of my responsibilities to administer this program called "Justice and Social Change." It was a program designed by the LCA to acquaint its membership with the realities of urban crisis. Justice and Social Change was to be presented at all LCA Synods. It was their contribution to an age of black discontentment. They asked me to take the program into white churches. It was a cut and dried program, calling for open discussion, slide presentations, and an explanation of the Kerner Report on white racism. The program had a teacher's manual and a participant's workbook. Prior to going into the churches with the program, I had begun to present the program on campus to the students. The general design of the program was intellectual. However, one of the suggestions in the teacher's manual was shockingly different. After introducing the problem of the nature of prejudice, the program leader (who was delegated to be white) was to give way to his assistant (a black) who would be encouraged to take fifteen minutes to "tell it like it is."

The purpose of the fifteen minutes was—as the leader's guide explained it—for whites to allow the black to speak from his own experience, how he or she had been discriminated against, so that all white participants could obtain a "feel of what it is like to be discriminated against."

When I first read that, I was amused by the irony that a white person was to be the leader, while the black person was invited to spill out his guts so that the whites could examine them. The first thing I knew was that any black who would dare "tell it like it is" would be met with massive white resentment. So, from the beginning, I was determined not to "use up" a black by placing such a suicidal venture upon him or her. Since I was a black, and not a white program leader, I saw that it was necessary to change the program from that orientation. I began, from that premise, to conduct a six-hour Justice and Social Change Seminar on the campus for all students and faculty members who volunteered to attend.

The first seminar met with minor success, but I could observe no overwhelming desire for change. But a few changes of attitude did occur, which encouraged me onward. The sessions were held in a room called the "Nursery" at Hamma School of Theology. Thirty to forty whites packed themselves into that room. I began by playing a recording called "Just Like You," which was a part of the package, and it was not long before I noticed that each student or faculty member gave the same sing-song response to that recording. The voice on the record was unmistakably black. I knew it, they knew it; but when each participant was asked to identify the voice, the whites, with few exceptions, would not acknowledge in their comments that the speaker was a black man. Why?

The next part of the program required the participants to write down in their notebooks, which they were to keep for reference after the program, the answer to this question: "What do you think is the basic cause for the problems that blacks have in America?" Few, if any, whites would write down "white racism," "white discrimination," or record any sentence that would indict white people.

In administering this program, I made three discoveries that stirred the fire in my bones: whites' denial of their own prejudice ("Are you prejudiced?" "No."); their belief that a person's race or color is irrelevant ("I see no color"); and their refusal to accept blame for the inequities of the black experience. Why?

Old and young, teachers and students, administrators and faculty—all echoed the same evasive refrains. The greatest shock and disappointment of all was that the few blacks who attended those sessions echoed the whites. Why?

Over the years I discovered the reasons for this, but during the early stages of the program's development I was stumped, stymied, perplexed—feelings that gradually turned into outright anger. The problem, I later learned, was that in a situation where whites and blacks are together, in a nonthreatening or nonemotional setting, both races seek to adjust to each other. Conflict is to be avoided; emotions are not supposed to surface. Whites know that blacks are not treated equally, and blacks know that whites discriminate, which denies them equal opportunity. Yet when they meet in a social setting, both races refuse to be honest. The blacks do not challenge initially, for to do so would create a hardship for survival and acceptance in a white setting. So they play the game that whites play: "Let's pretend that we all have the same problems."

Whites have wrapped around their evasions of truth and reality a thin veneer of respectability: feigned ignorance, deliberate dulling of the senses, self-imposed blindness. All this with the knowledge that blacks are powerless to combat them, challenge them, and win. Behind the veneer are the historical role models who gave them the song to sing, compelled them to memorize "My Country 'Tis Of Thee," and from all visible social and economic evidence, bequeathed them their sweet land of liberty. That is the essence of racism, institutionalized deep in the marrow of their bones. Worse yet, the delusion so long practiced, so long denied to surface, becomes eventual truth. The superior posturing becomes a state of being, of belonging to the exclusive club in which entrance depends strictly upon the paleness of the skin, the projection of majority rule, the inherited legacy of getting their "First with the Most." The refusal to indict self is a normal human reaction as well as a constitutional safeguard, undergirded by a judicial system that declares a man innocent until proven guilty.

As a black man, I began to peer into the white psyche, recognizing the cage in which they had confined themselves. Emerging from those cages would leave them vulnerable to the pain of racism's extinction. It would cast them helplessly in a jungle like lions without claws, elephants without tusks, tigers without teeth. To submit to the truth and reality of their own racism would mean to condemn the fathers and mothers who bore them. Families would be split, friendships demolished, and opportunities denied. White racism uses the crutch of sameness, lest the ties that bind be broken, and those loosened from those ties become outcasts on islands of forgetfulness. White women's racism was solidified because the perpetuators of the system were their own sons, husbands, and fathers. To reject them, or even to reject their way of life, was to cast away their hopes of love, passion, and sexuality.

I could not prevent my outrage at those white entrapments,

when I contrasted them to the massive destruction of a race of people. No longer could I even try to understand or rationalize white behavioral patterns with debate, nor could I listen to their argumentations. Condemnation remained the only course to take, biting and bitter sarcasm the only injection for such a deadly disease. Their pulses had to be quickened, their consciousness pricked, their lies exposed. Nowhere else in the world was a race of people enslaved to the pride of another race —under the guise of freedom. Blacks were chained to a perversity, eaten alive by spiritual cannibalism. Somehow I knew that understanding those perversities and attacking them would give me back the manhood that was snatched away from me by years of subduing the fires of resentment, being taken in by promises, being cajoled by liberals and coddled by white Christians.

After my chance discovery of the effectiveness of "encountering" whites with my black anger, "tell it like it is" became a pivotal phrase in the Justice and Social Change program—not as a fifteen-minute outburst but as a permanent weapon to flay the flesh of the lies that emerged from white lips. The "tell it" became a continuous flow, uninterrupted and unrelenting in its scope. I found myself saying all of the things I had always wanted to say. I was the leader. I was in charge. They had hired me to bring into their clean white world the dirt, pain, and obscenities of ghetto life. I obliged them.

As I traveled throughout the state of Ohio under the auspices of the Lutheran Church's race relations program, I changed the name from Justice and Social Change to "Black and White Encounter." But the mysterious change that was taking place among white students and faculty members at Wittenberg and among white Lutheran church members began to create a feeling of apprehension within the state and national LCA leadership. A small army of whites had begun to question why I hadn't been extended more opportunities to express myself within the Lutheran Church. As my white support increased, so did my blackness and my arrogance. I began to feel heady with a new sense of power in the white world. Even out-

side the Encounter program, I began challenging racist statements and attitudes in all settings—social and otherwise. I
began to think egotistically of my mission as messianic.

At first, my fellow Hamma Seminary professors found it
extremely difficult to explain me and my methods to their colleagues and other church leaders. But that problem was solved
once they had gone through the Encounter program. Dean
Luther Stirwalt and his wife Frances; Dr. Wayne Marsden and
his wife Jean; Dr. Ben Johnson; and finally Dr. Fred Wentz,
president of the seminary (my boss)—all went through the Encounter experience. I had been seen as a wild man, a destroyer
of values, a spoiler of youth, anathema on the Wittenberg campus. But as my support among the Hamma faculty and the individual churches grew, my detractors and discreditors found it
increasingly difficult to erase me and my methods from their
institutions. As the Encounter movement spread on campus
like prairie fire, I decided to train other blacks in the method to
assist me. Mark Thomas, a senior student, soon became able—
without my assistance—to challenge and change white attitudes. George Williams, who was later to become the director
of the Springfield, Ohio, Human Relations Commission, and
Sherman Hicks, a black theology student, both learned and
became accomplished in the method. Debbie Soergel, John
Pelligrino, and Katherine Woods—all white—became part of a
campus staff that assisted me and the other black Encounter
leaders in our efforts to eradicate racism.

I concede that my methodology always has precipitated
controversy. But the most rigid and hard to crack of all white
institutions proved to be the white Christian church and its
leadership. My early use of the Encounter method, I later came
to realize, was crude; it was like a lump of coal compared to the
polished stone that it was to become. At that early point I conducted it without the sophistication of a second day, a day of
reconciliation following the first day of black anger, which I
added to the program as I was refining it. So the program was
too abrasive for some people, and some of these people were ex-
pressing themselves to the LCA leadership. An example of the
kinds of excuses many white church leaders used to try to dilute

the growing effectiveness of the Encounter program is the following letter, addressed to Dr. John Rilling, president of the Ohio Lutheran Synod.

February 18, 1970

Dear Dr. Rilling:

On Friday evening and Saturday morning, February 6-7, Mr. Roy Carter (our Social Ministry chairman) and I attended an "Encounter" session entitled "Justice and Social Change" at the Sheraton-Dayton Hotel. We were two of six participants from the Lutheran congregations of the area. Mr. Charles King, Jr. and three students from the Wittenberg-Hamma student body were our leaders.

I waited to this point to write, so that I would not in haste or anger say something which I later would regret. Yet at this time I feel much the same way as I did 11 days ago.

My biggest complaint was the fact that Mr. King early in the evening reacted emotionally to a comment by saying "shit." When one of us, Mrs. Kay Stitz, of Trinity Lutheran, Dayton, seemed to wince, he sensed this. Then he asked if it bothered her. She said, "Yes." Then he began a tirade of words—shit, bullshit, fuck, this will grab you by the balls, etc.—indicating that we would be hearing this time and time again. Each time he used such a word, he turned to her asking if it bothered her.

Our words were interpreted and twisted to suit him; he cut off the one negro participant whenever she tried to say anything which would reflect a moderate negro's attitude; everything we said and did reflected that we were white racists; the negro had no faults in any of this; the negro alone (not the Jew, the American Indian, or other American minorities) had been really persecuted. At midnight he announced that we were through for the night, and that we could talk informally, go to bed, join him at the bar, etc. When the six of us went to our rooms to retire, we were reminded the next morning that this showed our white racism and lack of concern, for we should have stayed up with the staff until 4:00 discussing the problem.

Maybe this is the approach that some feel is necessary to shake people up, make them see themselves for what they are, and change. But I am afraid that it "turned me off completely."

Mr. Carter and I went to this program hoping to find something which we could bring into St. John's, since this community and congregation have many, many people who are anti-negro and want to keep them out. Both of us are opposed to using this with our people.

244

May I assure you that I feel that the negro is equal to the white man. I feel that he should be allowed, and I would welcome him, to live, work, study, and be everywhere that I am. I am grieved that this race has been mistreated for so long. I have preached hard-hitting sermons which have offended some of my members. I helped lead in putting on "White Vandalia and The Black Man," a seven week program by 5 Vandalia congregations, which was an attempt to meet the ignorance, misconception, and hatred in this area.

But I honestly feel that if this program were offered to the majority of our members—both those who have great prejudice, and those who are very lovingly concerned—it would hurt rather than help. (And I am not trying to shield my parishioners—for I have shaken them up and disturbed them often by my words and actions.)

I thought that the participant's book was fine; the record I considered excellent; I have not seen the leader's guide. My main concern is that my vote would be against the synod spending money for partial salary and expense for a person like Mr. King to go about putting this program on IN THIS WAY. I have the firm conviction that if Jesus Christ were carrying out his physical, earthly ministry today instead of when He did, that such language and methods would not be used by Him. It would shake me greatly in my faith to come to the conclusion that the Holy Spirit at work in the Church and in all areas of life could not bring about change and reconciliation without using this approach.

May God bless you, the synod, all Christians, and the Church during this Lenten season.

Most cordially,
Glenn F. Clauser

The reason Rev. Clauser's letter grossly exaggerated and misinterpreted my actions I now understand. Whites tend to emphasize the negative aspects of interacting with black people to diminish the need to respond to the positive black indictments. The manner in which I conduct Encounter is indeed oppressive. The idea is to effect a role change whereby the whites can feel the unfairness produced by institutional controls exercised by a race other than their own. In that way their mindset can be reversed to understand *and feel* the black experience.

Dr. John Abma, Chairman of the Psychology Department at Wittenberg University at that time, was more analytical of the Encounter process. After a two-day exposure to the program, he wrote his reflections:

REFLECTIONS ON BLACK-WHITE ENCOUNTER

I participated in the encounter program of the weekend of February 14 and 15, Friday night and Saturday morning. I would like to react in three interrelated ways. First, to the techniques employed—that is, to the expertness of group leadership; second, to the goals of the group experience; and third, to the probable effects, as I see them.

The best feature of the encounter was that an atmosphere existed in which the expression of strongly-held views was possible in a direct and appropriately emotional way. By all we know, this is essential for emotional growth. On the negative side, the needed atmosphere of trust within the group was disturbed somewhat by the technique of using confederates within the group. These helpers, black students for the most part, were cooperating with the leader, but this fact was not announced to the naive members of the group. This was an oversight in group leadership technique.

The material presented in the group was generally effective. Recordings, lecture material, wall pictures, and booklet were all good. However, details of content could be improved, in my estimation, as follows:

1. More accounts of black life both within and outside of the ghetto might be given. This would open the eyes of many whites who honestly don't know the conditions and experiences that define discrimination.

2. Better use could be made of techniques that did not work too well in our group. For example, members formed a circle and joined hands. Another member was instructed to break the circle. It would help if each member could take the role of outsider, and gain the experience of being excluded from an in-group. In my encounter sessions, this was done only once, with confederates chosen to "fake" certain reactions.

3. There is the opportunity here to give whites a sample of the black experience. Whites could be given a first-hand introduction to some of the insults and disadvantages that black people know only too well. There are anecdotal accounts indicating that this is a powerful experience for white people, and one which inclines them toward eliminating white racism.

4. The group should not run over the scheduled times, either on Friday night or Saturday morning, unless by unanimous group consent. (My group was extended by over an hour

beyond the announced times, at both sessions.) Also, group members probably should not continue their individual encounters in private late Friday night, as some have done (but not in my group). Lack of monitoring of such interaction at such an emotional time would be risky.

The major goal of the group encounter is excellent. The intent is, of course, to do something, *anything*, about the grossly unjust treatment of blacks in our white culture. All whites should know and feel the extent to which whites continually mistreat and exploit blacks. Inaction on our part is inexcusable and immoral. This point is made well by the group encounter.

A feature that disturbed me about the encounter was the development of a gulf separating blacks and whites. I don't know whether this was a goal of the encounter or not. However, I never used to speak of "Blacks" and "Whites," but, after encounter, I do. It seemed that sincere gestures of friendship, sympathy or good will were rejected by the blacks present. The rejection seemed to be on the basis of whiteness, without regard for individual characteristics or degree of guilt. The argument of the blacks seemed to be, "Do not try to relate to us as people. You cannot possibly understand us anyway. Instead, go to your own white racist brothers and make them stop persecuting us." My counter-argument is, "Can we not do both? Let us relate to you as black people AND insist that white culture be changed now to end the mistreatment of black people."

The probable effects of encounter are many and varied. I will list a few short-term effects that I observed, ranging from the most to the least desirable.

1. Some whites appear to be truly converted by the experience. They are ready to confront other whites with objections to discrimination in all forms.

2. Some whites appear to be truly confused. They don't know what hit them, but they are frightened by threats of black violence. They don't know what to do or say. They don't know why the blacks judge them, as individuals, so harshly.

3. Some whites are guilt-ridden by the experience. They will do anything and say anything just to get off the hook of guilt. Guilt is not the most durable or dependable of motivators. There are too many ways of escaping guilt that are not truly constructive.

4. Some whites may return the apparent hatred of blacks with resentment of their own. They may decide to do nothing, since anything they might do would not be valued anyway by the black community.

5. It is difficult to see that the black participants benefitted as individuals from the encounter. They did not seem to become more mature in their understanding of the problem. There was no hint of a growing capacity to forgive or to be reconciled, even in the distant future.

In conclusion, I believe steps must be taken against white racism. I also believe that those steps, whatever they might be, should not alienate or depersonalize black and white people. I would hope that reconciliation might be a part of the ultimate plan.

John S. Abma

As the Encounter method expanded beyond the college and seminary campus, I began making changes in it to remove or lessen some of the least favorable aspects mentioned by Abma and other features that generated the most criticism. I learned not to socialize with or even greet participants before a session began, not to use black confederates within the group, and to have whites respond to white racist attitudes within the group—that is, not to have all the challenges to them come from me or the other blacks. So, as I conducted my Encounter seminars, I continued to refine the program into the most effective vehicle for the changes I knew were needed in white attitudes.

CHAPTER 27

The Urban Crisis Center Is Born

WHILE MY WITTENBERG EFFORTS WERE BEGINning to bear fruit, a small town nearby, Middletown, Ohio, was experiencing a racial crisis. Sporadic racial incidents had been occurring, and more massive disorders were both feared and predicted. On an impulse, I went to Middletown, contacted the city officials, and informed them of my Encounter technique. I asked them to try my program as a way of re-establishing harmony in their town. Black leadership in Middletown agreed to participate, but the whites were reluctant. It was Mary Lord, a white councilwoman, who convinced white officials that it would not hurt to try out my services. So I conducted a one-day session with black leaders, police, council members, and the city manager.

When I left Middletown, things had changed, and I was elated. The process had worked. All participants agreed that a trust had been established, and black leadership agreed to hold off their demonstrations. A biracial council was formed, and my student assistants and I were to assist in formulating a system of resolving black grievances and analyzing for the city the adequacy of its responses. When I reflected on it, the implications of what the Encounter method had accomplished were staggering. During my years in Gary and on the Kerner Commission I had learned of the urban crisis in America; and during my Wittenberg years I had virtually stumbled across the Encounter method. But it took the small town of Middletown, Ohio to be the catalyst for the thrust of the rest of my career.

I returned to the campus of Wittenberg with a new concept. I immediately told my colleagues there what had happened and began to implore them to assist me in getting the LCA hierarchy to see how Encounter (my adaptation of their program for the church) could be directly applied to the urban crisis in American cities. As a result of the Middletown success, the city manager of Dayton, Ohio made a request for a similar exposure in that city. Taking my university staff to the city, I conducted the full, gruelling two-day sessions for the city manager, chief of police, and the other city department heads. Once again, success.

I could now see clearly the strangeness of my past focus on sensitizing the white church and young white students. I was now convinced that the Encounter program was not only needed by the cities and their officials individually, but was needed to decrease the possibilities of racial disorders. Here was a new mission, a new thrust, a new hope for change.

I traveled to New York to attend a conference on how to better implement the Justice and Social Change program within the LCA. As each white priority leader gave his report, I was shocked to discover that most of them were not engaged in eradicating racism—the program's alleged purpose—but attempting to increase black-white fellowship, love, and consideration for each other. It was the old white balancing trick: "Let's not rock the boat." To make matters worse, with the exception of a black minister who served on the National Board of Social Ministry for the LCA, I was the lone black present. My anger increased when I learned that the budget for the Justice and Social Change program was in jeopardy and would certainly be curtailed. I was informed that Dr. Marshall, president of the National Synod of the Lutheran Church in America, was opposed to the Priority Program, and that the monies would have to come from the local churches in the future, not from the LCA. Once again, the white church was backing away from blackness.

Heady with my successful experiences in producing white attitudinal change, I decided to "encounter" the whites at that conference table. I let my wrath and disgust flay at the shame of their activities.

"This program works!" I shouted at the conferees. "How dare the church back away from a program that produces white change?" And as I continued my challenge to them, I could see that several of the conferees were catching on to the hope of the new mission I was proposing. Jim Nichols, assistant to Dr. Rilling of the Ohio Synod, had accompanied me to the conference, and he spoke in support of the new direction. Jewell Jessup, executive director of the Board, took a vote. The King proposal for a new direction was passed.

I had won! The whites had been "encountered." And the excitement over what the LCA was about to embark upon found even the fainthearted of the group of forty facilitators buzzing about the potential. But it was agreed that, without the support of Dr. Marshall, my proposal could not succeed. And to get such a proposal through Dr. Marshall, I knew, would be a major task. He had not impressed me with being enlightened on the need for justice and social change.

I had discovered that fact only a few months earlier at Capital Seminary in Columbus, Ohio, where Dr. Marshall spoke to a mass meeting of Capital and Hamma Seminary students and faculty members. The gist of what he said was that a pastor must not go beyond his people, for if he goes too far beyond them, he will lose them. His meaning, in essence, was clear: Don't rock the boat. Again, as the only black in that gathering, I had risen to my feet during the question-and-answer period, and challenged Dr. Marshall's advice to the white seminarians. As a black, I reminded him that, if white ministers refused to rock boats on his advice, then they would be aiding and abetting racist practices that dehumanized blacks and left them at the mercy of institutionalized racism. Would he, then, reconsider his admonition? If this church was to be at peace with itself, then who should wage the war against racism?

I sat down to much applause from white seminarians, frowns from LCA dignitaries on the dais, and smirks of glee and pride on the faces of the Hamma professors. Before Dr.

Marshall replied, he stepped back from the podium and conferred with Dr. Fred Wentz, president of Hamma, evidently to inquire who this outspoken black man was. He returned to the podium and responded:

"Dr. King, please don't take my words out of context. That's not what I meant. . . ."

"But that's what you said," I replied from my seat. Dr. Marshall's face turned red as a beet as laughter filled the hall. He eventually succeeded in agreeing with the need for change, but not if it meant dividing the church of God. My silence at his last explanation was the occasion for other white seminarians to point out to him the contradiction of both the teachings of the Bible and of Christ to such thinking.

That had been my introduction to Dr. Marshall. Now I was being informed that my proposal would need his blessing.

"Let's call him up and inform him that we need to see him on this" was someone's suggestion. Jewell Jessup agreed to call. Jim Nichols suggested that I also speak to Dr. Marshall.

It was a noncommittal Dr. Marshall who listened to my explanation. Yes, he agreed with the concept but questioned how the LCA should do it. Yes, he was open to the formation of a delegation to put the proposal into writing in the meantime.

The proposal was written, and a committee to implement it was formed, consisting of: Dean Dahl, representing Wittenberg University; Robert McCord, representing the Ohio Synod; Jewell Jessup, representing the national Social Action Committee of the LCA; and myself. The proposal asked for $50,000 to establish an Urban Crisis Center on the Wittenberg campus for one year. The Center would invite city officials from around the nation to participate in the Encounter program, which would be followed by an analysis of their racial problems and suggested solutions to those problems. I was to be the director of the Center, and the University would provide space, computers, and departmental expertise wherever and whenever needed. Fees from participants would augment the budget from the LCA.

The committee presented and explained this proposal to the state executive board, and they approved it. The state convention of the Ohio Synod was next on the agenda. At that convention, Dr. John Rilling, president of the Ohio Synod, introduced me to the virtually all-white delegation.

"This," I informed them, "is the happiest moment of my life" (and it was). "For years," I continued, "I have been highly critical of white institutions, particularly the white church, for their lack of attention to the urban crisis of this nation. What your vote will do today, I hope, is prove me wrong. God bless you."

I wept as the applause from hundreds of religious white delegates rained down on me. It was extremely difficult for me to keep my composure and modesty as delegate after delegate requested permission to speak and testified how their lives had been changed and enriched by their experience in my Encounter program. They spoke of how their churches had become involved and sensitive to blacks and other minorities, and that the proposal for an Urban Crisis Center, with Charles King as director, would establish an example throughout Christianity that the church was and should be involved. It was no longer a question, said one delegate, of "What can I do?" It was now a commitment: "This we must do!"

Through all of this Dr. John Rilling was noticeably passive. His face was stoical, hard, and unsmiling. He stood to remind those who still desired to testify of other items on the convention agenda.

"All those in favor. . . ."

"Aye" was the thunderous response.

"Those opposed . . ."

The "nays" were faint, far off in the distance.

"Passed."

I recalled the time, more than two years before that moment, when Jim Nichols of the Ohio Synod and Luther Stirwalt, dean of Hamma Theological Seminary, had personally come to Gary to urge me to accept Wittenberg, Hamma, and the Ohio Synod as my new career focus. I had been interviewed by them and offered a position by letter. I had not responded to that offer. Fred Wentz, president of Hamma, had called me wanting to know why. I had informed him of the crisis of the cities, including Gary. I did not want to abandon my efforts to resolve issues that involved my people.

"What better way than to get us involved?" he inquired. I was still hesitant. Then came the personal visit and appeal from Nichols and Stirwalt. And I finally agreed to accept.

After the vote at the Ohio Convention, I walked over to shake hands with Jim Nichols, Fred Wentz, and Luther Stirwalt. The church, at long last, was now involved in the urban crisis.

*   *   *   *   *

That summer of 1970, requests for the Encounter seminar came thick and fast. But it would not be until fall, and possibly winter, before the Urban Crisis Center would be ready for operation. I was impatient. I foolishly had brochures printed up advertising the establishment of the center on the Wittenberg campus. Dr. Andeen, the university president, was furious; and so was Dr. Rilling. Fred Wentz cautioned me to move more slowly. I was reminded that final approval had to come from Dr. Marshall and the national LCA Convention.

In the meantime, requests for my services came once again from the city of Dayton. Dr. Wayne Carle, superintendent of the Dayton Public School System, wanted to know whether I could put on an Encounter seminar for him and his staff. So I did. Of all the persons I have ever encountered, Wayne Carle, a Mormon, was the most effective white agent for changing white attitudes and racist systems. It was not long before he had reversed the trend of the Dayton schools by insisting on complete desegregation of the schools. Against the wishes of a conservative school board, he mandated that all of his administrators and more than 700 teachers undergo the Encounter experience. He sent me from school to school throughout that summer and fall of 1970, sensitizing teachers, administrators, and even parents. He was determined to eliminate racism wherever it was in his power to do so.

254

Wayne Carle became both a student of and a missionary for my program. Blacks who had formerly seen Dr. Carle as a white racist were amazed at the change that took place after he had completed the Encounter program. Ignoring white critics, he not only spoke directly to whites about their racism, but he acted out his convictions with policies and procedures that brought forth dramatic and meaningful changes. Members of his staff were also impressed with the Encounter program. The following letters indicated the importance of setting up the Urban Crisis Center at Wittenberg.

Dear Mr. King:

The opportunity to be a participant in the Black and White Encounter was greatly appreciated. I will long remember the experience, and hopefully I will be a better man because of it.

The problem is almost overwhelming, but with people like you working so diligently I feel sure that some day all men can live in harmony. I sincerely hope that I will be able to do my part in turning the tide of prejudice into love for all mankind.

May God bless you and give you strength so that you can be successful in this most important venture.

Sincerely,
Gene Hodson

Dear Charles:

My attention was called to a prize-winning article written by you in *Nation's Cities*. I'm not surprised, but I would like to assess the article for myself. I know you have several copies of it available, and would appreciate having one fired out to me. . . .

Reports from your encounter sessions are all positive. I assume the proper authorities will be in touch with you again very soon if such is not already the case.

Keep in touch.

Sincerely,
William H. Watson
Assistant Superintendent
Urban Education

Dear Dr. King:

The Black-White Encounter was a useful and inspirational experience for all participants. Each comment has indicated the need for extended service in this area.

It is quite possible that we will provide an opportunity for all principals and central office staff to be involved in a workshop in August. We feel that your contributions will be a valuable asset in this area. . . .

Sincerely,
Phyllis B. Greer (Mrs.)
Director
Equal Educational Opportunity

I forwarded these and other letters to Dr. Rilling and the LCA Board for Social Ministries. I was hoping that they would realize the scope of my work, its effectiveness, and the need to hasten the process.

I also reminded them that I was on my way to Atlanta to receive national recognition at the annual meeting of the American League of Cities. I had been selected by *Nation's Cities*, the official magazine of the League of Cities, as the person who had made the most effective contribution to urban affairs that year. Accordingly, the Louis Brownlow Award was presented to me that summer by the American Society of Public Administrators. The presenter of the award was then mayor of Indianapolis—now U.S. Senator from Indiana—Richard Luger. John Erlichman, President Nixon's chief of staff, rose to his feet and shook my hand as hundreds of mayors and city officials applauded the presentation. I was asked to speak a word.

I spoke. But it was not a nice or diplomatic statement. In 1979 there were only two black mayors and a handful of black city officials. As I looked out over the thousands of delegates' faces, I could see no black faces at all. And that fact sickened me. The article for which I had won the Brownlow Award was entitled "Discriminatory Systems Must Be Challenged and Changed." I reminded the convention of this title, and that the absence of blacks in their gathering emphasized my concern and their failings.

There was no applause. As I sat down to deadly silence, John Ehrlichman was introduced to explain to the mayors the Nixon program of revenue sharing for the cities.

*   *   *   *   *

Back at Wittenberg, I cursed myself for being so caustic at the League of Cities Convention. I had blown a prime opportunity to let every major city and its officials know of the establishment of the Urban Crisis Center at Wittenberg.

Then came the shock. It was a letter from Dr. Rilling:

July 10, 1970

Dear Mr. King:

I am genuinely glad to hear of the award which has been made to you by the American Society for Public Administration. I am glad to learn too that the reactions to your Dayton City Official Encounter were so positive that you are now following up with a program designed for high school principals and department heads in that city.

In further response to your letter seeking clarification of your employment status with the Ohio Synod Priorities Program, I would state that the Executive Board engaged your services for the period of one year beginning September 1, 1969 to August 31, 1979 on a half-time basis. As you know the curtailment of the Priorities Program on a national level has led to the curtailment of employment by coordinators in most of the synods.

Reactions to the Encounter Program in Ohio have varied but I do not believe that its most enthusiastic supporter would maintain that the effort to implement the program in the 350 congregations of the Ohio Synod has met with measurable success. At the Executive Board Meeting which you attended several months ago you stated your conviction that the Encounter Program in congregations was not really a live option and your proposal therefore was to move away from the congregational program to such programs as you have implemented at Middletown and Dayton. It is the conviction of the Synod Staff that in the light of the action taken at the Minneapolis Convention synods should urge congregations that have not participated in an encounter program in the congregation be encouraged to do so. It is now our intention to approach the program on a pan-Lutheran basis using existing urban ministry organization in the various sectors of the state.

When the proposal was made for the establishment of an urban training center on the Wittenberg-Hamma Campus the Executive Board did not realize the restricted nature of the Board of Social Ministry's commitment to such a proposal. At Minneapolis it was made clear to me that the Board of Social Ministry's commitment, if the project were approved, would be for seed money only. After an initial grant fiscal responsibility would be entirely the responsibility of the Ohio Synod. A figure of

$50,000 was stated as the kind of money which the Ohio Synod would have to produce for a program of the scope you were proposing. In a day when church funds are diminishing rather than increasing I do not believe the Executive Board will commit itself to such a proposal.

Since it appears to me quite unlikely that the Executive Board will commit itself financially to this kind of funding and since Dr. Andeen has also made it clear to you that Wittenberg's own program is already operative and does not envision using your services for such a project, it would appear to me wise for you to accept any other opportunities of employment as seem to be available.

Sincerely yours,
John W. Rilling
President

Dr. Rilling's letter left me numb. This was unbelievable. It was obvious that the trinity of Drs. Marshall, Rilling, and Andeen had coordinated my dismissal from the Synod's Priority Program and, against the vote of the Ohio Synod, scrapped the entire concept of the Urban Crisis Center. I knew that Dr. Wentz and the professors at Hamma stood fully behind me. And I knew that my proposals had broad support throughout the Ohio Synod. In the wake of Rilling's letter, Hamma and Wittenberg students began to flood the Ohio Synod's office with letters of protest. One such letter, which typified the support I received from the student body, dramatically expressed what the Encounter methodology had meant at Wittenberg:

Dr. Rilling,
Please overlook the informality of this letter, but what I have to say just won't seem to fit into a business letter.
Last weekend I participated in an Encounter session under the direction of Mr. Charles King. Now, please understand, Dr. Rilling—I went into that room with an attitude, maybe a typical one, of self-improvement. I had bandied the symptoms of white racism about, had come to recognize it in at least its more outspoken forms. Now I wanted to intensify my perception, sharpen my responses to black needs, pattern my actions about a more personalized sensitivity. Do you see what I was saying?
Although I did not recognize it at the time, *I* was the target of my efforts—I was completely preoccupied with *my* role in the *game* of white racism. Oh, naturally I professed a deep concern

for Black America—otherwise I probably wouldn't have gone to Encounter. But the concern I felt was the comfortably removed indignation for the injustices of the white system against blacks. A comfortable position—and an utterly ineffectual one. Like most white liberals, radicals, and the "concerned" church, I had been copping out, through verbiage.

So, the Encounter began. For my own part, I was familiar with the rhetoric, knew the right words to say. Quickly I learned that, because I am part of their white world, because I know how their minds work, I was able to evoke emotive responses from the other whites in the group. But by late Friday night I had begun to realize that, although I could *generate* feeling, I was not *feeling* it at the stark, gut level. In sixteen years of formal white schooling I had become an emotional gelding.

By Saturday morning I was frantic. I had to be challenged, I had to be forced to feel. I was not disappointed. The moment came when all the carefully chosen words in the world meant nothing without action, without instant, unthinking feeling. Like most of the group, I failed miserably. I analyzed, I conjectured, but I did not *feel* until that terrifying moment when all my well-cushioned inadequacy was ripped open, right in front of me. "Man, you're *killing* me," King sobbed, "you're killing blacks with every word." For the first time, I knew what he meant—felt what he meant. Dr. Rilling, please believe that the painfulness of this kind of realization is excruciating. Unspeakably. Anguish, Dr. Rilling. Not rhetorical anger, not self-righteous indignation. Sheer anguish. And there sat a man who hardly knew me—I'm kidding myself—he knew me well—and he felt an agonizing human compassion for me—for me—the likes of which I have probably never felt for anyone. I was shattered. My whole being rested with an emotionally dying man (he was—and is—and we, Encounter after Encounter, are numbing him more and more), with an uncompromisingly human, black student, and with a giant of a black mother.

It has now been nearly a week since Encounter. I am free to go back to my old life, to my old ways. But I can't, Dr. Rilling. I'm carrying a roomful of people around with me, everywhere I go. And at every living minute there is a numb pain. Stubborn, impossible to ignore, indescribable. A pain. I wonder if it will ever go away—I am hoping it won't. You see, for me Encounter was not a pleasant experience. Even after the sleepless nights, the crying out has subsided, the pain remains. And that's exactly as it had to be. Charles King did more for me in two days than a legion of intellectuals have done in a lifetime. And when I try to imagine the pain magnified, exploding to an intensity beyond belief, fed at every second by blind white eyes, I honestly wonder how any black man lives from day to day.

That, I guess, is the black man's crime: he possesses a natural, immeasurable human compassion—a feeling which cannot be turned off or relegated to comfortable intellectualizing at will. And so, Dr. Rilling, you and I are killing Charles King, killing his people, and we can't even feel the death throes all around us. Can you feel what I'm saying?

On the people-cluttered floor of a Hamma lounge, surpassing all the stupidity, the mindlessness, the insensitivity I had to offer, when I deserved to burn and was only beginning to feel that, Charles King gave his heart to me, to all of us who would accept it. Please don't take that—or him—away from my foolish, stumbling race. He is our last hope. And you and I both know it.

> With heartfelt thanks,
> Michael Smith

To my surprise, theological students issued a demand to the Synod executive board that my contract be renewed. Dr. Ben Johnson and others of my colleagues at Hamma traveled to Columbus and picketed Dr. Rilling's office—in the rain. Furthermore, an "Ad Hoc Coalition concerned about Charles H. King, Jr." was formed and circulated a petition demanding my reinstatement.

> August 3, 1970

Dear Member of the Ohio Synod, L.C.A.,

We have organized an Ad Hoc Coalition concerned about Charles H. King, Jr. The enclosed petition states our concern over the failure of the Executive Board of the Ohio Synod to renew his contract as staff person for the Priorities Program.

This petition will be presented to Dr. John Rilling on behalf of Rev. King on Thursday, Aug. 6, 1970. We request that you join us in this Coalition by signing this petition yourself and by encouraging other individuals and your congregation to sign it also. Please mail the signed copy to the Synod Office and a post card to us indicating that you have done so and the number of signatures.

If we can further explain our stance in this matter to you or others whom you know, please feel free to contact us.

Thank you.

> Yours truly,
> Ad Hoc Coalition
> Clifford C. Smith, Acting Chairman

PETITION

We the undersigned hereby express our disappointment and indignation that the Ohio Synod of the Lutheran Church in America has not renewed the contract of the Rev. Charles H. King, Jr. We feel that this decision was irresponsible in that it was:

1. Lacking in an objective consideration of the man or the program and the decision was made in an emotion-filled context. The stated reason for not renewing the contract can be refuted with fact.

2. Contrary to the expressed wishes of the members of the Ohio Synod who seemingly endorsed *both* the proposed Urban Crisis Center *and* the Rev. Charles H. King, Jr., at the May convention in Dayton.

3. Symbolic of the lack of commitment to solving the Black/White crisis and a clear indication of the weakness of the Lutheran Church, Ohio Synod, to realistically deal with Black Humanity.

4. An insult to the Black minority of members of the Ohio Synod. The decision seems to say that there is no place in the Lutheran Church in America, Ohio Synod, for a Black man.

5. A symptom depicting the administrative ineptness of some of the members of the Executive Board of the Lutheran Church in America, Ohio Synod and the President of the Ohio Synod in dealing with their own white Racist postures.

6. Not respecting of the man, nor of his professional ability.

Therefore, we the undersigned hereby demand the following:

(1) The immediate reinstatement of the Rev. Charles King, Jr. as Director of the Priorities Program (Encounter) for the Ohio Synod L.C.A.

(2) An immediate *public* apology for his irresponsible dismissal.

Letters from Lutheran pastors throughout the state made their disappointment and anger known. One week after the petition had been circulated and presented to Dr. Rilling, and had received no satisfactory assurances from him, the Ad Hoc Coalition issued the following open letter to the pastors in the Ohio Synod:

August 10, 1970

Dear Pastor,

We, too, are concerned about the crisis in Synod, referred to by Dr. John W. Rilling, in his letter of Aug. 7, 1970. In order that the Rev. Charles King's half-time contract renewal might receive a fair consideration, we wish to call the following facts to your attention and solicit your assistance.

1. We *are* in an Urban Crisis.

2. The Synod in Convention voted for the Urban Crisis Center and therefore for Charles H. King, Jr. as its director by implication, since the center and program were King's proposal.

3. Dr. Rilling indicated King's separation from Synod (July 10) without consultation with either the Task-Force Committee or the Executive Board.

4. The Executive Board *in closed session* (July 28) ratified the action of the President, also, without consultation with the Task-Force Committee or the minority (Black) member(s) of the Board or Synod.

We are requesting support for a fair and open hearing before the new "Standing Committee on Justice and Social Change" and the "Executive Board" on behalf of the Rev. Charles H. King, Jr. and his Synod ratified program. Will you please express your request for such a hearing to Dr. Rilling by phone or letter immediately.

In the spirit of King's work of reconciliation between Blacks and Whites, we pray God's grace will prompt even greater understanding among us all. . . .

Sincerely,
The Ad Hoc Coalition
Clifford C. Smith, Acting Chairman

I had wanted to fight back myself; but others fought for me, sparing me the pain of open confrontation with the president of the Ohio Synod. Dr. Rilling had opened a Pandora's box with his letter. Quizzed by the press about the matter, he found himself continually answering up to the charge of committing a racist act. His defenses were pitifully weak. When I saw the volume and magnanimity of the responses in support of me and my program, I decided that it would be diplomatic to express my confusion and disappointment to Dr. Rilling in a conciliatory tone. I sent him the following letter:

Dear Dr. Rilling:

Again, I want to thank you for the long discussion we had relative to my status with the Ohio Synod. I want first of all to assure you that my interest remains in the area of the furtherance of progressive programming of the Priority Program with or without my leadership.

Since talking to you last, I have been made aware of two facts that shed additional light on the problem of my contract renewal. It was in the form of a recommendation given to you by Jim Nichols, of your staff and the immediate supervisor of my work. Jim's recommendation, according to him, and which I understand, was predicated upon attempting to free me from Synod structure with the hope of the Task Force assuming the responsibility of the program. Knowing Jim as I do, I know he considered this to be in my best interest; unfortunately, your letter and subsequent conversations did not carry through with the full intent of the non-renewal decision. Your letter to me of July 10th, and the subsequent action of the Executive Board, did not address itself to the issue of my future with the Synod; in fact, the last sentence of your letter indicated that I "should seek employment elsewhere."

After the action of the Executive Board was read to me over the phone by Secretary Welborn, I specifically asked him if such action precluded my being considered as the potential director of the Crisis Center. He stated that this matter was not discussed, and, in his official letter which followed a few days later, he wrote to inform me of my future with the Ohio Synod: "The action of the Board supports the earlier letter of the President of the Synod."

What puzzled me, then, was the fact that the idea of the Crisis Center, which I had conceived, worked on, promoted, and gathered materials on was still being considered by the Synod, while at the same time I was being asked to seek other employment.

What further puzzled me was the fact that the Crisis Center was virtually unanimously endorsed by the Ohio Synod in Dayton. It followed in my thinking that my personal involvement and relationship was inextricably tied together with the Center. With the understanding that the Synod's approval was a mandate for continuing to work with cities, and with the Task Force directing me to continue my experiments in Dayton and Middletown, I continued those activities with enthusiasm. In fact, I requested and received assistance from Lee Westley, director of the National Priority Program, and from the Board of Social Ministry in the Dayton city officials' Encounter.

The success of those encounters with 60 department heads of the city is attached in the form of a letter from the city manager. The success of the Encounter sessions with the Dayton school officials is attached in the form of a letter from the superintendent of the Dayton school system, Dr. Wayne Carle. Other attached letters indicate requests for additional services of the Encounter program, sessions that would reach a total of 220 school officials and teachers. They asked and received permission to conduct the same on the premises of Wittenberg University.

After the action of the Executive Committee, and the subsequent publicity, the Dayton school system cancelled out. The disappointment of this action is indescribable, suffice it to say. It was my personal opinion that the LCA program could indeed induce immediate change in cities with urban problems, and the carrying out of the school system's Encounters would have provided conclusive documentation.

Considering the evidence on hand, supplemented by the submitted interviews with Encounter participants who are high officials in the Dayton schools and city government, any effort to impede or deny the validity of an Urban Crisis Center at Wittenberg University flies in the face of reason, concern for solving the problems of blacks in cities, and the stated commitment of the LCA to seek justice and social change.

What, then, prevents the Crisis Center from being a fact?

From my personal vantage point, I see the obstacles being those persons who have never participated in Encounter, who do not understand the process or the program, and remain adamantly opposed to the Center. I see officials and educators, long accustomed to tradition and uninformed as to the real and present crisis in the cities, shying away from involvement. The tragedy is that the type of involvement requested *is not even a personal one*. All that is required is *permission* to use facilities and the address of the university for a badly needed service.

The intent of this letter is twofold: first, to reassure you that I hold no grudge or malice concerning the events that have unfolded; and that I personally respect and hold in esteem your role as president of the Synod, with a growing understanding of the problems that such a position entails. Secondly, I have discovered our isolation from each other, and that the communication links have been both faulty and nonexistent. I am aware that the problems of race, racism, protest, and conflict are foreign to your nature, background, and experience. These factors, plus my own intense emotional concern and consistent involvement in areas distinct from your own, have led to the strange mixture of confusion and seemingly stalemated positions that tend to increase polarization.

On my part, I am breaking through in gaining a better insight into the inner workings of establishment proceedings, as I am sure that you are now observing the workings of activists dedicated to eradicating all vestiges of injustice. In the long haul, it is this type of mutual confrontation and understanding that will bring about solutions, and it is this focus which is the essence of the Encounter Program.

I am sending copies of this letter to those who are actively engaged in seeking change, with the hope that their future actions and activities in my behalf, and in behalf of the program, *must* be predicated upon possibilities for reconciliation, and that no reconciliation will ever be possible unless love, respect, and an understanding of the dynamics of black, white, political, and protesting forces all work toward the admitted positive objective—justice and social change.

It is my further hope, based upon our discussions on this matter, that whatever the results or outcome of the decisions that follow, the Ohio Synod, under your leadership, will be solidified and harmonized.

Sincerely,
Charles H. King, Jr.

The reactions to Dr. Rilling's letter had come from a small arm of Lutherans—students, teachers, and pastors—who had, through the Encounter experience, been made aware of institutionalized white racism and saw that it could be changed within themselves. But all of this support for me and my program, including my own letter, did not have the effect of changing the minds of the higher-ups in the Ohio Synod. My termination stuck.

I sat down and wrote a more personal and reflective response to my dismissal as a Priority Program leader and the loss to Wittenberg of the Urban Crisis Center. This response I entitled "White Man, Black Man . . . and God," and I sent a copy of it to John Rilling.

Welcome, black man, to the white world. Come, full of spirits and hope. Watch the white-strained expressions of greetings, and listen to the weak-voiced promises. You are black, entering a white world that suddenly offers to pay you for your presence. Years of black absentia from white institutions are, in a moment, made electric; the institution throbs with excitement and fear. Now, with a showcase black, perhaps the ghetto will be silenced. The aching pain of the cities will be massaged gently with this far-reaching effort to make "one of them" important—if not equal.

265

The black ghetto witnesses the departure of the black man and offers a thin line of farewell. How well it knows the white world, its patterns, lures and hypocritical welcomes. "Farewell," the ghetto speaks fondly to the departing black, who is ready to make his entrance into the white institution. "We will see you later."

The last expression is not totally lost to the showcase black. For if he is to carry his blackness into whiteness, he must prepare to hide a part of his dignity, a part of his heart, and much of his soul. The battle before him will be awesome; no longer free, he will be forced to smile meaningless smiles, quiet his roaring guts, and speak in tones that mimic the politeness of the white world. No matter that his friends and relatives left in the ghetto are perched on the razor's edge of disaster, he must rationalize his departure to himself and to all blacks who question him: "It's an opportunity." The door long shut silently cracks open, and as he enters that door, the sight before him is awesome.

Gradually, the black man learns the new language of diplomacy; patiently he begins the task of intellectualizing the pain of his people. White stupidity becomes his cross, and he bears it hopeful of their and his own redemption. Suddenly, the dawn of truth; the white world he has entered is unreal, its people insensitive. "Tell us more," they ask mockingly, "we are trying to understand." But they can't . . . and never will *as long as the black man acts white.*

Oh, gentle Jesus, now I understand Gethsemane—the garden, sweet-smelling white classrooms, churches, schools, filled with buds of innocence and the faint odor of decay. These people, these strange, isolated, decaying bits of humanity have no feelings, no soul. The ghetto beckons once again, but the black man must delay his flight. He knows that unless he can kindle the fire that burns in all men—the fires of hope—the ghetto will burn.

Thus, Encounter becomes his weapon. In his person *all* blacks must leap into life. He must arouse, alarm, shock, quicken white senses. "Listen," he screams and shouts, "I am black, do not take that away from me, for only by remaining black can I bring to you the rest of the black world. Let the ghetto speak through my lips and its stench ooze from my person. Smell me, touch me, even if you cannot love me . . . know me. The white classroom becomes alive; the young flowers, once withering, perk up. The scream, the shout, the pain of blackness penetrates to their bones, and the spark of new awareness soon leaps into flames. The crimes of their fathers and the white institutions' hypocrisy and sterility become apparent. These children, spawned in the sea of whiteness, suddenly discover that the water through which they have been swimming is polluted with racism. The black man now holds high his head and his voice becomes softer as he thanks God for the gift of black persuasion. With this weapon the black people will no longer need to riot. They can now put away their rocks and sticks.

A new day dawns with each encounter. A new religion is discovered. A new faith. White people, when exposed to the raw edge of suffering, become people without color. Basking thus in the new-found world of people who have found their souls, the black man publicizes the news. He hastens to report to the ghetto. "White can be right, they do have souls, they *can* feel. . . . hold back the burning, black brothers and sisters, a new world is coming." Really? The black man rushes back to the white institution. "Dammit, white man, please don't fool me this time. I have sung the praises of your growth, I have discovered your hidden humanity. God does exist, he is not dead, you have shown Him to me."

The ghetto is wary, but the black man presses on with his blackness. He becomes arrogantly certain of his presence; white rules and standards he now discards. No system can hold him or control him; recklessly he plunges deeper into white racism's waters, approaches the core, the heart of the system. No classroom this, for at the core is the seat of power, prestige, and influence. Cock-sure, stupid black man. God cannot be found in that setting. Long since gone . . . . 300 years. The black man discovers that he has moved too fast. He beats a hasty retreat too late—he is caught in the swirl of his own making. The waters he disturbed overwhelm him; the hope that was throbbing and alive dissipates. He is drowning.

Help! A few whites hear the scream, but white power overwhelms them. "Let him drown; after all, he stinks. He refuses to be white. His language is offensive, his manner and his style are nothing more than old-time religion. He's not a good administrator. Besides, we have been checking on him, and our microscopes reveal that he has human frailties, too human to be in a white world. Let him drown . . . or throw him back into the ghetto. Our budget will no longer carry him."

"Let him drown! He manipulates. This insolent black man has found certain keys to the system and used them to help his people. How terrifying! How dare a black man use white political strategy without permission, without checking, without going through the laborious steps?"

"Guilty," the black man answers from the stream that engulfs his future and the future of the ghetto. He has used language that is offensive while engaged in encounter. "Guilty," the black man acknowledges. There. The black man's guilt is out in the open, he has confessed to the sins of manipulation, words, and human frailties.

What now, white world, white man? Dare you confess your guilt of manipulating 22 million black people into the slums, destroying black manhood by condemning them to the trash heaps of mediocrity by refusing to employ them? Insulting black women by depriving them of husbands and sons who are driven to crime, dope? Dare you confess that in all of your synods you have fewer than 17 black clergymen? Have you looked at your pews lately and observed that they are white as the driven snow?

"Let him drown. You see, white world, how he speaks, how he talks, how he insults, how he upsets. Get rid of him. Back to the ghetto with him, let him go. If we keep him, our churches will refuse to give more money to the Synod. We can then build more stately white mansions while black babies are starving, and black youths are preparing to burn down our cities. We misnamed this program when we called it 'priority.' "

Oh, gentle Jesus, it is the Church, your church, that speaks in that manner, and the institutions of learning that were constructed in your name. The black man, hurt, confused, disillusioned, now looks longingly back to the ghetto. The ghetto beckons fondly. In that setting, screams need not be contained, and the whacking at the walls of racism would be accepted as legitimate actions from people frenzied with the passion of survival—and violence.

Should he return to his people? No. White world, stupid white world, ready or not, here I come again. I must come back again, screaming, yelling, filling your halls, your churches, and your classrooms with the rage of my black brothers and sisters.

Why?

I have discovered your hidden humanity. God does exist. He is not dead; you have shown Him to me. I refuse to give up until you can find Him in me.

*   *   *   *   *

After the termination of the Urban Crisis Center concept by the Ohio Synod, I was asked and I consented to remain for one more school term to teach black history and black theology at Hamma. After that, I decided to reenter the urban arena and use the Encounter approach full-time in the secular world. I opened up an office in Dayton, Ohio, and thus was born the Urban Crisis Center, Inc.

CHAPTER 28

Military Encounter

WITHIN THE ARMED FORCES BLACKS HAVE always had difficulties. After spending a total of ten years in the armed forces (Navy, Air Force, Army), I knew of the stresses of being a part of the nation's fighting forces, supposedly safeguarding democracy, and still being a second-class citizen. I remember well the year 1948, when President Truman signed the executive order integrating the services. Blacks would no longer serve as a separate, segregated part. We were to be fully integrated into all areas and bases, companies, divisions, on shore or on ships. As one of the early participants in desegregating the services, I witnessed many of the initial incidents in the Air Force in 1948 that could have led to violence. It had been predicted, in fact, by then General Eisenhower, who testified opposing integration, that violence within the services would result. Cooler heads prevailed, men checked their prejudice and their racial passions, and armed forces integration was accomplished without a hitch.

However, the outbreak of urban disorders in the midsixties, in a large measure, kindled the bitterness that was latent in the black breast. The disciplined life of the military is able to curtail many personal habits, desires, and needs. But the military could not, in spite of its controls, cut off the rising tide of blacks who demanded their identity. Military commanders could not understand the new blacks entering the services. They were accustomed to the blacks of the 1940s and 1950s, of a time prior to the black revolution. Those were the blacks who fit the mold, who conditioned themselves to traditions and served well, abiding by every order and command. Not so the black youth of the post-Civil Rights era. They had entered the services voluntarily to escape from joblessness and hopelessness. A large share of them came from urban America, and they were recruited into each branch with promises of a better way of life. It was not long before these black youth experienced a kind of racism they had never been exposed to. For one thing, many were having daily contacts with whites for the first time. From a segregated past into an immediately integrated present was a shock to both blacks and whites who came from those insulated backgrounds.

To those in the Navy, aboard ship, the problems of race were even more intense. On long cruises or maneuvers there was no escape from each other. The day-to-day duties and activities, without shore leave, were a frustrating enough way of life. Include the dynamics of race, and an explosive mixture can develop. Thus the Navy, in particular, was extremely vulnerable. Its solid traditions were racist to the core. For decades it had used its black sailors only in the capacity of mess attendants—"stewards' mates," we were called. I served as a steward's mate during World War II. In the late 1940s, when I enlisted in the U.S. Air Force, it was the memory of those dehumanizing Navy days that convinced me to switch branches of service. It was the U.S. Navy that had introduced me to both the insidiousness and overtness of white racism. My boot camp training during the war was at Bainbridge, Maryland, where my dream of being a war hero was shattered by being trained as a mess attendant. I learned how to set tables, pour coffee, serve meals, cook short orders, shine shoes, make up officers' beds, and clean.

After the war, at Virginia Union University in 1946, I met a black man who had also served in the Navy. He was one of the first blacks who received a Naval Commission to become an officer and a gentleman. We attended classes together, played on the basketball team, and joined Kappa Alpha Psi fraternity. Samuel Gravely at that time was an ensign in the Naval Reserve. Reentering the Navy after the war, Gravely steadily climbed up the Navy ladder from commander to captain, and ultimately he became the nation's first black admiral. Other blacks in the Navy did not fare so well. But Samuel Gravely was an exception to the rule, as was General Benjamin Davis in those days, the first black general in the U.S. Army.

Later I was to learn that all "first blacks" become conditioned to racism and do not allow it to intrude upon their missions or goals. To become a "first black," one had to force himself to accept bias as a way of life, to wink at it, blink at it, and become blind if necessary to its dehumanizing methodology. White institutions readily accepted such blacks who could ignore the ravages of color prejudice. Mission orientation became first and foremost, and blacks who became mission conscious and established that as a priority rose rapidly in white institutional ranks.

On the other hand, those young noncommissioned blacks who had enlisted in the Navy in the sixties to escape the ghetto existence refused to adapt to racism. They were the sons of the black revolution. They had entered the Navy from cities that had burned with the fire of protest—Los Angeles, Detroit, Newark, and Chicago. The hot fever of protest had not died in them, and it became stirred up by Naval practices of its traditions. The bell bottom-trousers and the huge collar were throwbacks to two centuries of design that symbolized the rigidity of customs and traditions. Aboard a Naval vessel the Captain was the law: his authority was unquestioned, and on many occasions he set his own rules and regulations on how his men should dress, act, and think. To many whites, such an existence was a natural and normal one; but to blacks unused to a continuous white institutional enslavement, it became exactly that—enslavement. A simple matter such as wearing their hair in the Afro style became the symbol of the revolutionary ideas of blacks in the Navy. To many blacks, the hair shaped in the form of the African past—full, rounded, tall, piled high—was the mark of black identity. As with Samson, it was a black source of strength and pride, a support system for a raped identity. Riots and disorders began to occur throughout Naval commands just over the refusal of blacks to cut their hair. Aboard the *U.S.S. Kitty Hawk,* blacks who rebelled against the Captain's orders to cut their hair were disciplined, court-martialed, and jailed. The word of the *Kitty Hawk* injustice spread. Soon other blacks aboard other ships joined in the protest. The Navy was experiencing revolt in its ranks.

Why the U.S. Navy and its officers could not understand the problem of the need for identity for blacks at that time astounded me. It was so natural for blacks, so unnatural for whites. I began to piece together the reasons. Identity to blacks, particularly blacks of the late 1960s and early 1970s, was a new and relevant issue. The older blacks had fought and struggled for equal rights and opportunities; as a race, we had advanced from "Nigra," to "Colored," to "Negro," to "Black." It was a long journey through that terminology, from slavery to Supreme Court decisions and the Voting Rights Act. It had been a stormy past; but with each acquisition of a right, so long denied, came a new concept of self-worth, a growing dignity, a recognition that this was indeed becoming a land of opportunity. The opportunities were not yet equal, but at least the nation had codified that hope into law, with penalties to be imposed upon those who denied us those rights.

As blacks acquired this new status of identity and self, whites who had never made such a journey into self-concept remained ignorant of both the meaning of identity and its relevance to the new black experience. They had reluctantly accepted the premise of equality of opportunity, but that acceptance, forced by law, blinded them to any other consideration that should be given to blacks. In other words, since whites were born free, with opportunities guaranteed, there was no need to struggle to obtain self-concept, worth, or dignity. It was automatically there, a given right.

I saw immediately that the program of encounter I had developed at Wittenberg University was a vital necessity for the Naval Command. I envisioned that if Navy captains and admirals could be exposed to the two-day program, changes could take place, disorders aboard ship would cease, and. . . .

I picked up the phone and dialed Washington, D.C., and after a half hour of bureaucratic procedures, I was able to speak to Vice Admiral Samuel Gravely. One day later I was seated in his office. Sam was resplendent in his uniform. I marveled at the trappings of power that surrounded him: a white aide, secretary, and receptionist—everything and everybody white. On the walls were his commendations and pictures in color of the ships he had commanded, ranging from tow tubs to U.S. cruisers. His chest was adorned with ribbons, and there were stars on his shoulder boards. Sam had made it to the top, and I was proud. We talked of the old days, our teachers, and the basketball team. I was his guest for lunch at the senior officers' mess in the Pentagon.

I had briefly informed Sam why I wanted to see him; but when I brought up the scope and meaning of my visit, I was surprised to see that he was disturbed.

"We already have a program in place," he informed me. "Besides, I am in charge of Naval Communications; what you are asking is outside of my command function."

Those were not his exact words, but I picked up that meaning. I tried to explain to Sam that the problems the Navy was having stemmed from institutionalized racism. He disagreed. It was the conduct of blacks who refused to conform to Navy traditions. I was appalled. Samuel Gravely, the first black commander of a destroyer, first black captain, first black admiral, was talking to me out of a white perspective. He had assimilated within himself the Navy tradition. For two solid hours I tried to break through Sam's institutionalization to reach and touch his hidden blackness, which had been virtually erased. I insisted that his career had been an exception, while he insisted that any black in the Navy could similarly achieve. I was almost moved to anger, but I realized that I was fighting nearly twenty-five years of white conditioning. I was stripping away his armor, the protective shield that made him move with ease through a world that he thought was oblivious to his race.

I was almost ready to give up and leave when he reached out to me. "What's wrong with me?" he asked. "How do you size me up, and why can't I understand all of this?" It was an honest reaction. After two hours, Samuel Gravely was conceding that he had been out of touch. This handsome, masculine man had buried the consideration of race, fought through the ranks, excelled in his career, reached the top rungs of the ladder—alone. Keeping himself free of race, he had blended, mixed, and congealed his identity right into the hands of those who respected his brains, his dedication, his allegiance to the Navy. The real Samuel Gravely—the black man—had been buried. I poured out to him what I saw in him, what had happened to him, and why. We no longer argued. I explained that he did not have to take up the black cause as a crusade, but that he could, from his strategic position and rank, point me to the right avenues where I could help bring change.

As I knew he could, Sam pulled some strings. The next day I was ushered into the office of Admiral Charles Rauch. I outlined my program of encounter to him and explained how I knew it could solve some of the traumatic racial strife present in the Navy, especially among its top officers who needed sensitivity training. Admiral Rauch was a seasoned career officer. He was pleasant in demeanor but remained deceptively quiet. He depended on a black lieutenant commander, his aide, to do all of the questioning and respond to my presentation.

Rauch's aide was one of those slick, articulate blacks who, like Samuel Gravely, was dedicated to the Navy tradition. He also was on his way up to be a "first black" something or other. We fenced back and forth. He had me understand that programs such as mine had to be presented as a bid to be evaluated with others. In fact, they had just awarded a bid to a minority consulting firm. That firm had more experience than did I, a better track record, plus their program was noncontroversial.

That did it. I exploded in that room. I knew that what I had they needed, that I was not going to give up trying, and that I didn't appreciate being talked to as if I were trying to hustle dollars. The least they could do was try the program. Besides, I added, I didn't come to Washington to be lectured on procedures by a "colored" aide. If Admiral Rauch was in charge of the program for race relations, why was he sitting there allowing a black man to put me and my program down?

It was obvious from the moment I walked in that I was to

be allotted fifteen minutes: five minutes to explain and ten minutes to be tactfully dismissed. I resented that and wanted both of them to know it.

The admiral's face turned red. "And I resent you," he said. The black aide, keeping his cool, asked me to leave. I left my anger in that room.

Back at my hotel, I called Sam. I explained to him what had happened, how I felt, and that if that was the kind of reception the admiral in charge of race relations gave blacks, then I could understand why the Navy was in trouble.

"I tried," Sam told me. "Where do we go from here?" When Sam said "we," he had suddenly become black. He laughed when I informed him of that.

"Let's go right to the top. I would like to see Admiral Zumwalt himself."

Looking back, I can see that Sam Gravely pulled small miracles for me. Whatever he needed from the white institution, he got. Now he was putting his reputation, his career, his blackness on the line for me. That night he was on the phone calling me back. I was to be in Admiral Zumwalt's office at 10 a.m. the next morning.

Zounds!

The next morning I entered the spacious offices of the man who was ignoring Navy traditions and humanizing the service. Admiral Zumwalt had been elevated to the post of Chief of Naval Operations over the heads of more than 200 senior Navy officers. And he made changes, drastic changes. A liberal thinker, a revolutionary operator, he knew and acknowledged the existence of white racism and was doing all he could to eradicate it. I was met by one of his senior aides and told that the admiral had been informed of my treatment the day before. Zumwalt wanted me to know that he would appreciate any new approach I had and that I was to set up a date and he would send two representatives to go through the two-day course. He could think of no two better representatives than the two men I had complained about: Admiral Charles Rauch and his black aide.

Zounds!

I set the date. I knew that if I could convince Admiral Rauch of the effectiveness of my program, I could make a breakthrough into the entire Navy command. I sent letters to members of the Army, Air Force, Navy, and Marine commands located in the Dayton, Ohio area. I informed them of the importance of my expected visitor and asked if they could also attend the two-day session. Since these were lower grade officers, I surmised they would leap at the chance to spend two days with an admiral. They did. The weekend for the black-white encounter arrived. All the participants showed up except for Admiral Rauch and his aide. It had snowed, and their flight from Washington had been canceled. The admiral phoned his regrets, but from the tone of his voice I gathered that he was glad it had snowed. After the session, the following letter was sent to him, signed by representatives of the Army, Navy, Air Force, and Marines. I was no longer alone.

Rear Admiral Charles F. Rauch, Jr.
Department of the Navy
Bureau of Personnel
Washington, D.C. 20370

Dear Admiral Rauch:

We were among the military and other participants in the black/white encounter in which you were to participate this weekend. We regret the weather conditions that prevented your landing in Dayton, and we want to convey to you our hope that you will have an early opportunity to be in a similar session with Charles King.

To describe our experiences over a sixteen-hour period would be difficult, but we stress that it profoundly changed our understanding of the black experience in America and our commitment to changing the system.

We believe that the process and techniques would be invaluable to you and your colleagues. This grows out of both the general thrust of the program and our specific discussion of racial problems in the military.

As a group we are asking Mr. King to contact you again, and we urge you to invite him to set up another session—preferably in Washington—where a number of your top staff could participate with you.

We would be pleased to have you contact any of us by telephone if we could be of assistance to you in assessing the potential value of this program to you.

Sincerely,

LtJG W. L. Williams, United States Navy

James F. Lovejoy, Assistant Education Advisor,
Patrick AFB

Gy. Sgt. Roy C. Laird, United States Marine Corps

Major John R. Edwards, WPAFB Social Action Officer

A few weeks later, Rear Admiral Charles Rauch and his aide responded to that invitation. I was able to assemble a few local citizens to participate. My objective was to convince the admiral that the program worked—that it was much better by far than the current program used by the Navy.

In a small room with about fifteen participants, including a white woman married to a black, the program began. The admiral, typical of a man of his rank, remained aloof and cautious, with an air of objectivity through the early hours. Present in the session was Dr. Wayne Carle, superintendent of the Dayton School System, who had also persuaded Father James Pointer, superintendent of the parochial schools, to complete the Encounter experience. Through Father Pointer I had received a contract to sensitize over 200 Catholic teachers, priests, and nuns to understand the black experience. As Admiral Rauch faced the problem of racism reluctantly, it was Carle who challenged him to become seriously involved in the session, and Carle's reaction to the admiral had a profound effect upon the latter. As the day progressed, I pulled on every sinew, nerve, and emotion within me to convince Admiral Rauch that white racism was the basic cause of the problem, that his attitude and concept of the problem were at variance with truth and reality. Even as the other whites slowly began to get the message, Charles Rauch held out. But finally he came through; and how that came about is a story in itself.

Anna was a handsome, stately white woman who spoke with a heavy Italian accent. During World War II she had fallen in love with an American soldier stationed in Italy. He was a black man. She had met many white American soldiers after V-Day, but she had found that her feelings for the black man surpassed those toward the whites. He asked for her hand in marriage, she consented, and they were married. However, she was not able to accompany him when he was shipped back to the states. Each day he would write her telling of his love and how difficult it was to work through the bureaucratic red tape that would bring her across the seas. What he did not tell her in his letters was that the problem was far more complex than red tape; it was white racism. Anna could not understand why other Italian women who had married white soldiers were able to join their husbands in America while she could not. Her husband's protests against the Army's refusal to allow his wife to join him were loud and profuse. His wife, he wrote to Army officials, was pregnant. Somehow, he was finally able to convey his problem to a higher-up. Anna then received the welcome news that she could sail to her new home in America.

Anna was deeply moved by the sight of the Statue of Liberty and deeply moved by the warm reception she received from her husband's family and friends. Unable to speak English upon her arrival, she slowly picked up enough of the language to observe and understand white reactions and comments when she was with her husband. Her white gynecologist was a warm, sincere man when she first visited him. That was until her husband accompanied her on one of her visits. When her doctor discovered that she was married to a black man, she observed that his warmth disappeared and in its place he deliberately imposed the stoniness of a glacier. He recommended her to another doctor, but her next doctor was no better. She tried to ignore the stares from whites when she was with her husband. But inside a quiet rage developed. She began to hate white Americans, for she knew that the child in her body would be forced to live among them, to be subjected to prejudice, to be discriminated against.

Anna would never forget the day she was rushed to the hospital to be delivered. Her husband drove her there and stood by her bed comforting her. She noticed the coldness of the nurses, how they spoke to him as if he were something less than human, all because she was white and he black.

As Anna told her story, I noticed that Admiral Rauch had become intensely involved in it. He leaned forward in his chair. Tears began to build in Anna's eyes as she brought her story to its bitter end.

"My son was born that night," she said. "I saw him; he was alive and kicking. I held him in my arms. They took him away, alive and warm. I went to sleep that night, feeling that all was well. . . ."

At this point Anna stood up, her facial expression having turned from soft sorrow to hardened rage.

"They killed my baby," she screamed, "they killed my baby." She walked briskly over to where Admiral Rauch was seated and in a burst of outrage she shouted in his face, "Don't tell me that you don't believe that interracial marriages matter, that it is not a problem. They killed my baby because I am a white woman and my husband is a black man."

Before she had begun her story, Admiral Rauch had voiced his disbelief at what I had said to him earlier—that white sexual hang-ups on race were a basic cause for their rejection of blacks. I had stated that their fear of black males mating with white women was a predominant reason behind white racist behavioral patterns.

"Nonsense," he had replied. It was at that point that Anna began to tell her story. Charles Rauch was transfixed as Anna's story concluded.

"The next morning, I asked to see my baby," she choked, "and it was then that they told me my baby had died during the night. They killed my baby. . . . killed him and told me he died."

Toni Weaver, my assistant, took Anna's hand and comforted her. All the whites in the group stared at the floor, in shame, at the horrible implication of what Anna had alleged. Admiral Rauch slowly rose, went over to Anna and took her hand to comfort her. She snatched her hand away from him. He returned to his seat and sat down, wiping tears from his eyes.

From that moment his skepticism disappeared, and at the end of the two days I knew that he had been touched, that he was well aware of white racism and the black experience.

"You'll be hearing from me soon," he promised. "These are two days that I shall never forget."

As he left, I dared to risk a question. "Admiral," I asked, "how does this program compare to the one the Navy is now using?" His reply to that question was prompt and almost committed: "It's like comparing a Chevrolet to a Cadillac," he said without a smile, "and yours is the Cadillac."

CHAPTER 29

The Kiss

BACK IN WASHINGTON, THE ADMIRAL MOVED swiftly. In a matter of mere weeks, I was sent on a "sole source" contract. The contract called for me to train twenty-four civilian and military race relations facilitators. They were to be sent to Dayton for eight weeks of training. I greeted each one as he or she arrived at the hotel where the training would take place. They came in pairs—one black, one white. They were to learn my methodology as teams, and if the method was transferable, the Navy would adopt the Urban Crisis concept throughout its entire command. The potential rewards of accomplishing that objective staggered my mind. I knew I had performed with the method, and I knew I could teach them how.

Most of the trainees did not share my optimism. In fact, some of the facilitators had been sent against their will. Others had never been trained or assigned duties in the area of race relations. When I learned this, I was appalled. I had been told that the class would be composed of skilled facilitators who had volunteered for the course. Noting some initial resentment, I began to doubt my ability to transfer the method to them. But the training began.

It was not until after the first week that enthusiasm began to wax. After putting the class through the oppressive stage, I began to see results. One by one, the participants gleaned insights into my method of exposing and diminishing white racism. The blacks in the class—almost one-half—became blacker and more certain of their identity as the weeks rolled by. We grew close, the blacks and I. We would hold all-night

281

sessions, far beyond the eight-hour class day, as they practiced on their white counterparts and on each other. The whites, once they were rid of their own racism, hang-ups, and fears, joined in with the blacks until all of us were speaking a common language—a language that would help us understand the nature of white institutions and learn how to challenge and change white attitudes. By the end of the fifth week, we were inseparable. We had become a family. Our class had become an example to me of what this nation could become if racism would be acknowledged and understood.

Each week a dignitary would come from Washington, D.C. to examine the class's progress. He witnessed twenty-four persons—black, white, and two Hispanics—interlocked into an inseparable bond of friendship that was unshakable. After each visitor left, we laughed at him. We laughed at the racism, the foolish questions, the pep talks. The visitors felt uneasy; somehow they picked up the fact that our group was unusual. The communication was honest and the challenges articulate, free from the diplomatic jargon traditionally imposed by the hypocrisy of racial adjustments.

It is important to note at this time that the initial purpose of the training of the twenty-four naval officers, enlisted and civilian personnel, was to compare our human awareness program with the existing program design of racial awareness (RAF) that the Navy was currently using as a mandatory twenty-hour course. Our contract specified this, laying out in minute detail the manner in which the comparison should be made and evaluated. The Urban Crisis program was to be videotaped at Charleston, South Carolina, and a team of facilitators was to simultaneously conduct a twenty-hour course that would also be videotaped. Comparisons were to be made by the team of evaluators, and they would determine which method produced the better results. Letters had been sent to various corporations, schools, police officials, and businesses who had used the Urban Crisis program in the last four years. These questions were asked: Was the program effective? Did changes take place in their institutions as a result of the Urban Crisis program? Would they recommend the program to the Navy?

There are on file affirmative letters from the respondents indicating detailed and philosophical agreement from officials throughout the country who have recommended the Urban Crisis technique and the changes that took place as a consequence of the program. Copies of a few of those letters were sent by the writers to the Urban Crisis office. A number of Navy bases were asked to submit similar documentation of changes that had taken place in those installations as a result of the existing racial program(s) conducted by the Navy.

The next step was for our teams to conduct the first twenty-hour course on the Charleston base. Three teams trained by Urban Crisis were to conduct twenty hours each so that the evaluators could ascertain whether or not Urban Crisis had transmitted to them the skills and techniques of an already acknowledged effective design. I was to conduct an initial two-day seminar with my assistant, Toni Weaver. After that, two of my teams were to conduct monitored seminars to determine whether I had successfully taught them the method. Once this information, tapes, etc., were evaluated, the evaluation team was to submit a report and recommendation no later than December 7, 1973.

At the end of the seventh week in Dayton we were ready for Charleston. At the Charleston Naval Base we were to be met by a team of naval psychologists and psychiatrists and a specially chosen board of examiners. I was to choose the first team of facilitators to conduct an encounter program, and the board was to choose another team from the remaining twenty-two people. Both teams were then to be given a class of twenty participants, and simultaneously, under television monitoring, they were to demonstrate whether they could duplicate my ability to confront and change white attitudes.

The first day on the base, we ate, sang, and gave testimonials concerning what those seven weeks had meant. I was nervous: this was to be the Super Bowl and I had to choose the first team. I felt like a coach who had to pick a starting lineup from a team of all-Americans.

One team was composed of a black woman, Geneva

Curry, GS-12, and a white male assistant, Dr. Bud Trimble (a clinical psychologist), both from the Washington office of civilian personnel. Another team consisted of a black chief petty officer, Frances Antoine, and a white woman, Diane Barbera, a civilian transportation specialist, both stationed at Warminster, Pennsylvania.

The first team of leaders, Curry and Trimble, was videotaped and observed in action by the Navy evaluators. It was after that first eight hours that the evaluators and all of us realized that the training had been successful, that that team was able to effect attitudinal change, and that the Urban Crisis technique was effective and transferable. That was the one vital proof that the entire pilot project was aimed toward. The second team, not videotaped, was also successful in producing racial understanding and attitudinal change, according to questionnaires.

It is difficult to describe the elation and joy expressed among all of the trained facilitators and the evaluators once it was observed that the method was transferable. Most facilitators knew that it was a result of the first two weeks of the course in Dayton. In Dayton, Geneva Curry had accomplished the same results with students and teachers from a white high school. We knew it could be done. Further certification of the method was also documented to the facilitators by two other members of the Urban Crisis staff, Dr. C. T. Vivian, well-known civil rights leader and former strategist and companion of Dr. Martin Luther King, and Mark Thomas, a black theological student from Hamma School of Theology in Springfield. The Navy trainees had studied hard to master the method; in fact, the classes, scheduled in Dayton for five days a week, had actually been prolonged by their own requests and enthusiasm to a full seven days a week during the three-week period.

The two training teams were to return the next day to complete the two-day course. But something happened that caused the elation to turn to bitter disappointment and despair.

*   *   *   *   *

Toni Weaver is a beautiful woman, inside and out. She is married to a professional photographer, Larry, and they are the parents of four children. When I established the Urban Crisis Center in Dayton, Ohio, it was Toni who volunteered to assist me as a full-time administrator. Her interest in eradicating white racism stemmed from her first exposure to one of my seminars. From that day forward—even to the present—she has dedicated her life to that end. As an administrator without salary, she spent her hours in those early days ensuring that the Urban Crisis Center would succeed. In addition to the administrative duties, she traveled with me, serving as a facilitator to church groups who requested seminars. Her keen insights, personality, and expertise in group dynamics were of immeasurable value to me and to the program. When I received the contract from the Navy, it was Toni who attended to every administrative detail. And as a member of the Urban Crisis staff, she participated in training the twenty-four naval students.

Toni Weaver is a white woman. In our travels, we would be the subject of stares—some hostile, others bewildered. The sight of a fat black man and a shapely white woman was one that bigots loathed, conservatives were disturbed by, and liberals questioned. We laughed at them all and had fun analyzing what each kind of stare meant and what each kind of person must be thinking.

Toni sat beside me on that first day in Charleston as she had for scores of other seminars. She was magnificent. As all of our students watched us via the television monitor, we were on target. Attitudes, as always, began to change. But one white man in particular refused to participate at all. I thought I knew why.

"Why?" I asked him.

Silence.

"Is it because you don't like Toni and me working together?"

"No."

His "no" did not ring true, and we both knew about his racist hang-up: white woman, black man. On other occasions when that hang-up surfaced and was denied, Toni and I would publicly embrace and kiss—a long, lingering kiss. Then we would ask the group what feelings they had when we kissed. The answers ranged from "no comment" to "disturbed" to "angry" to "nothing." Toni would then discuss with the group the foolishness of being disturbed by the embrace of two people, neither of them known to anyone in the group, merely because she was white and he black. It was our way of revealing one of the foolish symptoms of white racism.

The purpose of this part of the program is to develop an awareness on the part of both blacks and whites that the underlying problem between the races is based on the emotional levels of fear in the white majority and anger in the black minority. The "kiss" serves to catalyze the emotional response. Gunnar Myrdal, a Swedish scholar who conducted an exhaustive study of the black-white problem in America, found that at the top of the list of white fears of blacks in the society was one fear that could simply be labeled "sex." What that means is illustrated below.

Many whites in an Encounter session, of course, argue against that conclusion, and several will declare that the study has no validity for them because they do not have that number-one fear. And they argue their points vociferously. The "kiss" is used to refute those denials and reveal to them their subconscious prejudices. After the black man and white woman have kissed, they ask the person who has denied prejudice: "How did that make you feel?" It is at that point that most participants will recognize, whether they acknowledge it or not, that they resent black-white sexual contact and that they indeed have a hang-up on the subject.

This is the only purpose of the "kiss." The program does not advocate black-white sexual relationships or interracial marriages; for, as the course teaches, those are individual matters between two consenting adults, and none of us has the right to approve or disapprove what is normal and natural to the human race. The leaders then show that it is only the color of the persons kissing that causes that emotional reaction; for if a white man kisses a white woman in a class to illustrate a point, the action is met with laughter, sly remarks perhaps, pleasure, and humor. Whereas when a black man does it, the group's resentment, frustration, and anger are clearly observable.

This, then, is the subtle essence of the racial problem. This underlying fear establishes a barrier that, when crossed by blacks, brings down upon them many forms of punishment devastatingly applied. White women are taught to be fearful of black men, to avoid them. Myths are created and stereotypes expanded to such a degree that when blacks and whites are together in social contact, the fears arise and the myths are remembered, and the cultural "violation" of ethnocentric behavior is magnified out of proportion.

The "kiss," when it is correctly applied and when the full intention and explanations of the varying reactions are noted, is a tremendous training instrument. It helps all participants understand themselves and other people. It raises the question of whether or not black men can be accepted as men equal to white men. It presses the issue of whether white women have the opportunity to exercise their rights of choice and companionship, because the "kiss" displays the oppressive nature of sexism where males feel obligated to protect white women. It makes blacks in the group aware of the hypocrisy of whites who declare that they have no prejudice, yet are bothered by the "kiss." It explains to all why white America allows racial inequities to continue: for a white to take up the black man's cause would subject him to the rejection of his peers; and when he continues to argue in defense of his progressive opinions, he is met and stopped cold with one question, "Would you want your daughter to marry one?" That is the question that stops him because with it he must face his deepest prejudice—the barrier of sex.

The "kiss" opens up these insights into the nature of the inner white man heretofore unknown or unrevealed. It is a magic moment for many whites because it helps them understand the devastating effect their fears and resentments have on the dignity of the black race as well as their own freedom. They begin to understand why over 12,000 blacks in America have been lynched for the rape, or alleged rape, of white women;

why black men on death row for that crime have always out-numbered white men by about five times. It brings home the miserable, damnable fact that of all the men executed for the crime of rape, no black man has ever been sentenced to death for raping a black woman, and no white man has ever been sentenced to death—or even received a life sentence—for rap-ing a black woman.

The "kiss" also develops new insights into the cause of women's liberation. It exposes the oppressive white male who has always practiced segregation in the streets while slipping down into the ghetto at night to pay for integration between the sheets. He denies to himself and the woman he feels compelled to protect that he operates freely on both levels, while denying to her, and to black men and women, the same full expressions of their personages.

Of course, the "kiss" is not always a necessary part of the Encounter program. It can, and often does, go unused. The Encounter leaders are fully aware of the initial reactions it pro-duces, and at times—according to the attitudes of some partici-pants with hard-closed minds—it is not the best technique to be used. The reason it is not used at those times is because of the deep feeling and hope that somehow those persons can be reached before they are driven away. If they have shown a deep-seated view of blacks as subhuman, the exhibition of the "kiss" will do nothing more than fire the inner violence that erupts into subtle everyday practices and statements.

On the occasion in Charleston, Toni and I kissed in an ef-fort to draw out the one reluctant participant. As usual, Toni discussed latent attitudes and their effects, and the group understood. We moved on to another part of the session.

But it proved to be a deadly kiss. The commanding admiral of Charleston Naval Base, Rear Admiral Graham Tahler, was told of the "kiss" by his secretary after our initial seminar. He was furious. He said that the program could not go on after the training teams' first day. And despite explanations and pleas from the board of evaluators of the program, he responded with a resounding "no." "No black man is going to kiss a white woman in my command" were his exact words to the board. We were, in essence, ordered off the base. The program was stopped.

Admiral Tahler's statement, "No black man is going to kiss a white woman in my command," became the kiss of death to a program that was already producing change in attitudes in the Navy. He spoke not as a single admiral but out of the sickness of inherited white racism. By stopping the program, he destroyed for over ninety persons within his command the full dimensions of human growth and potential. He killed our dreams by shouting out of his own nightmares.

It is extremely difficult to forgive him for this, but ultimately I believe I shall. For it is only by understanding him, the culture, and the nature of white racism that any of us shall ever understand the death of the black race that is implicit within those words: "No black man is going to kiss a white woman in my command." He never will understand that with that remark he stole from Toni Weaver—mother of four children, wife of a devoted husband, humanitarian, fighter for human rights—her birthright as a person and the shaper of her own destiny. By her own understanding of the lessons involved, the kiss became her own expression, her contribution to make her race aware of its racism. Thousands of witnesses who have experienced the program have acknowledged to us that that one illustration has set them free from inner fears and bewilderment over the problem of race.

* * * * *

I was certain that an appeal to Admiral Kidd in Washington would be heard. So I made a midnight call. A sleepy Admiral Kidd informed us that it would be best if we left the base.

"We don't want to make this program controversial," he told us. He said that he would get in touch with Admiral Zumwalt and inform him what had happened.

What do we do? The group decided to fight back, refuse to leave the base, hold a press conference, and expose Admiral Tahler.

"Let's go down swinging!" Larry Law said, and most of the trainers agreed. But I dissented. I was fearful that the whole program would be lost in the swirls of controversy.

Admiral Kidd called back. The twenty-four trainees were to all go back to their home bases, but the entire group would be able to reassemble and continue the program at the Philadelphia Naval Base within thirty days.

"It's a trick!" one said.

"We'll never get together again."

"No, no, no, no!"

I convinced them that I thought the admiral's way was best. I urged them to return to their home bases and wait; and if nothing happened within thirty days, I would raise holy hell around the nation. The farewells were teary. The family was breaking up.

*   *   *   *   *

Larry Law was one of the white enlisted men sent to Dayton by the Navy for the eight-week course. As a chief petty officer and Southerner, Larry's background made him an unusual student in the course. Initially, I found it extremely difficult to relate to him; so did the other blacks. He was strictly Navy, by the book, and the rigidity of his personality gave him an air of insensitivity. But as the weeks went by, it was Larry who gave me, out of his own thinking, the inner thoughts of white males in regard to race and sex. It was as if the course had purged his soul. To him, the trip to Charleston Naval Base was almost a religious crusade. He and his black co-trainer Cheesman, stationed at the same naval base in California, were fully prepared and ready to exhibit their ability to change white attitudes. They were never given a chance.

The "kiss incident" completely shook Larry up. The nature and feeling of the white male were well known to him. Somehow the "kiss" had plunged us all into the depths of despair. After we were ordered off the Charleston Naval Base, all the trainees anxiously awaited word from me as to what action they should take to implore their commanders that a tragic mistake had been made and that the program should not be curtailed. During that interim period Larry called me. He was furious. Upon his return, he had been ordered to make a report of his training. He was ordered to appear before a committee to explain the program *without Cheesman*. What the Navy did not know was that it was a different Larry Law they were dealing with. His letter to me and his report of that meeting (printed below) were very incisive, as he plunged head-on into the attitudes of his white brothers.

> Dr. King,
>
> As you remember, I called you on the evening of 8 December in Dayton, to ask your permission for Mr. Cheesman and I to jointly answer questions about the program!
>
> Well, Mr. Cheesman was not allowed to join me in that meeting! I was ordered to carry it out by myself!
>
> I was interrogated for six hours about the program.
>
> I want you to know what did happen. Please read the handwritten opening and handwritten closing statements very closely.
>
> My CO was given this same folder on 10 December. I have heard *no* feedback and cannot gain any insight into their thinking or feelings on the subject.
>
> This may be of help to you!
>
> God speed,
> Larry

Larry Law's statement:

Please consider what is happening here!

Here I sit, a military man of 18 years. You want my views, my impressions of a joint military-civilian, black-white training program.

You five Master Chiefs are military men with combined military service of close to or over 100 years. And you will make a judgment and recommendation to the Captain based on what you hear, see, and feel in this room this morning.

Can you see yet?

1. My views: Are views of a *white military man!*
2. My opinions: Are opinions of a *white military man!*
3. Your questions: Are questions of *white military men!*
4. My answers: Are the answers of a *white military man!*
5. Your judgments: Are the judgments of *white military men!*
6. Your recommendations: Are the recommendations of *white military men!*

7. Our Captain: Who will receive your recommendations, based on your judgments from my answers to your questions to gain my views and my opinions, is a *white military man!*

This program is a joint military-civilian program. This command sent *two men* to this training to be trained as and operate as a *team*. A two-man, military-civilian, black-white team!

My teammate and I were informed that he *could not* attend this meeting! I asked if my department head, Mr. Lionel Serating, could attend. I got the same answer. I asked if Chaplain Smeland and/or a medical officer could attend; again the answer was *No!*

Captain Young stated that if I knew of any discrimination at this command, he wanted to know about it.

Look around you!

Where are the civilians?

Where are the blacks?

Where are the women?

Where are the other minorities?

Where is my team partner?

This meeting, this investigation, this interrogation—this is the black experience! This is what it means to be black! This is how you go about making a white man into a black boy!

This morning is discrimination against Mr. Cheesman, myself, and the program. It also discriminates against the civilian work force of this command. Yes, and all the blacks of this command, both military and civilian. All the women of this command! And all the other minorities of this command!

Yes, there is discrimination at NWS Yorktown, Va. We, all of us, myself included, have proven that here today. It sickens me that I allowed myself to be a part of it!

This meeting has been with the wrong people! More important, the questions have been addressed to the wrong person! Mr. Cheesman is the trained team leader, the facilitator. I, "Chief Law," am an analyst. I am to assist Mr. Cheesman. Again, a black man is suffering a loss of personal dignity!

Do you want my recommendation? If you really want this command, this Captain to really know what this training is all about and what it can really do, you will use your influence to persuade Captain Young to go to Dayton, Ohio, to the Urban Crisis Center at #4 West Third Street. The institute is holding Seminars for CO's and high-ranking civilians of Navy bases on the 7th of Jan., 4th of Feb., and 4th of March.

Again, I take full responsibility for this statement and I stand accountable for it!

Larry D. Law, GMMC

We continued to wait. The thirty days passed, and nothing happened. Had we indeed been tricked?

CHAPTER 30

To the Top of the Command

I DECIDED TO ACT. IT WAS OBVIOUS TO ME THAT I
had been conned. Admiral Zumwalt had given me his
word, but my respect for his forthright approach to race relations was becoming diluted. I knew that the liberal politics and
actions of the admiral had already rubbed the Armed Forces
Committee the wrong way. However, my zeal for continuing
the project and the knowledge that the personnel I had trained
were being subjected to severe inquisitions spurred me on. I
knew that the "kissing incident" was newsworthy. Up to that
point I had held my peace, even though my silence and lack of
protestation was a drain on my pride. The promise that the
success of the pilot project could lead to a lucrative contract also
pricked my conscience, while I held my tongue. No more.

Checking into the Washington Biltmore Hotel, I strate-
gized my approach. I prepared a press release that explained
what had happened to me, and how the Navy was sacrificing a
successful race relations program, merely to appease Admiral
Graham Tahler.

In retrospect, I can now see that this issue to the Navy was
more than an offense to an admiral; it was reintroducing controversy into the already shaky and highly criticized liberal
policies of Admiral Zumwalt. On this issue the Navy needed
breathing room; the leadership was already short of breath,
and I was threatening to cut off their wind entirely.

I called the *Washington Post* and informed the city desk that
I was scheduling a press conference for 10 a.m. the next day.
"What about?" they asked. The Navy had cancelled my con-
tract, and the reason for the cancellation would be given at the

conference. I also called the *Washington Star*. I received non-committal responses from both papers. I sat down to think of another approach. The approach I decided on was to contact the Secretary of the Navy, John Warner. Perhaps if his office knew of my attempt to protest, they would make a decision in favor of continuing the program. I called. "There is no way for you to see the Secretary of the Navy," I was told by his administrative assistant, "but if you would put your reasons in writing . . . I will see that Secretary Warner gets it." Thanks, but no thanks.

I called Bud Trimble, a clinical psychologist; Bud had been a member of the pilot project. Bud and the twenty-three other Navy personnel had informed me that if ever the time came for me to challenge the "kissing incident," they would back up whatever decision I would make. I outlined to Bud my strategy. The bottom line was for the Secretary of the Navy to order the program to continue, or I would publicize the fact that we were ordered off the Charleston Naval Base as a result of the "kiss."

"I think I know how I can get Warner to move," Bud informed me. How? It turned out that Bud and Senator Mark Hatfield, both born-again Christians, were close friends. Bud picked me up at the hotel, and we were on our way to Hatfield's office. The Senate was in session, but Senator Hatfield came hurriedly into his office. Bud outlined to him the entire problem in five minutes. The Senator was magnanimous; he assured me that he would make it possible for me to see the Secretary of the Navy. He advised me against holding a press conference, that such a move would not do me any good, nor would it be good for the Navy. He added further that, if my race relations program was as good as he was led to believe it was, I owed it to the Navy to save it from controversy.

I informed Senator Hatfield that what he advised me to do to save the program was exactly what Admiral Zumwalt, Admiral Kidd, and Admiral Rauch had told me. It was my honest conviction, I told him, that the admirals were responding to political pressure, and that they had written off the program entirely. The Senator understood my frustration but asked me to please trust him. At that moment, I had not considered the fact that I had worked a minor miracle. Here I was, on my first day in Washington, in the office of a U.S. Senator, who was promising me an audience with the Secretary of the Navy on that very same day. Through Bud's connections, I had bypassed aides, telephone calls, letters, and appointment calendars. The entire Washington bureaucracy had been circumvented—all because a black man was ready to reveal what had happened to him because he had kissed a white woman. A U.S. Senator, ignoring the flashing red light that was summoning him back to the Senate floor for a roll call vote, was imploring me not to tell. I felt a headiness that almost redeemed my lost pride when I was ordered off the Charleston Naval Base.

It was with that heady feeling that I went back to my hotel room. There, I was promised by Senator Hatfield, I would be contacted by the Secretary of the Navy. Back in my room I knew the U.S. Navy was frightened by me: I had placed them in a vulnerable spot. I called the reporter from the wire services whom I had earlier informed of my press conference. Unlike those at the *Washington Post* and the *Washington Star*, he stated that although he would not be able to make the conference, if I would give him the story over the phone he would use it the next day. Foolishly I saw in hindsight I had told him the entire story before I had met with Senator Hatfield. He had pointedly asked me to notify him in the event that my attempts to meet with officials before my press conference were successful. Would I do that? I promised him that I would.

I called him to say that I was to meet with the Secretary of the Navy, a meeting arranged by Senator Hatfield. He laughed. "How did you accomplish that?"

"They were evidently afraid of the story," I informed him. He agreed. It was quite a story, and he hoped I would still hold the press conference; as a matter of fact, he wanted to come over to the hotel and talk with me. I refused, but told him that he would be the first to know what the results of the meeting were. He promised to keep in touch.

The phone rang; it was Admiral Kidd. A chauffeur was on

his way (8:30 p.m.) to pick me up. The Secretary of the Navy had agreed to meet with me; but prior to meeting with the Secretary, Admiral Kidd wondered if I would go over with him first what I intended to discuss with Secretary John Warner. It might well be that the entire issue could be resolved by him to the satisfaction of everybody. This was going to be an attempt to compromise, I thought; and I was right. In fact, it was more than a compromise.

"Secretary Warner believes this matter can be best handled by my office," Admiral Kidd said smilingly when I appeared.

"But I was promised an appointment with him; I want that appointment."

"Dr. King, your program is one of the best we have found. I would like to suggest a way in which you can continue to work with us."

"But what about the people I have trained; will they be able to use my program?"

"That's the problem," the admiral sighed. "That's going to be extremely difficult at this time."

"Why?"

The admiral stood up. He was pained by my question and hurt by its implication. On the wall behind him was a huge oil painting of his father, the Pearl Harbor admiral at the time of the assault by the Japanese. The gold braids, stars, ribbons— all traditions were to be upheld. Standing now in the office of his son was a black man who was threatening those traditions. I had struck a vital weakness of institutional racism: the male ego, the foundation and emotional cause of prejudice. I had trained twenty-eight Navy and civilian personnel how to challenge those prejudices, to challenge without compromise, and to win in the process. Those men and women were depending on me to fight for their rights to implement that training, to bring the program into the Navy.

Admiral Kidd was very nervous. His black aide, civilian Nathaniel Stinson, who had convinced Kidd to back the program, was also in the room. However, he remained silent; he had a disturbed, frustrated anger on his face. It was obvious to me that communication between Kidd and him had broken down. I soon found out why.

Kidd turned to Stinson and asked, "Did you relay my decision to Dr. King?"

"No, sir," Stinson replied.

"Why didn't you do like I asked?"

"I didn't because I didn't think it was right."

The air in Kidd's office was electric with Stinson's last remark. His tone was defiant—compellingly, unmistakably, resonantly defiant. To me, Stinson had always seemed the cautious, pleasing black, seldom upset. It was he who had convinced me to trust his immediate supervisor, Admiral Kidd, to stand by the pilot project in spite of the kissing incident. Stinson had been proud of the admiral's attitude toward blacks and minorities, and he had relayed to me the admiral's admiration for my work and the fact that he had already passed on to the Navy Command his endorsement. But here and now, in this room, not only was Kidd backing away from the program, but he had evidently attempted to get Nathaniel Stinson to pull me away from a showdown. Later Stinson told me about the political forces that were at play, but I was initially bewildered at what it was that he had refused to convey to me.

"What was he to tell me?" I asked Kidd, to take Stinson off the hot seat.

Kidd and Stinson glared at each other; it was as if I weren't in the room. Admiral Kidd came slowly from behind his desk, went to a window, and looked out into the night, his hands clasped behind his back. I looked at Stinson, and he gave me a silent message to keep the admiral on the hook.

"If Nat had given you certain information, perhaps we could have called off this meeting."

"Why should we call it off, Admiral?"

"Because it would be greatly beneficial to you," Kidd said quietly.

A bribe? Could this be a bribe? I was way ahead of the admiral: the way he said "beneficial" alerted me that I was to be tendered an offer that I "dare not refuse." I looked back at Stinson, who now held his head down, looking at his shoes. It was an embarrassing moment. Whatever pressure had been placed on Kidd must have been tremendous. He strained out his next words, still looking out the window.

"Dr. King, you have a unique program, a unique talent, and the Navy doesn't want to lose you or your program. We have a concern, an honest concern—at least others have—that what you do can only be done by you."

"That's not true," I interrupted him. "Sir, that's what the pilot project was supposed to prove, and we did prove that: every psychologist and examining board assigned to this project came to that conclusion before we left Charleston. . . ."

"I know, I know, but we cannot use the people you trained," Kidd said wearily.

"Why, Sir, why?" I shouted.

"May I be excused, Sir?" Stinson asked when I shouted out.

Kidd did not respond to Stinson, and he did not respond to my "why." He began with a delicate approach.

"How large is your center in Dayton?"

"I work out of hotels," I told him. "I don't have a space large enough to hold thirty people at my office."

"How would you like to expand, lease a large training space so that your work could expand?"

"I would like that; it's one of my hopes."

"I think, Dr. King, that that dream can be realized," Kidd's voice became stronger, more convincing. I had bit on the bait. "I'll see to it that the people under my command will continue to receive training under you."

The implication of what Kidd was offering was far greater than I had ever imagined. Stinson quietly went out the door and *slammed* it shut.

"Great, that would really be something," I answered.

"I want you to get with Nathaniel, and we'll work out the particulars."

"Fine," I said. I looked at the clock on his wall. It was 10:00 p.m. I became anxious.

"What time am I supposed to meet with Secretary Warner?"

"Oh," said the admiral, "he's waiting for me to call him. It might well be that we have settled the matter."

"Settled the matter? Nothing has been settled until the pilot project is complete. . . ."

Then I caught on. Damn! I had been tricked. It now became clear to me what had made Stinson angry. Kidd had evidently asked Nat to inform me that if I would drop the "kissing" matter, they would give me Navy personnel to train in Dayton on a continuous basis. I could make a lot of money and expand my operation. The deal would be to forget about the pilot project, forget about the twenty-four people I had trained, and forget about the U.S. Navy using my technique within the service. It would be best for all concerned if I would leave Washington quietly, fold up my tent, and silently steal away. Warner had obviously attempted to have me stopped cold in Admiral Kidd's office. He did not want to see me. In fact, at that very moment he was waiting in his office to receive the necessary word that I had been paid off and, most importantly, that there would be no press conference.

The implications of what was going on left me dumb. No wonder Nat Stinson had left the room: he did not want to be a witness to what the admiral was going to ask of me. Nat had fought hard to keep his commitment to me, and to keep the twenty-four military and civilian trainers alive. Time and time again he had bucked red tape to speed up the training process, travel vouchers, paychecks. He had made numerous trips between Washington and Dayton, serving as liaison between the top brass and ourselves. It was Stinson who kept up our spirits after Charleston. It was he who convinced us that the "kissing incident" would pass and that the Navy would not leave us in the lurch. Whatever the Secretary of the Navy had ordered the admiral to do, the admiral had told Nathaniel Stinson to do. But Stinson did not have the heart to make such an approach to me. He conveniently forgot the assignment, and the admiral himself was left with that task.

"Admiral," I asked softly, "am I to understand that this expansion of my work will replace the project? That the twenty-four people will not be used by the Navy?"

"Yes, that's what I've been trying to make you understand."

"In other words, if I agree to that . . ."

"If you agree to that, the Secretary of the Navy will personally assure you of a prime contract with the Navy—to hold Human Awareness seminars with the supervisors. They will come to Dayton to receive the two-day course . . ."

"What will happen to the twenty-four trainers?"

"They will be used in the same capacity, but not utilizing your technique . . ."

"No soap!" I suddenly felt heroic.

The shame of what was taking place showed plainly in the admiral's face. He was cutting a deal with me. I knew that what he was proposing was inconsistent with his character. The pressures were on him as an institutional robot, and he was following orders. I knew that he knew the offer would be thought of as a bribe—because it was a bribe. There was no way of calling it anything else but that. Outside the door, Stinson knew it. The Secretary of the Navy knew it.

My "no soap" was not altogether a response of integrity. I flirted with the temptation to yield to the huge dollar signs that I began to see. I had even rationalized in my mind that this might be a better deal: I could get hundreds, even thousands of supervisors. But each time I thought of those twenty-four people who had become almost as close as family, I could not go on flirting with the bribe. They *were* family. They were waiting to hear from me, believing in me, and knowing that I would not give up. That's where the "no soap" response came from.

The admiral picked up the phone. It was 11:00 p.m., December 5, 1973, that I was ushered into the office of John Warner, Secretary of the U.S. Navy.

I was not prepared for what I was to face in the Secretary's office. It was as if I were entering a room where a council of war had been summoned: there were approximately twenty high-ranking Navy officers—captains and admirals—in this room. I was asked to sit outside the room for a few minutes, while Admiral Kidd went in alone to make his report. His mission had failed. For fifteen minutes they must have been devising a backup plan, or a new strategy to confront me with. I was laughing within myself—all this because I had kissed a white woman! Nat Stinson sat beside me. I had insisted to the admiral that he accompany me when I met with the Secretary of the Navy. The admiral asked me why.

"Because I want someone black with me," I explained. What I did not explain was that I wanted Nat with me so that I could remain honest—*and black*. Nat and I sat side by side. He was in high spirits. He was proud of me, and I of him. He had risked a lot.

"You've got them now," he whispered to me mischievously. "Don't let them snowball you in there."

We grinned at each other in mutual appreciation for the moment of truth. I felt the high that comes only when you know that you have all the aces, with only two showing. When summoned, we both walked in; we were the only blacks.

Secretary Warner, erudite, handsome, and suave, greeted me warmly. He appeared pleased to meet me.

". . . heard so many good things about your program." Meet Admiral this and that, Captain so and so, and on he went. After the introductions, he sank back into a deep leather chair, puffed on a pipe, and asked, "What can I do for you?"

The artificiality of the moment was overwhelming. All of the admirals were smiling. They had shaken my hand as if I were a lost but now newly found friend. They were grinning the grins of the pleased, smiling the smile of the contented. Never before, I imagined, had so many top brass assembled together to welcome a black man whom they all knew had kissed a white woman. Admiral Kidd was the only one not smiling. His assignment had been to keep me out of that room; he had failed.

I suddenly realized that I had no pat speech, no thought-through method of presenting my case. On the spur of the moment I decided to use my encounter technique to put them all on the defensive, to take charge, to let them all know, including the Secretary of the Navy, that I was a black man who refused to plead or beg. I was there to demand justice—immediate justice.

I told them that I had been ordered off a naval base by Rear Admiral Graham Tahler. My program had been curtailed, my manhood denied. Twenty-four people had witnessed the dehumanization that white racism imposes. Those twenty-four people, black and white, were fully prepared to wage a war against racism within the Navy. They could be the nucleus for change throughout the Navy. They had faith in the Navy, and what did the Navy do? Slapped them in the face, told them to go back where they came from and forget all they had learned. Those twenty-four people were angry, and rightfully so. I was also angry, outraged, and disgusted that a blatant racist like Admiral Tahler would be allowed to stop a program. He should be relieved of his command. Furthermore, Admiral Zumwalt had promised that the program would continue at the Philadelphia Naval Yard. Somehow, the Secretary of the Navy—or someone—had refused to allow him to keep his word (that information had been given to me by Nat Stinson). All of this had occurred because a black man had kissed a white woman, who, incidentally, was an employee, a staff member of his organization.

By this time all the smiles and grins had disappeared. The only smile in the room was the one on Nat Stinson's face.

"We have been betrayed, lied to, tricked, *and bribed,* and I don't intend to leave Washington until justice prevails."

Secretary Warner, surprisingly, kept his cool. The captains and the admirals were plainly upset by my manner, attitude, and lack of decorum. I intended them to be so, and I gave notice to that fact.

"Right now," I said, glancing at each of them with a hard stare, "all of you are upset with me, angry at me for daring to speak to you this way; and that's the key to understanding your own racism. For I have spoken the truth; it hurts you, but you want us blacks to be nice and quiet, while you kick us.''

"I'm not upset with you," Warner said, quietly puffing on his pipe. "Does that mean that I'm not a racist?"

"No, sir, it does not. You are the kind of white man who stays cool, calm, and collected; you are in control. You have to make a decision. That kind of white evaluates black anger but refuses to let emotions get involved."

"Is that good or bad?" Warner asked me.

"Bad!" I replied. "Any person who puts his emotions on a back burner becomes strictly institutional and has great difficulty feeling empathy or compassion."

Warner's approach seemed to invite other questions from some of the top brass. I answered each question lucidly, calmly, intellectually. The anger was gone. I explained the nature of prejudice, racism, sexuality—and they were hooked. I glanced at Nat. I had done it. He recognized that I had applied the technique of arousing them and then feeding them information from my expertise, to get them to understand.

It was 1:00 a.m. when I left. John Warner promised that I would hear from him soon. He had taken note of all my requests and demands. I felt good, clean, vindicated. And suddenly I felt magnanimous. I had to give back to them some of the dignity I had taken away. Perhaps, just perhaps, the Secretary of the Navy would reinstate the pilot project. It was obvious that he was impressed. All of the anger had gone out of me. Some of the admirals and captains even asked when and where my next seminars would be held, and I passed out cards. I decided not to hold the press conference. I informed the Secretary of the Navy that I would wait to hear from him, and I thanked him for the meeting. The press conference concerning the "kiss," I told him, would not take place. We shook hands all around and I was chauffeured back to my hotel.

In my room the red light was blinking. Messages. The *Washington Star,* the *Washington Post,* U.S. wire services. I had forgotten about them. What to do? I called the reporter from the wire service.

"How did it go?" he asked.

"How did what go?" I inquired.

"Your meeting with the Secretary of the Navy."

"Oh, yeah. Well, O.K."

"Did you get your program back again?"

"Well, in a way. I can't tell yet."

"What about the press conference?"

"It's off."

"Why?"

"I decided not to have it."

"In other words, you made a deal."

The horror of his statement struck home. I had indeed made a deal. I had been charmed by John Warner, flattered by his captains and admirals. I had forgotten temporarily the twenty-four people I had left hanging on a promise. I had indeed been bribed. This time, unlike in Admiral Kidd's approach, it had been more subtle: the change in me had occurred *after* I had expended my anger. Always, at that point, I seek reconciliation. I had become a victim of my own technique. I had given back to the whites "something of value." Indeed, up to that moment I thought I had done well—that I was on top. But reflecting back on what had happened at the Secretary of the Navy's office, all I had given them was what they needed most: time. Time to somehow find a way to get rid of me.

"You made a deal, right?" the reporter repeated.

"Yeah," I replied, "a deal was made, and part of the deal was no press conference. I promised them that."

"What do you get back in return? How much?"

I felt tired, ashamed, and disgusted. I unloaded, told the reporter the entire story. Of course, he knew most of it already. Whatever John Warner was planning for me, for the twenty-four, would go down the drain if the kissing story were told. I knew that, and the reporter knew that.

"It's a good story," he told me, "so I'm going to run it. Okay?"

"Frankly," I told him, "I don't give a damn any more." At least twenty-four people and Nathaniel Stinson would know that I went down swinging at racism.

True to my promise, I did not hold a press conference. I did not have to. Most papers picked up their major stories from the Associated Press wire service:

> Washington (AP)—The Navy has suspended a pilot race relations program, in part because it was decided the emotions of the participants were rubbed too raw to continue.
>
> Accounts vary, but the black civilian organizer of the program says a Navy admiral objected to demonstrations designed to deliberately arouse latent prejudices among both blacks and whites.
>
> Charles H. King, Jr., who heads Urban Crisis Inc. of Dayton, Ohio, said he kissed a white assistant during the training program at the naval base in Charleston, S.C.
>
> The act drew a protest from an irate woman participant, King says, and the Navy suspended the program.
>
> Navy officials say the kissing incident was only part of the objection to King's program, which could have developed into the principal source of race relations officers for the Navy.
>
> A series of major racial incidents aboard Navy ships in recent years, including a full-scale brawl aboard the carrier *Kitty Hawk,* has prompted the Navy into an extensive attempt at race relations training in the fleet.
>
> King, who has trained school teachers, policemen and business executives, said he holds a $27,000 contract to develop a pilot program for the Navy.
>
> He said 24 civilians from a number of Navy bases went through what he described as a "creative racial confrontation." King acknowledges using techniques intended to anger and provoke participants so their deepest racial emotions are stirred.
>
> The kissing incident led to a complaint from a female Navy employe to Rear Adm. Graham Tahler, commandant of the Sixth Naval District.
>
> King said in a telephone interview that Tahler summoned Navy officers working with the program and ordered the training halted immediately even though King had another four days to go in his contract.
>
> Navy officials in Washington say King raised myths about the sexual prowess of blacks and used such strong language, that the Navy is not prepared for King's kind of confrontation, however true to life it may be.
>
> King and the Navy agree his program will get a new examination to see if his methods can be applied. Meanwhile, the 24 persons already trained have returned to their old jobs with no

promise that what they learned will be put to use toward easing race problems in the military.
12-06-73 09:28EST

CHAPTER 31

Encountering Success

S INCE MY INITIAL DISAPPOINTMENTS IN TRYING
to bring the Encounter methodology to the church and
the military, the Urban Crisis Center has gone on to conduct
racial awareness seminars for numerous corporations, cities,
and colleges and universities. Even the military eventually
came through, and I have conducted seminars for the Army,
the Air Force, and individual Navy installations. One note-
worthy seminar was at Redstone Arsenal in the heart of the
South, Huntsville, Alabama, for major scientists and military
personnel under the command of General Vincent Ellis.

Over the past two decades, the pursuit of white racism has
led me through a maze of whites that has established, at least
for me, that white America is susceptible to my message and
potentially changeable. That fact—at first only a hope—distills
my lingering anger and increases my pursuit. It has been a
lonely journey. Few if any blacks have been able to witness
with their own eyes the series of victories that have convinced
me that white individuals, scattered throughout the nation, can
be led to see themselves in unflattering but revealing light.
Changing the attitudes of white people, which I began in the
late 1960s on the campus of Wittenberg University, is now my
full-time occupation. My style and methodology in accomplishing that goal has varied little over the years. The fact that it has
been done, and that it can be done, has become a religious venture, a crusade for a just and equitable future for blacks in
America. True, the years have not shown any massive movement to certify my hope or even to demonstrate that what I
now write is true. This nation's 200 million whites remain vir-

tually untouched by the nation's blacks, physically or emotionally. We are still a people apart, uniting only in those few places that whites have not wanted to or—for economic reasons—been unable to flee.

The response to my approach has swung from extreme rejection by an insensitive media (who more often than not highlighted the initial conflict and abrasive style of my seminars) to white and black officials who are profusely thankful for my work. My appearance on the Phil Donahue Show and T.V., "America: Black and White," led to scores of invitations to lecture and give seminars at colleges and universities. I am now on that lecture tour as I write these words.

The proliferation of my activities and national exposure have also led to an unexpected and welcome bonus: black recognition. The years of my work, the fire released from my bones, was normally confined to small rooms of whites. The few blacks in attendance knew—but the masses of blacks did not know—of my efforts and success in changing whites' attitudes. Television changed that. Requests for speeches, conventions, schools come now from blacks. Young black men beg me for training, for exposure to the process; they too want the fire released from their bones. The most pronounced and flattering plea came from a source most welcome—Martin Luther King, III. Martin's son accompanies me on many of my seminars outside the city of Atlanta. His name and the fame of his father have not affected his humility. As he gradually grows in strength and increases the insights into the methodology of producing white change, I can predict that great things are yet to come from him and for the nation. I love this young man, whom I see slowly building into an awareness of an almost mandated destiny. I am both proud and flattered to have MLK's son as a student of my method, a method that he now sees as an emphatic need. It is the need to understand and eradicate white racism.

*   *   *   *   *

The evolution of the awareness program has been stimulated by two black men, profound thinkers and interpreters of the black experience. They are the former mayor of Atlanta, Maynard Jackson, and Dr. Benjamin Mays, president emeritus of Morehouse College.

In 1973, when Maynard Jackson was running to become the first black mayor of Atlanta, he attended one of my Encounter classes in Dayton. What he observed, he later revealed, stunned him: white attitudes were changeable. He made an impassioned and eloquent statement to the whites who completed the course. Deeply moved by the experience, he publicly announced that, if elected, he would do everything in his power to move me and the Urban Crisis concept to Atlanta. He won and I moved.

At Jackson's urging and support, school officials, the chamber of commerce, bank presidents, and law enforcement officers in Atlanta became graduates of the two-day awareness program. I had earlier dreamed that if city leaders, white men of power, could be exposed to the full dimension of their own racism and sensitized to the black experience, cities could be saved from blight and white flight, and blacks and whites could live and work in peace. Atlanta began to see my dream come true.

Since the early days of my arrival, the graduates of my course, men of power have included: Alan Kiepper, General Manager, Metropolitan Atlanta Transportation system, who completed the course and eventually contracted with me to train over 400 of his managers, administrators, and employees; the board of directors of Trust Company Bank; Dick Kattel, then president of the largest bank in the south, C&S, who encouraged over ninety of his administrators to complete the sixteen-hour program. In my nine years of labor in Atlanta, the concept of my approach and the fire in my bones have reached over 600 police officers and 350 firemen. John Portman, internationally known architect and builder of hotels throughout the world, wrote about the Urban Crisis approach: "I see this program as one that should be utilized in every major city. It makes a tremendous difference." Other cities began to take notice as the program was supported and endorsed by the Atlanta Chamber of Commerce. The entire city of Portland,

Oregon engaged my services for three weeks. Leadership Memphis asks me each year to return to sensitize seventy of its leaders. Each year over seventy-five Leadership Atlantans have completed the sixteen-hour course. City managers and police chiefs are beginning to see and understand the importance of their administration's being exposed to the urban awareness approach.

Dr. Benjamin Mays, one of the best-known black educators in the world and the recipient of over fifty honorary degrees, proved to be a sustaining force early in my initial Atlanta efforts. When I moved to Atlanta, he was chairman of the Atlanta Public School Board. When I heard that he was inquiring about me and the Urban Crisis program, I personally called him and invited him to attend the sixteen-hour course. I desperately wanted him to evaluate my approach and to witness the fact that white attitudes could be changed. He accepted the invitation. The fact that he was about to become a student and not an educator awed me. Patiently and with quiet dignity, he observed my every move, monitored every expression. I knew that my approach was foreign to his nature and perhaps to his philosophy. For years his task had been to emphasize the need for black education over and against the problems of white racism. His years as President of Morehouse developed hundreds of black leaders and ministers, including Martin Luther King, who called Benjamin Mays the man who had most inspired him. Now he was sitting in one of my seminars. I did not spare an emotion that first day; I let it all hang out. The uncompromising truth came from my lips. When the session ended, I could see that I had succeeded: the whites understood; change in attitude had taken place. I was fiercely proud at the end of the seminar, because I had displayed my talent to one of the world's best-known and most respected blacks. What were his thoughts?

He spoke openly to the group, which was composed of white educators, civic leaders, and chamber of commerce types. I felt a blessing coming. Instead, Dr. Mays took that occasion to speak of how he had felt through the years, traveling through America attempting to gain money from philanthropic and powerful whites for Morehouse College. He spoke of the pleas that had come from his lips, when he had wanted to shout out his disdain at the attitudes he met—racist in nature, racist by design, and unknowingly racist. It was his religious shorings that had sustained him in those years. His anger—and it was always there—was contained, invisible, unuttered. He was glad that the whites in the room had been exposed to the full essence of black anger. He emphasized that "that young man," pointing at me, had verbalized all of his inner feelings and, in fact, philosophy as well. He detected a meaningful theology in my approach and a love for mankind that my anger failed to hide.

I felt blessed. Tears sprang into my eyes as we all left that room. Later, when I was alone, they spilled out completely when I remembered his last words to me that day: "Boy," he had said with a small, knowing smile, "you are something else."

CHAPTER 32
White People Must Change

*T*HE FUTURE OF BLACKS IN AMERICA ACTUALLY *is* a matter of survival. And it is not just a matter of what blacks will do; the real question is what whites will do about the problems of blacks in the future. Our entire destiny is tied up with the nature of white society's reaction to those problems.

I detect among most blacks a sense of despair and anger—not outwardly expressed anger but an inner hostility. This is particularly true among young blacks in colleges and universities who are looking at the institutionalized operations of white systems that will not allow blacks to exist within them. These young blacks are turning again to black unity and seeking survival within the concept of blackness. And I consider that a one-way street—and suicidal.

My purpose is to convince white people to change. If they don't change, it actually spells the end of a future for many, many blacks. Now, some blacks will survive—maybe even the majority—by acclimating themselves and becoming part of the system. But I fear for the future of millions of black people who no longer want any part of white America. And that is where the trend is going, particularly since we have separate secondary school systems. The blacks who now go to all-black schools will never grow up knowing white America. And when they find out about it, it will be too late. That is when I believe we could have a resurgence of riots, as blacks try to survive in a world in which they cannot see the end of the rainbow.

I do not think it will be the kind of violence that occurred in the past. And I do not wish to make predictions, because they have a tendency to become self-fulfilling. I wish to say what I fear *might* happen unless changes are made. Some blacks like to use violence as a threat to whites to change. But what I want to do is face whole, hard, pragmatic realities: one cannot expect black frustration, hostility, and despair to stay canned up. It must have an outlet. When and where that will take place, I do not know. It may not be in out-and-out violence, but it may be catastrophic in that blacks all over the country may catch that despair.

The catastrophe may come in the form of more people being placed in penitentiaries. It may come in the form of a large contingent of black people being taken away to old-time concentration camps in the name of national security. Most people do not realize that the McKarran Act—the law that allowed this country to herd Japanese people into internment camps because they were considered a threat to national security—still exists. That law is still on the books. The possibility does exist that blacks who will not conform, and who will thus be considered dangerous, may as a result of some movement on the part of the government or on the part of blacks come to the point of conflict and catastrophe. Many blacks express a vague fear (some actually well-defined) of just that kind of internment. When one looks at the teeming, angry feelings of blacks now contained in the ghetto, one can see an explosive mixture.

White people will often say, "But look at the number of blacks who are now part of the middle class. Doesn't this show a trend that things are looking brighter for the future of black people?" The answer is No. There is no trend. As a matter of fact, that serves as a blinder to both blacks and whites to the real problems of the future. Whites see blacks as having better jobs, shopping in the same supermarkets and department stores, holding positions in large corporations. This allows them to think that blacks are making progress. They are not. Those are merely examples of *individual* black progress.

One-third of all blacks still live on or below the poverty level. Thirty-five percent of all black families are matriarchal, and most of these matriarchal families are on welfare. Almost five million black children from welfare families are in segregated school systems. Seventy-five percent of all men in prison are black; 65 percent of all female prisoners are black; 70 percent of all the crime in urban areas is committed by blacks. We cannot allow the sight of middle-class blacks who have been assimilated into white culture to blind us to the problems that lie beneath those horrifying statistics.

When white people typically comment, "Well, you have to admit that there's been progress," my reply is: "If a knife is in a man's back four inches, and you pull it out two inches, how can you ask the man who still has a knife stuck two inches into his back to acknowledge that there has been progress?" We have to deal with the unsolved problems of the vast majority of black people, not the handful of blacks who have acclimated themselves beyond the point of the masses.

No matter what kind of success a black person has, no matter how high that black person goes in the white social or economic institutional structure, he or she still faces racism all the time. That makes it impossible for black people to reach back and help their brothers and sisters who are less fortunate. Blacks in America suffer discrimination on all levels, whether in the middle class or on welfare. In either position they are subjected to the slings and arrows of outrageous racism that prevent them from ever achieving a full sense of dignity or even hope that the future holds something better. Successful blacks are actually motivated to make the next step upward. But they never expect to become presidents of companies, or be on the board of directors, or be directors of banks, for example. High positions are denied to blacks in deference to the seniority of whites above them and as a result of traditional discriminatory methods by which they are kept on levels beneath the masses of whites.

The same problem holds true in the political arena. The fallacious assumption was that, once blacks had the vote and were able to elect black representatives to city hall, particularly in urban areas, a solution had been found. But that proved to be misleading. Black mayors are powerless to specifically help black people because their concerns are in raising money, collecting taxes, and ruling blacks and whites alike. A black mayor particularly must maintain the image of being the mayor of all the people; therefore, he or she cannot devote full time, as black leadership used to do in the 1950s and '60s, to erasing inequities.

Now these blacks who are in positions of what I call "futile power" must exercise a public image of being fair to all people. And the problem is that one cannot treat blacks and whites in a balanced way. There has been so great an imbalance that if one institutes a balanced approach—as if color made no difference—blacks end up with the short end of the stick. The first priority is to remove inequities, not to treat everybody alike.

My method and message is first of all to get white people to acknowledge that this imbalance does exist—now. But their response, as I have mentioned above, is often that things have changed in the 1970s and 1980s. Many white people are victims of institutional thinking. And I can fully understand why. Most white people grew up believing the American ideal that this nation is a melting pot, the land of the free and the home of the brave. That no matter what a person's background, he can, if he works at it, become President one day. But they are talking about white people when they say these things, although most whites grew up thinking that it also applies to blacks. So when they see blacks responding to inequities, they feel that blacks are just complaining. After all, "everyone in this land has an equal opportunity." They believe that America's idealism holds true for everyone because it holds true for them.

White people have never been taught to face the fact that color indeed makes a difference. They have never been told that white people on the whole discriminate against black people. They have never come in contact with or struggled to understand the problems of being a minority person in a majority society. So they think in terms of the majority—how they themselves act—and think this is also true of black people. Racism actually is not prejudice alone: it is prejudice that is institutionalized to such an extent that the patterns and traditions of the majority group will have an adverse effect upon a minority. You cannot expect a minority people to have the same motivations, skills, and hopes as do the majority, because the whole system is built for and conducive to the majority. Society's benefits are geared toward the majority, which in this country is white.

During the 1960s and '70s, a good deal of federal money was sent to the cities to solve the obvious urban problems. But it did not work. What that money really did was buy off black leadership. It killed the militancy of the black leaders; they began to be the directors of this or that program. The money took the cutting edge off black frustrations temporarily. The money that came to the ghetto did nothing more than stifle black progress by successfully locking in black leaders as administrators of programs that were designed to fail. Too little, too late.

*   *   *   *   *

So, what *is* the answer?

The answer is in the hands of white Americans. The solution cannot come from black people. Expecting an answer from them is like expecting the lion to look at the lamb and say, "What is the answer to your fear and frustration, little lamb?" We know what the problem is; it has been well outlined statistically and historically. The problem is white racism. The problem is discrimination. The problem is racial prejudice.

Now, what is the answer to the problems of black people? The answer is in the will and power of white society and white institutions to change. They *must* change.

In addressing the problems of blacks, white society must first of all ensure that every child in America receive a decent education. The public school system is divided geographically, and black schools are inferior not only in material resources but in attitudes as well. In an all-white system, the child will grow up with a superior attitude; in a black school system, the child will grow up with an inferior attitude.

I keep urging the necessity for desegregation of school systems because I believe it would cut in half the hopelessness I see for the black future. There is hope if we can catch children while they are still young and place them together in decent surroundings, doing away with ghettoization. The school system remains the only institution in America where black-white togetherness is possible, because children must go to school by law. And unless black and white people are brought together in the next decade, we will have twin societies—one white, one black. If we are having trouble now between whites and blacks, think of what will happen in the future when the white suburban children who will have the power face a hostile group about whom they know nothing at all.

I do not want to imply that everything will stand still until we desegregate the school systems. A simultaneous step should be taken toward the reordering of the systems' priorities. It costs more than $13,000 a year to keep a man in prison. Rather than working to reduce the causative factors of crime, we subsidize him in prison. In the state of Georgia alone, $60 million is going into the building of new prison facilities. What could $60 million do in a job program for unemployed black people? We could create lives with new meaning, dignity, and hope. Our priorities are reversed.

What really frightens me is that, on the same day that the federal government sent $2 million to Atlanta for the investigation of the child murders, the Reagan administration cut the AFDC (Aid to Families with Dependent Children) staff program by $635 million; it cut $525 million from the food-stamp program; and it cut the CETA (Comprehensive Employment and Training Act) program entirely. That put more than 117,000 poor blacks and whites out of work. After these hundreds of millions of dollars were taken away, the administration saw fit to give two million of it back to one city, disregarding the fact that the same environmental circumstances out of which the murdered children of Atlanta came are present in every major city in this country: Chicago, Los Angeles, Detroit, San Francisco, Houston, Newark, Gary, New York.

The Reagan administration now says that the priority should be to relieve the stress on the private sector, to give them tax incentives and tax breaks so that the economy might grow and eventually employ poor people. That will never happen. It is completely insensitive to ask poor people to wait until big business is ready to beat their economic problem. The point is that, even if big business does prosper, black people will still face their number one problem: discrimination.

I say that the answer to the problems of black people is in the hands of white society because white institutions hold the power. Blacks are powerless. Period. Blacks own less than 2 percent of the national wealth.

If a black mayor were to do something that the white community thought was detrimental to its interests, the governor and state legislature could meet in session and take away that city's charter. There is no place in this country where any black could do anything that would wholly benefit blacks without having the power sweep down upon him or her. Blacks must still operate within that unjust balance; they cannot apply power directly on their own behalf. In the face of these conditions, blacks are powerless financially, politically, even spiritually. You cannot pray down the white man.

But blacks will survive because they are used to surviving. A suffering people has the capacity to develop long patience and endurance, and to look on the fact of blackness as a cross to bear. And we bear it quite well. But my fear is that in this generation we have been unable to transmit to our young people the need to bear crosses. They refuse to bear the cross. And that is the basis of my fear for the future.

EPILOGUE
I Tire of Being Black

*I*T WAS A TOWN TUCKED AWAY FROM THE TWO-
lane, bumpy tar highway. The kind of town where no gas
station is open at two o'clock in the morning. I had one eye
glued to the gas needle that was dipping dangerously toward
"E" and the other one glancing right and left when a gas station sign popped up: "Pop's Place—Open 24 Hours." The
year was 1952, long before the Civil Rights Bill; the place was
Mississippi, long before civilization. Pop was typically Ku
Klux Klannish, and the gas he pumped appeared to go into my
Hudson reluctantly. My wife of a few months squirmed in
pain, needing to visit the rest room. But Pop had informed me
that he had no rest room for "nigras."

The pump had clicked out six gallons when the ludicrous-
ness of the situation struck me. "Dammit, that's enough," I
told the insolent Pop. "Didn't you say fill it up?" he inquired
as the pump clicked seven gallons. "Take it out—stop!" I
demanded. "It ain't full yet," Pop replied sarcastically. Suddenly my wife opened the car door, leaped from the car, and
ran a few paces toward the edge of the bushes beside the
restaurant. She couldn't make it though, and there, in full view
of Pop, she relieved herself.

The humiliation and dehumanization forced upon us that
night is hard to describe. The memory is so deeply etched in
my mind that each time, even now, that I stop at or pass a station that resembles Pop's Place, I quiver with rage. It was a
time in which black anger was contained, when black manhood
was drained by the white South, when protest was futile, and
violent reaction meant death. I recall those years not to instill

guilt in whites, nor to stir up the past for blacks, but to remind us all that the song "We Shall Overcome" refers less to the outward condition of the black experience than to the inner strength, less to the demise of the Klan than to the gradual growth of whites who today would not tolerate a Pop.

Small white gasoline stations have been replaced, to be sure, by ten-pump stations with self-service islands and highway rest stops that ensure equal accommodations. Yet, in spite of my own growth and advanced perspective on the social order, Pop has left me with an inner paranoia, a poison that refuses to drain off, and a target that refuses to appear.

Time has washed away the fury, the helpless rage I felt at that incident, and time supposedly heals all wounds. Yet I am left with the scar of that night that refuses to heal. It is perhaps the only outlandish, racist act that distorts that part of my soul that refuses to be set free. This despite the fact that I have weathered the storms of a past cluttered with the debris of discrimination in the belief that the Pops are dead or no longer in control. I have long since retrieved my manhood and long since refused to shake in silent fury or be blinded by copious tears while fleeing from battles with racists. I have spent most of my adult life fighting against white racism, trying to achieve equality for blacks. It has been a strange and meandering road. For many stretches I have marched in the company of hundreds, while on others I have marched alone. The most important things I have learned from my walks on this road are that blacks and whites must learn to understand each other and that both races must acknowledge the poison of white racism and work to eradicate it.

To be black is a confusing proposition. Not the color itself, but the complexities brought to it by the cold, harsh realities of a nation filled with all-encompassing whiteness. We are caught in the briar patches of white power and institutional controls, and there is no escape. The sun rises and the sun sets on our blackness. Twilight, dusk, and midnight refuse to produce keys that will release, and even our dreams are surrounded by a stifling haze that dwarfs the hope. No man or woman escapes this blackness, for from the first cry of birth to the last sigh of death, black we are and black we shall be. Understanding this, each black must be prepared to fight—not the violent, bloody battle of suicidal proportions, but the insipid, creeping racism that strips and peels away the thin layer of an identity so recently acquired and so easily lost in the forest of whiteness. This declaration of war seeks not independence but release from dependence on the crumbs from the master's table—for an equitable share of the meal. Do we tire of this effort? What manner of people would not tire of being caught in the swirls and tides of racism, perpetually swimming upstream to spawn.

I tire of wearing blackness as a badge, as a shroud, with the predictable negative incidents that emphasize the low esteem in which I'm held. Yet even that serves as the foundation of motivation, the extra spurt necessary to compete—to win. My blackness then is both a curse and a blessing, twin images of life, creating a dichotomous existence that refuses to congeal or to blend. Would to God that I could forget my skin, my lips, my hair that refuse to conform to the institutional demands of white conformity, or, better still, that the eyes of the discriminator be temporarily blinded when I pass by, or plucked out entirely when black visibility creates white insensitivity to the dignity of our persons.

I tire of the bewilderment that the twenty-eight dead and missing children of Atlanta could arouse a nation to the high passions of anger and grief—but subside far too quickly and too late to encompass the millions of black children still alive but destined to die too early. I tire of walking the streets of this nation's ghettos and viewing the dirt, the filth, the broken bottles and lives, shattered by racism's double-edged sword that cuts and recoils at the sight of the blood it has caused. The bitter cold wind that pushes itself beyond the rags stuffed between broken pane windows—awaiting repair from the Housing Authority's false promises of summer. The huddled masses of the black poor, sleeping in heaps to conserve the brief sparks of warmth still left in their bodies.

And there are the drugs, pushed, then gently inserted in my people's arms, arms available for jobs—if jobs were accessible—uplifted arms, clutching fists, not to fight, but to pop out veins as a road map to searching needles . . . and death. Death comes early to my people: the slow death of incurable depression, eyes closed to hope, blinded by the brilliance of well-to-do Caucasian twilights, the gleaming finery of white opportunism so long denied to those whose skins are tinted or tainted by color. From that source come this nation's killers; by now their composites may be considered uniform.

I count myself one of those, never free of their chains that are also mine, linked inextricably to a common umbilical cord impossible to sever. The fire in my bones achieves white heat, consuming my joy at individual successes, stunting the growth of love toward all who are not of my hue, stifling the very air considered to be free.

Being black is like skating on ice but not knowing the location of the thin places, going to war without weapons, holding a hand grenade and searching for a target beyond the ten-second interval allotted after pulling the pin. Weary of life, too fearful to die, clutching on to white ice, trying to survive in the cold waters of racism, while those on the shore refuse to throw you a line, alleging by their inaction that, while drowning, you still have the strength to swim to the shore.

And there are the schools with a dominant black presence, where black policemen patrol the halls to remove those who refuse to learn and to contain those who are unable. Black educators who boast of a 5 percent rise in reading ability contrasted to last year's dismal statistics. Without money, without tax base, without white concerns, far too many black schools become tombstones to mark the spot of the demise of educational achievement. Schools turned all black have black teachers too tired to teach; and those who really care and try are burned out by the sheer exhaustion of meaningless efforts. The children leave those schools, untaught by white teachers who fear them, kicked out by principals who soon grow to hate them. These are the ones who are considered disturbers of the status quo, prone to violent eruptions and profane utterances.

I tire of choking back the tears at the sight of black high school graduates unable to read or fill out applications for employment, devoid of the graciousness of speech, dress, and personality that should accompany those applications. At the sound of the calls from fatherless homes whose mothers plead for help for their incarcerated sons, for lawyers to defend them or to eke out qualities of mercy from prosecutors and judges politically mandated to stash them away.

Cold, cruel, insensitive white institutions continue to build and grow tall on the broken backs and spirits of a people unable to stand erect. I am so tired of begging, pleading, shouting into the winds of a nature so perverse, so immune to compassion, that my burning is an ultimate consequence of a self-fulfilling message of disaster. My skin becomes my torch, and far too soon, the shroud for my grave—where I shall tire no more.

Begone, black child. Return to the streets that spawned you, and learn on your own to swim upstream against the strong currents of the unemployed. The psychological raping and educational slaying of black youth lead them to criminal behavior. The ranks of the police swell in proportion—and so do the taxes on those who are left in the city, unable to pay, unable to run. The whites who flee, bleached whiter by fear, look behind them in flight, abdicate their holdings, the tall buildings built with the skill and the toil of their fathers, the immigrants of old. Unlike the blacks, they were met on the shores at the end of their long journey with, "Give me your tired, your poor, your huddled masses, yearning to breathe free. . . ."

Today there are no harbors for blacks, no Statues of Liberty. Black statues are the desecrated, deserted buildings that were erected by the immigrants. Broken windows, bricks devoid of mortar, open doorways, dark urine-stained walls stripped of just glories and human occupancy, decorated with crass graffiti. Occasionally, wrecking balls batter at those walls, sending down into the dust that which was but is no more. The buildings that remain, in the heart of the city, stare back through dirty window panes too high up to be stoned.

This is the land that blacks inherit. Black politicians stake a claim on that territory, to rule and control that which has finally become unruly and out of control. They fight each other for power, begging for bread and meat from the capital. That help seldom comes, and the have-nots, who no longer care, are too weak, too disenchanted even to despair. Blinking blue and white strobe lights, blasting stereophonic sounds fill the air. Defeated black Americans stand on street corners in the chill of early evening, waiting with sixty cents in change to catch filthy buses. They will empty those buses into homes sold to them by white-flighters at exorbitant prices, on contract, and enterprising white realtors who have instituted blockbusting . . . or into high-rise slums erected by whites on the Housing Authority, which pile blacks high rather than allow them the freedom of open land and precious space. Thousands of blacks, in every major city, jostling each other out of the limited space allotted. Contained, they tick away like time bombs.

I cry aloud for release from these walls of pigmentation, this prison of color. But who will hear, and who can change the handiwork of God? Perhaps He alone—but even He will not budge to dip his brush in the initial oils of the earth from whence I sprang. To be black is beautiful, I inform myself, for that fact fails to spring from any other source. I am the sole interpreter and definer of my own existence, the maker of my own mirror, the resounding echo of my own songs, whether they be blues or a hymn. "Just As I Am, Without One Plea" I come. I am here. Accept me as I am and seek no praise for your efforts; reject me and kindle the flames of my slow burning anger that, when distilled with my blackness, creates an atomic and bionic being who is unconquerable, impenetrable, invincible. White institutions make of me a warrior, ready to do battle, hammering incessantly against those practices and customs that eat the heart out of my existence. What you have not known, cruel white world, is the steel beneath my sinew and muscles, and the untapped reservoir of my brain. Unknown because black strength in labor or within the economy has never been listened to in its fullness, untapped because the creativity of black talent and aspirations has never exploded within your culture.

I tire of wearing blackness as a badge, but I have worn it so long, so well, that I've caught that second wind, that mysterious force that propels me onward and upward. It is this mystic power that anoints my bushy head with a tenacity unpossessed by any other race of man under the heavens, or outside or inside the gates of hell. Blackness dwells on both terrains, and there is no in-between. To float on the misty clouds of black history or to sink in the slime of today's ocean of racism is the totality of the black experience. Our heads and our minds are bursting with the knowledge of ourselves, and weirdly enough, with the knowledge of whiteness. You see, we know the man, but the man doesn't know us. And that puts us on top. Wake up, white folks, black giants are walking in your forest, cutting paths out of thickets, blazing trails, jumping over ditches, marking pitfalls, swinging from vines, erecting bridges, and fashioning spears into pruning hooks. We are a people determined to make it, not in spite of our blackness, but because of it. Historians will record it, social scientists will be astounded by it, and civilizations will be magnified by it. Our race is not with time, but with eternity, when we shall no longer tire.